"Barrick takes us on an engaging tour of the social and linguistic challenges facing Bible translators, as they move between language systems to make the Bible accessible to common people in their heart language."

—George Athas, Moore Theological College

"With a vast array of fascinating historical realities and colorful word pictures, Barrick takes us into the complicated—yet essential—world of Bible translation, and puts us in the driver's seat to see how God is faithfully preserving and spreading the gospel of Jesus Christ through his written Word. Every church must have a copy."

—David Beakley, Academic Dean, Christ Seminary, Polokwane, South Africa

"This book is intriguing, challenging, and comforting. This book is designed not only for Bible translators, but for all perceptive believers who want to understand the challenges involved in bringing a translation to fruition. Bill Barrick so beneficially 'pulls back the veil' to allow his readers to see what translators struggle with and how decisions are made."

—Stephen J. Bramer, Chair and Professor of Bible Exposition,
Dallas Theological Seminary

"Bill Barrick has masterfully applied his expertise as a Hebrew scholar, coupled with his years of experience as a Bible translator, to make a compelling case for translating God's Word in the common language of the readers."

—Dave Brunn, International Translation Consultant, Ethnos 360

"This volume is an important contribution in clarifying the issues of Bible translation. It also inspires us to join in and/or support the lofty endeavor of making God known to every nation, tribe, and tongue."

—Abner Chou, John F. MacArthur Endowed Fellow, The Master's University

"With clarity of explanation and an engaging style, Bill Barrick walks the reader through the interpretive steps necessary to render the text of Scripture faithfully and clearly from original language to target language. Readers of this volume will come away with a better grasp of the diligence and care required to provide readable and accurate translations, and will likely catch Barrick's excitement for the task along the way. Unique contributions include a refined matrix and principles for assessing popular English Bible versions, first-person accounts of the feats and challenges of missionaries on the front lines of Bible translation, and a detailed sketch of the qualities and training needed to be an effective Bible translator."

—Kyle C. Dunham, Associate Professor of Old Testament,
Detroit Baptist Theological Seminary

"In reading *Understanding Bible Translation*, I felt like an apprentice sitting at the elbow of a master artisan, watching him perform his craft with excellence. Bill Barrick masterfully demonstrates what is involved in translating the Bible with both clarity and accuracy."

—Daniel J. Estes, Distinguished Professor of Old Testament, Cedarville University

"Whether you are a senior pastor tasked with weekly teaching or a student of Holy Scripture, this book is a must-read! This new work of Bill Barrick will broaden your understanding of biblical translation."

—Jason D. Falzarano, Dean of BABS, Calvary Chapel University

"Bill Barrick covers all the essentials in a long-awaited and accessible book on Bible translation that will suit both college and seminary-level readers, as well as lay-readers. Barrick's very high regard for the Bible, and adept handling of some very difficult subjects [illegible]
complemented by his own personal experience on the [illegible]

—Stephen T. Hague, Professor of Biblica [illegible]

"Bill Barrick writes for the seasoned Christian about the importance of Bible translation and points out challenges that such translators face. Included in this book is an evaluation of English Bibles and encouragement to churches regarding how to support Bible translators. Lastly, Barrick gives guidance to those interested in becoming Bible translators."

—Gregory Harris, Department Chair and Professor of Bible Exposition, The Master's Seminary

"Using the personal experience of fifteen years in Bible translation and missionary work in Bangladesh, Bill Barrick writes winsomely—and in a compelling manner—about the value and importance of Bible translation. He explains both the joys of an accurate and readable translation and the tragedy (sometimes humor) of the inaccurate translation. Numerous instances of good, better, and best translations pepper Barrick's text, especially when he writes about the history of Bible translation."

—Joel D. Heck, Professor of Theology, Concordia University Texas

"*Understanding Bible Translation* is full of practical examples of how 'good translators take an interest in every aspect of life and culture,' as Bill Barrick makes the convincing case that 'the Bible's cultural, geographical, and historical details must be left intact.' The text emphasizes the need for accuracy and clarity in translation, and a strong case is made for relying on the original biblical languages in translation work."

—Bill Katip, President, Grace College and Seminary

"This is by far the most up-to-date and well-written book on the subject. I have always shared with my students the use of synchronic word studies when determining the author's word usage in its context. This takes it even further."

—Stephen R. Lewis, President and Professor of Biblical and Theological Studies, Rocky Mountain Seminary; and Adjunct Professor, Jordan Evangelical Theological Seminary

"*Understanding Bible Translation* takes a highly technical endeavor and makes it obtainable for all. William Barrick has given the church an exceptional, firsthand, heartfelt book that will carry this great need and wonderful privilege into the next generations. This book is a thoroughly enjoyable and deeply rewarding read."

—Stephen M. Lonetti, Missionary and Pastor, Beacon of Hope Church; Founder and Executive Director, LifeGate Worldwide; and Bible Translator Emeritus, New Tribes

"Bill Barrick meticulously explains the complex task of Bible translation in an easily understandable manner for us non-translators. Using multiple biblical texts as illustrations of proper translation, Barrick compellingly urges his readership to appreciate anew the translation process/history for the Bible they read in their own language and to encourage their support for Bible translation projects."

—Richard Mayhue, Research Professor of Theology Emeritus, The Master's Seminary

"This volume is the overflow of Barrick's rich history of teaching Hebrew, and his experience as an exegetical consultant for the *Standard Bengali Common Language Bible* and the *Muslim Bengali Common Language Bible*, as well as a number of other local languages. One of the facets of this book that makes it such a captivating read is how the author beneficially integrates germane biblical texts and his firsthand experience as a Bible translator and consultant in Bangladesh into the fabric of this work."

—Robert V. McCabe, Retired Professor of Old Testament, Detroit Baptist Theological Seminary

"In a day of the proliferation of new versions of the Bible and translations of the Scriptures, we need a useful tool to help us properly assess them. Having read it with much personal benefit, I heartily recommend this great work."

—Alex Montoya, Pastor of First Fundamental Bible Church, Whittier, California; Professor of Pastoral Ministries, The Master's Seminary; and President, Seminario Biblical Fundamental of Southern California

"Decades of personal experience in each of the relevant disciplines related to this subject (international missions, Bible translation, pastoral ministry, and seminary training) make Dr. Barrick uniquely qualified and his work a must-read for anyone in or preparing for any of these roles. His exegesis is thorough. His tips and insights for translators and exegetes are invaluable. Most importantly, his love for Christ and absolute commitment to the accurate and faithful handling of God's Word resonates consistently throughout."

—Bryan Murphy, Associate Professor, The Master's Seminary; and Pastor/Teacher, Roosevelt Community Church

"If you want to learn how Bible translation works, wouldn't you want to learn from a faithful Christian scholar who has been teaching people to translate the Bible for more than fifty years, who spent fifteen years translating the Bible into Bengali, and who has helped translate English versions such as the ESV and NET Bible? Bill Barrick has so much wisdom to share."

—Andy Naselli, Associate Professor of New Testament and Theology, Bethlehem College & Seminary

"For two decades I have told my students that William Barrick is the top biblical exegete I have known or read. In this volume, Dr. Barrick establishes a new standard for works on Bible translation. His mastery of biblical languages and extensive experience at Bible translation in a foreign field permeates every page of the book."

—Douglas Petrovich, Professor of Biblical History and Exegesis, The Bible Seminary

"*Understanding Bible Translation* has given me new insight in understanding the biblical text better to help me prepare a New Reader's edition of the Bible in Bangladesh. This book is a valuable resource for Bible translators and those in the arena of theological studies."

—Shamsul Alam Polash, Chairman, International Bible Church Trust

"*Understanding Bible Translation* reads at times like a biographical thriller, a humorous cultural guide, an exegetical manual, a pastor's personal diary, and a well-planned textbook where intriguing experiences provide the backdrop for addressing important issues. All who aspire to be faithful messengers will be fascinated and informed by this helpful book."

—Tim M. Sigler, Provost & Dean, Professor of Hebrew and Biblical Studies, Shepherds Theological Seminary

"I have praised God many times for his grace in sending Dr. Barrick and his family to Bangladesh to meet the need of the ABWE Bangladesh Field Council. His knowledge of Hebrew and related biblical languages, and his faithfulness to accuracy in our translation of the text, were invaluable for accomplishing that project over the course of about sixteen years. His book, *Understanding Bible Translation,* gives excellent insight into all that is involved in translating the Bible into another language."

—Lynn Silvernale, International Translation Consultant, Retired missionary to Bangladesh, ABWE

"A seasoned veteran of Bible translation in multiple languages, Bill Barrick privileges *accuracy* and *understandability* in transmitting the sacred text to the everyday reader. This book is a gem of serious value for both the church and the academy."

—Mark Snoeberger, Professor of Systematic Theology, Detroit Baptist Theological Seminary

"As someone involved in an international ministry involving interaction in several different languages, I understand the need for careful approaches to understanding communication across language barriers in both oral and printed forms. Many such works have come on the scene over the years, but this one will provide the best balance to Bible translation. Bill Barrick, an experienced Bible translator at one time in Bangladesh, avoids the extremes of language translation: hyperformalism on one side that at times approaches a wooden literalism, and an approach on the other side that takes too much liberty in translation. Barrick correctly opts for the transfer of meaning more than form in the translation process from the original biblical languages. The real strength of the book is the identification of clear translation principles at several points in the process and in the many concrete examples for the purpose of illustrating such principles"

—Mike Stallard, Director of International Ministries, Friends of Israel Gospel Ministry

"If I were facing major brain surgery, I would certainly want to know that my surgeon had plenty of experience and knew what he was doing. *Understanding Bible Translation,* is by analogy, the chance to learn from a skilled master craftsman"

—J. Paul Tanner, Middle East Director for Biblical Education by Extension

"This veteran missionary turned seminary professor has mastered the art of Bible translation. Whether you are a novice or an expert, a layman or a pastor, a sender or a goer, if you want to better understand what's at stake in a good Bible translation this book is for you."

—Adam Tyson, Pastor, Placerita Bible Church

"Has God really said what I just read? Why are the King James Version and the English Standard Version different? What version should I read? Dr. Barrick has provided a marvelous resource to help serious readers, Bible students, and aspiring scholars understand the important and complex nature of translating the Bible into everyday language. I highly recommend this book for Christians serious about their faith. It will increase your confidence in the Bible, and your trust in the God who is not silent."

—Thomas White, President and Professor of Theology, Cedarville University

"This book is a must-read for any serious Christian, so that one will take God's Word with more seriousness—with the same weightiness as the translators engage in when they endeavor to translate God's Word in another language."

—Jan Verbruggen, Professor of Old Testament Language and Literature, Western Seminary

"Bill Barrick has provided a much-needed resource for future Bible translators, ministry students, and laity seeking a better understanding of Bible translations and the labor and challenges in ensuring the Word is faithfully preserved, and transmitted."

—David W. Whitlock, President, Oklahoma Baptist University

"Bill Barrick draws upon a lifetime of scholarship to challenge what I thought I knew about Scripture, humble me with gratitude for those who translated my Bible, and inspire me to support the teams who continue this sometimes thrilling, sometimes tedious work. You will not look at your Bible the same way again."

—Mike Wittmer, Professor of Systematic Theology, Grand Rapids Theological Seminary

"For fifty years, the author's reputation for biblical precision has been incontestably established. The scholarly footing and foundation of his current offering is another testimony to this reality."

—George Zemek, Academic Dean, The Expositors Seminary

UNDERSTANDING BIBLE TRANSLATION

BRINGING GOD'S WORD INTO NEW CONTEXTS

WILLIAM D. BARRICK

Understanding Bible Translation: Bringing God's Word into New Contexts

Published by Kregel Academic, an imprint of Kregel Publications, 2450 Oak Industrial Dr. NE, Grand Rapids, MI 49505-6020.

The Greek font GraecaU and the Hebrew font New JerusalemU are both available from www.linguistsoftware.com/lgku.htm, +1-425-775-1130.

ISBN 978-0-8254-2025-2

Printed in the United States of America

19 20 21 22 23 / 5 4 3 2 1

"A beautiful and at the same time a true wife
is as great a rarity as a good translation of a poem.
Such a translation is usually not beautiful when it is true,
and not true when it is beautiful."[1]

—Moritz G. Saphir

For my wife Barbara, who is both beautiful and true—better
than any translated poem can ever be.
She is beyond red coral gems in value (Prov. 31:10).
Of all my encouragers for this book,
she has always been foremost.

I am also thankful for the Bengali Bible translation team
members with whom I worked in Bangladesh (1981–1996):
Lynn Silvernale, Basanti Das, Polycarp Dores,
Shamsul Alam Polash, Harold Ebersole,
Vic and Joan Olsen, and Ron Perrine.
You all schooled me in the classroom
of Bible translation field work.

CONTENTS

ABBREVIATIONS

AB	Anchor Bible
ASV	American Standard Version
AYBC	Anchor Yale Bible Commentary
BCOT	Baker Commentary on the Old Testament
BDAG	Walter Bauer, Frederick W. Danker, W. F. Arndt, and F. W. Gingrich. *Greek-English Lexicon of the New Testament and Other Early Christian Literature.* 3rd ed. Chicago, 2000
BDB	Francis Brown, S. R. Driver, and Charles A. Briggs. *A Hebrew and English Lexicon of the Old Testament.* Oxford, 1907
BEC	Baker Exegetical Commentary
BHGNT	Baylor Handbook on the Greek New Testament
BHHB	Baylor Handbook on the Hebrew Bible
CCL	Chakma Common Language Bible
CEB	Common English Bible
CJB	Complete Jewish Bible
CSB	Christian Standard Bible
DBY	English Darby Bible
DRA	Douay-Rheims American
EBC	Frank E. Gaebelein, ed. *The Expositor's Bible Commentary.* 12 vols. Grand Rapids, 1979
EEC	Evangelical Exegetical Commentary
ERB	Rotherham Emphasized Bible
ERV	English Revised Version

ESV	English Standard Version
GKC	E. Kautzsch, ed. *Gesenius' Hebrew Grammar*. 2nd English ed. Trans. and rev. by A. E. Cowley. Oxford, 1910
GNT	Good News Bible (see TEV)
GNV	Geneva Bible
GWT	God's Word Translation
HALOT	Ludwig Koehler, Walter Baumgartner, and Johann Jakob Stamm, eds. *The Hebrew and Aramaic Lexicon of the Old Testament*. Trans. and ed. by M. E. J. Richardson. 4 vols. Leiden, 1994–99
HBI	Frederic Clarke Putnam. *Hebrew Bible Insert: A Student's Guide to the Syntax of Biblical Hebrew*. Quakertown, PA, 1996
HCSB	Holman Christian Standard Bible
HTS	Harvard Theological Studies
IBHS	Bruce K. Waltke and M. O'Connor. *An Introduction to Biblical Hebrew Syntax*. Winona Lake, IN, 1990
ICC	International Critical Commentary
ISBE	James Orr, ed. *The International Standard Bible Encyclopaedia*. 4 vols. Grand Rapids, 1939
ISV	International Standard Version, New Testament
JB	Jerusalem Bible
JPS	Jewish Publication Society Bible
JSOTSup	Journal for the Study of the Old Testament: Supplement Series
KEL	Kregel Exegetical Library
KJV	King James Version
LB	Living Bible
LEB	Lexham English Bible
LXX	Septuagint
MBCL	Muslim Bengali Common Language Bible
MIT	MacDonald Idiomatic Translation, New Testament
NAB	New American Bible, Revised
NAC	New American Commentary
NAS	New American Standard Bible
NASB	New American Standard Bible, Update
NCV	New Century Version

NET	New English Translation (or NET Bible)
NEB	New English Bible
NIVUK	New International Version (UK)
NICNT	New International Commentary on the New Testament
NICOT	New International Commentary on the Old Testament
NIDOTTE	Willem A. VanGemeren, ed. *New International Dictionary of Old Testament Theology and Exegesis*. 5 vols. Grand Rapids, 1997
NIGTC	New International Greek Testament Commentary
NIRV	New International Reader's Version
NIV	New International Version
NIVAC	NIV Application Commentary
NJB	New Jerusalem Bible
NJPS	New Jewish Publication Society Bible (see TNK)
NKJV	New King James Version
NLT	New Living Translation
NRSV	New Revised Standard Version
OBB	Old Bengali Bible (sometimes known erroneously as the "Carey Bible")
OTL	Old Testament Library
PNT	Bishop's New Testament
REB	Revised English Bible
SBCL	Standard Bengali Common Language Bible
SBLDS	Society of Biblical Literature Dissertation Series
TCL	Tripura Common Language Bible
TDOT	G. Johannes Botterweck, Helmer Ringgren, and Heinz-Josef Fabry, eds. *Theological Dictionary of the Old Testament*. Translated by John T. Willis, et al. 15 vols. Grand Rapids, 1975–2006
TEV	Today's English Version (see GNT)
TLOT	Ernst Jenni and Claus Westermann, eds. *Theological Lexicon of the Old Testament*. Translated by Mark E. Biddle. 3 vols. Peabody, MA, 1997
TNK	New Jewish Publication Society (see NJPS)
TNT	Tyndale New Testament
TNTC	Tyndale New Testament Commentaries
TOTC	Tyndale Old Testament Commentaries

TWOT	R. Laird Harris, Gleason L. Archer, and Bruce K. Waltke, eds. *Theological Wordbook of the Old Testament*. 2 vols. Chicago, 1980
v., vv.	verse, verses
WBC	Word Biblical Commentary
WEY	Weymouth New Testament in Modern Speech
WYC	Wyclif Bible
YLT	Young's Literal Translation
ZECNT	Zondervan Exegetical Commentary on the New Testament
ZECOT	Zondervan Exegetical Commentary on the Old Testament

PREFACE

SHORTLY AFTER OUR ARRIVAL IN BANGLADESH as missionaries, a Bangladeshi pastor visited our flat. After a time of pleasant conversation and a cup of tea, he said farewell, walked out the drive, and disappeared among the crowd of people on the street. Then our younger son exulted, "Wow! I didn't realize I could speak Bengali so good!" Swapon spoke English with an obvious Bengali accent—an accent quite foreign to our ten-year-old son. Our son mistook accented English for actual Bengali. If only learning a foreign language could be that easy. After joining the Bible translation team in Bangladesh, I soon discovered that translating the Bible can be a daunting task in which knowledge of the receptor language is but one of many difficult challenges a translator faces.

Bible translation might be compared to reconstructing and restoring a great palace from antiquity. The aim of reconstruction is to restore the palace to its original form and beauty so that present-day viewers might see it as it once existed when it reverberated with life and court officials pursued their administrative responsibilities within its decorated walls. The Bible is an ancient book written in languages surviving in similar, but not identical, forms to those spoken and written long ago. Translators employ linguistic analysis in an attempt to gain a clearer understanding of those languages as they were spoken in antiquity. They labor to reproduce the exact meaning of the ancient text. The Bible translator aims at helping the modern reader come as close as possible to understanding what the original hearers and readers understood when they interacted with the biblical text.

Bible translations affect their readers, whether for ill or for good. A clear perception of the principles and process of Bible translation provides a number of benefits:

- heightened awareness of resources for unlocking misunderstood or difficult to understand passages of the Bible
- fuller understanding of the ministry of Bible translation on mission fields around the world
- better evaluation of Bible translations for personal and congregational use
- better knowledge of what is involved in academic preparation for Bible translation ministries
- more solid basis for determining how one might become involved in Bible translation ministries

Fifteen years of Bible translation experience in Bangladesh contribute to my background for writing a book of this nature. Like many missionaries, I became involved in far more than I had originally intended. As well as Bible translation, I worked in the areas of training nationals, translating materials for Sunday school and for the Bible institute, church planting, and mission administration. Even in Bible translation, the primary project (the Standard Bengali Common Language Bible, SBCL) provided opportunities to be involved in other Bible translations. In one way or another (sometimes nothing more than helping to train national translators), I participated in the Muslim Bengali Common Language Bible (MBCL) and a variety of Bangladesh tribal translations for the Bawm, Chakma, Tripura, Mro, Marma, Garo, and Sadri. In addition, work began on a regional dialect, Chittagonian, and a revision of the older Bengali Bible translation originated by William Yates back in 1834 after William Carey's death. Since leaving Bangladesh, I have contributed to the English Standard Version (ESV, Job), the NET Bible (NET, Job and Leviticus), and Lexham English Bible (LEB, Job and Leviticus).

Fifty years have passed since I first started teaching biblical Hebrew. Preparing for and teaching Old Testament studies on the seminary level involves engaging ancient biblical translations like the Greek Septuagint, the Samaritan Pentateuch, Hebrew texts from the Dead Sea Scrolls, the Syriac Peshitta, and the Latin Vulgate. My exposure to Bible translation was expanded by comparing Bible translations in German, French, Italian,

Spanish, Arabic, and Urdu with the Bengali projects and teaching overseas. Short-term visits to speak or teach in Albania, Croatia, Germany, Portugal, Ukraine, Russia, South Africa, Brazil, Colombia, Honduras, India, Myanmar, Singapore, Hong Kong, Thailand, and the Philippines add to ever-increasing contacts with different languages and cultures. Translating extrabiblical materials from Akkadian, Ugaritic, Aramaic, Syriac, Greek, Latin, Moabite, Edomite, Ammonite, and Egyptian continues to increase awareness of translation practices and perils.

All of that experience and exposure has taught me there is much yet to accomplish in the realm of Bible translation. My prayer is that this book will capture the minds and hearts of people who will commit themselves in some fashion to the ministry of Bible translation. Our churches must take up the great and rewarding challenge of Bible translation. Evangelism and church planting cannot proceed without the Word of God in the language of the people whom the missionary desires to impact with the gospel of Jesus Christ. The church itself is founded upon Scripture (Eph. 2:20, "the apostles and prophets"). Every major incursion of the gospel into another culture, whether in China or among the Navajo, in Germany or among the Watusi, has focused on providing the Bible in the heart language of the target audience, for "faith *comes* from hearing, and hearing by the Word of Christ" (Rom. 10:17 NASB).

The writing of this book began over twenty-five years ago when our SBCL project coordinator, Dr. Lynn Silvernale, suggested I write a small booklet about our project and Bible translation methodology. Many drafts disappeared in the flood of changes over time as a full book began to emerge. My wife, Barbara, bore patiently the long hours I spent immersed in writing. Colleagues and friends (too many to mention here by name) offered valuable suggestions and advice. Shawn Vander Lugt and Laura Bartlett, my editors at Kregel, patiently walked me through the final formatting, edits, cover design, and promotion. A special thanks also to Dennis Hillman at Kregel who first encouraged the publication of this book and endured my seemingly endless delays long enough to see it to completion.

CHAPTER 1

BECAUSE THEY UNDERSTAND

A HUMID TROPICAL HEAT BLANKETS THE MOSQUE. Children chanting their lessons in Arabic lend an air of charm and mystery to the scene. In the distance the ringing of bicycle rickshaw bells punctuates the intermittent silence. Then a babble of children's cheerful voices cascades over the courtyard as they crowd into a single classroom. They settle into their cross-legged seating upon bamboo mats on the hard clay floor and a hush descends over the room.

Bustling into the room and confronting his visitors, a white-bearded mullah inquires, "Did you give this book to my son?"

"Yes," I replied. The book is a paperback edition of the Muslim Bengali Common Language (MBCL) New Testament.

"You didn't give me one," he protests.

"I will give you a more nicely bound edition for yourself," I promise.

As the principal, the mullah oversees the madrassa (an Islamic day school) housed in a suburban neighborhood mosque in Chittagong, Bangladesh. His son serves as one of the teachers in the madrassa. Squatting down beside me where I am sitting on the floor, the elderly gentleman holds the book in his outstretched right hand. "Can you read this book?" As he asks the question, he places the Bengali New Testament in my hands.

"Yes. May I choose the passage?" He tilts his head slightly to convey his positive response—a gesture common to all Bangladeshis.

Watching us intently are about forty young students between the ages of eight and fifteen. They sit on the floor around us, filling the classroom.

With a few softly spoken words, the mullah instructs a student to take the Qur'an off its stand in front of us. The student carefully removes the Qur'an and wraps it in a protective cloth. Then he gently and respectfully places it on a shelf in the wall.

My missionary colleague and I marvel at the alacrity with which the students obey their elderly principal. In but a brief minute or two, he summarily sets aside the scheduled reading of their highly revered holy book. Perhaps he is being extravagantly gracious and hospitable to two American missionaries. After all, we are not free to go until our hosts have served us some tea and "biscuits" (actually, we would call them "cookies"). Then again, he might be deeply interested in what this new book has to say.

Having obtained his permission, I open the book and begin. When I finish reading the passage, the seemingly quiet and gentle man proves how insistent he can be. He snatches the book from my hands—I'm thinking, "Now I've done it!"—and, amazingly, he continues to read aloud to the end of the chapter. This senior Muslim cleric has just participated in a public reading of Luke 5:12–39. It is but the start of an extended relationship providing years of opportunity to present the gospel to two of the madrassa's teachers. From the beginning, the Word of God displays its power to attract and to alter a person's mind and heart.

Communicating in the People's Vernacular

Five hundred years earlier, on the opposite side of the world from Bangladesh, an Italian duke desires to own a sparrow hawk for hunting. He writes in formal Latin to a village mayor requesting that a sparrow hawk (*accipetrem*) be captured, tied up in a sack, and sent to him. When the letter is delivered, it provokes a good deal of concern. The villagers take it as a demand for the seizure and delivery of their popular archpriest (*arciprete* in their common Italian dialect). They know of no reason why the duke should be so displeased with the priest, but feel compelled to fulfill his request. Therefore, they seize the bewildered priest, bind him hand and foot, deposit him inside a heavy cloth sack, and deliver him to the duke's palace.

At the palace the package baffles the receiving official. "Do you have a letter?" he asks. A quick reading of the letter reveals the nature of the villagers' misunderstanding. Being informed of the situation, Duke Borso, in a diplomatic move to preserve the villagers' face, returns the priest with a letter informing them that he has changed his mind and that they may free the priest. From that time on, the duke writes to his vassals in their common language, not in official Latin.[2]

Over and over throughout its history, the Christian church has, unfortunately, repeated Duke Borso's mistaken use of formal language to communicate with ordinary folk. True to the biblical commission to evangelize (Matt. 28:19–20), Christians rightly attempt to convey the gospel concerning Jesus Christ to every possible language group in the world. Too often, however, Bible translators choose to employ a formal literary language instead of a common vernacular (i.e., the common language of the common person). The elderly cleric in the madrassa enthusiastically received the translation of the New Testament in the Muslim Bengali dialect because it spoke to him in his heart language. Missionary and national translators did not select a Hindu dialect for reaching out to Muslims, nor did they employ Christianized Bengali ignoring common Islamic vocabulary. The madrassa principal could understand what was read and he could easily read it for himself. The translation spoke directly to him without any linguistic barrier.

By the Holy Spirit's enablement, the living and active Word of God is the only instrument that can convert the human heart (Rom. 10:17; James 1:18; 1 Peter 1:23–25). No matter how many testimonies of conversion an unbeliever might hear, testimonies can only attract. God employs only the Word itself to accomplish the actual conversion. That biblical truth provides adequate authority and motivation for the inclusion of Bible translation ministries in the gospel outreach of the church among all peoples and language groups.

> ***Historians agree that Scriptures in the vernacular acted as catalysts for the Reformation.***

In various eras of church history, Christian translators have too often avoided vernacular translation, resulting in a divided church. During the most extreme times of division, the scholarly, cloistered clergy stand on one side of the divide, while on the other side sits a biblically illiterate laity. In the time leading up to the Reformation the debate intensified between adherents to a formal language and adherents to a common language in Bible translation. Historians agree that Scriptures in the vernacular acted as catalysts for the Reformation. William Tyndale biographer David Daniell is very specific: "The energy which affected every human life in Northern Europe, however, came from a different place. It was not the result of political imposition. It came from the discovery of the Word of God as originally written, from Matthew—indeed, from Genesis—to Revelation, in the language of the people."[3] Vernacular translation, however, did not make its first appearance on the stage of church history at the time of the Protestant Reformation. In fact, the concept and practice of vernacular Bible translations was *re*emerging following a long dormancy. Before taking up that history, we must consider briefly the question concerning the necessity of vernacular translation.

Why should the Christian church produce vernacular Bible translations? Pragmatically, individuals benefit from being able to read the Scriptures for fifteen minutes without becoming bored or bewildered by the style of the translation itself. So, Bible translations must be readable. The fact that the Bible is an ancient religious volume does not require a modern English translation to sound as though the Venerable Bede (672–735) himself had been resuscitated to write it in the patois of the thirteenth century. Nothing within the teaching of the Scriptures requires that the receiving language be as ancient as the Bible itself.

Pragmatically, individuals benefit from being able to read the Scriptures for fifteen minutes without becoming bored or bewildered by the style of the translation itself.

Many Bible translations employ a Hebrew-flavored language for both Old and New Testaments. This fact is equally true whether the receptor language is English, German, Bengali, or Swahili. In the modern world, White House news reporters do not write, "The President of the United States opened his mouth and spoke," nor do sports reporters announce that "Steph Curry dreamed a dream last night." Why then should translators retain a rendering that is practically incomprehensible to modern English readers? Compare the following two translations of Amos 4:2–3.

The Lord GOD hath sworn by his holiness, that, lo, the days shall come upon you, that he will take you away with hooks, and your posterity with fishhooks.	"The Lord GOD has sworn by his holiness that, behold, the days are coming upon you, when they shall take you away with hooks, even the last of you with fishhooks.
And ye shall go out at the breaches, every *cow at that which is* before her, and ye shall cast *them* into the palace, saith the LORD. (KJV)	And you shall go out through the breaches, each one straight ahead; and you shall be cast out into Harmon," declares the LORD. (ESV)

Granted, the second might be a clearer translation, but is either version as understandable in its English to modern readers as its original Hebrew to those who heard Amos proclaim his message? Should the translator or the reader be satisfied with a murky rendering? Are there sound theological or linguistic reasons for obscurity in a Bible translation? As we proceed with an examination of the history of Bible translation, as well as the principles and practices of Bible translation, we will discover answers to such questions.

A Greek Old Testament for Greek-Speaking Jews

Even before the time of Christ, Alexandrian Jews translated the Hebrew Bible into Greek in order to make it more widely available to both Jews and Gentiles who possessed little or no knowledge of biblical Hebrew. Jewish translators gathering first in Alexandria, Egypt, in the middle of the third century before Christ, permanently changed the history of the Bible with their translation of the five books of Moses (Genesis-Deuteronomy).[4] For the first time in its history, men translated the Bible into what, at the time, was a nonbiblical language. Up until then, serious-minded Jews transmitted the text in its original languages (Hebrew and Aramaic). The rabbis point out that all three divisions of the Hebrew Bible (our Old Testament) contain portions in Aramaic. An Aramaic place-name is to be found in the Torah, or Law (Gen. 31:47); one verse of Aramaic is found in the Nebi'im, or Prophets (Jer. 10:11); and, a considerable portion is found in the Kethubim, or Writings (Dan. 2:4–7:28; Ezra 4:8–6:18; 7:12–26). "Let not the Aramaic be lightly esteemed by thee, seeing that the Holy One (blessed be He!) hath given honour to it in the Law, the Prophets, and the Writings" (Palestinian Talmud, *Sota,* vii, 2). Jews and Christians alike have come to refer to the pre-Christian Greek translation of the Hebrew Bible as the Septuagint, meaning "seventy" (often abbreviated by the Roman numerals LXX). Its title originated from the tradition that seventy-two

Jewish scholars had participated in the translation of the Torah (the five books of Moses).[5] Eventually, second-century Christian writers selected "the seventy" as a nice round number by which to identify the translation.

During the writing of the New Testament, the Septuagint reigned as the Bible of choice, since the Hebrew text was not as readily available.

During the writing of the New Testament, the Septuagint reigned as the Bible of choice, since the Hebrew text was not as readily available. Therefore, when New Testament writers wished to cite the Old Testament, nearly seventy-five percent of the time they chose to quote the Septuagint or its equivalent.[6] In the early centuries of the Christian church, the church fathers relied heavily on the Septuagint for citing the Old Testament in their theological treatises, commentaries, and correspondence. F. C. Conybeare and St. George Stock, in their *Grammar of Septuagint Greek*, make the following observation:

> St. Augustine remarks that the Greek-speaking Christians for the most part did not even know whether there was any other word of God than the Septuagint (*C.D.* XVIII, 43). So when other nations became converted to Christianity and wanted the Scriptures in their own tongues, it was almost always the Septuagint which formed the basis of the translation. This was so in the case of the early Latin version, which was in use before the Vulgate; and it was so also in the case of the translations made into Coptic, Ethiopic, Armenian, Georgian, Gothic, and other languages. The only exception to the rule is the first Syriac version, which was made direct from the Hebrew.[7]

The Greek language of the Septuagint is Jewish Hellenistic Greek.[8] Linguistically, Septuagint Greek is not really a separate dialect of Greek, because the translators did not choose to utilize strictly Jewish vocabulary or phraseology. Apparent Semitic influences in both grammar and vocabulary may best be explained as a reflection of either translation philosophy and technique, or cultural influence (an extralinguistic factor).[9] The translators normally chose to render the Hebrew text literally, employing legitimate Greek vocabulary and grammatical constructions. The resulting Greek is not a formal literary Greek as much as it is the spoken Greek of the Jewish community residing in Egypt in the third century B.C. The Septuagint might well be considered the first vernacular translation of the Scriptures. Therefore, the New Testament writers employed a vernacular translation when quoting the Old Testament, not a formal literary translation.

Vernacular translation, as opposed to a formal literary translation, prevailed for the first translation of both Old and New Testaments into an extrabiblical language, the Syriac Peshitta. "Peshitta" means "simple" or "common." The translation began sometime in the second century A.D. and came to its standardized form around A.D. 400. Jerome's Latin Vulgate (completed just a few years after the standardization of the Peshitta) was also in the vernacular—thus the title "Vulgate," meaning "vulgar" or "common." These three ancient versions (Septuagint, Peshitta, and Vulgate) laid the foundation for vernacular Bible translations. Most subsequent pre-Reformation translations adhered to the same translation style.

A Bible for English Ploughmen

Nearly sixteen hundred years after Alexandrian Jews translated the Old Testament into Greek, John Wyclif (1330–84), the "morning star of the Reformation," declared that the Scripture should be available in a language common people can understand. Before the Reformation had gotten under way in Europe, he argued that God gave the Scriptures for all mankind:

> Christ and His Apostles taught the people in the language best known to them. It is certain that the truth of the Christian faith becomes more evident the more faith itself is known. Therefore, the doctrine should not only be in Latin but in the vulgar tongue and, as the faith of the church is contained in the Scriptures, the more these are known in a true sense the better. The laity ought to understand the faith and, as doctrines of our faith are in the Scriptures, believers should have the Scriptures in a language which they fully understand.[10]

Spurred on by his belief, Wyclif pioneered the translation of the Bible into English. However, many of his countrymen did not share his vision. At that time, the Roman Catholic Church considered any Bible translation in the common language of the people to be heretical. Henry Knighton, a Catholic historian of Wyclif's day responded to the concept in the following manner:

> Christ gave His Gospel to the clergy and the learned doctors of the Church so that they might give it to the laity and to weaker persons, according to the message of the season and personal need. But this Master John Wyclif translated the Gospel from Latin into the English—the Angle not the angel language. And Wyclif, by thus translating the Bible, made it the property of the masses and common to all and more open to the laity, and even to women who were able to read . . . . And so the pearl of the Gospel is thrown before swine and trodden underfoot and what is meant to be the treasure both of clergy and laity is now become a joke of both. The jewel of the clergy has been turned into the sport of the laity, so that what used to be the highest gift of the clergy and the learned members of the Church has become common to the laity.[11]

It has been said that Wyclif's translation determined which dialect would become the standard for England. However, Wyclif did not directly influence the establishment of Midland English as the standardized common language of England. London's prominence and England's geography and demographics affected that development more profoundly than any individual like Wyclif.[12] On the other hand, it would be correct to conclude that Wyclif disrupted the tyranny of the clergy[13] and interrupted the dominance of their Latin when he took his theological reasoning to the common people in the common language.[14] The English vernacular's rise displayed "double significance. It was a victory of the people's language over the Latin language of the learned few, and at the same time it was the victory of a popular vernacular (English) over what in England was an aristocratic vernacular (French)."[15]

German Bibles for Germany

Yet another great Bible translator in the period of the Reformation was Martin Luther. Historians, artists, and filmmakers focus on the Protestant Reformer's bold and confrontational actions and words. As a result, the church's collective memory highlights the nailing of his ninety-five theses to the cathedral door at Wittenberg and his bold stand at his trial in the Diet of Worms. These colorful and memorable scenes tend to overshadow his role in the translation of the Scriptures. Luther, however, was not the first to translate the Bible into German. According to John Reumann, before Luther's German translation, there had been others:

> Ufilas had put the Bible into Gothic before he died in A.D. 383, thus providing the oldest literary monument in a Germanic language. There are frag-

> ments preserved of a Frankish translation of Matthew, dated A.D. 738. Some unknown "German Tatian" provided a harmony of the gospels through a ninth-century translation. By the end of the Middle Ages, German manuscripts of the Bible numbered in the thousands. What is more, there were also German translations in print before Luther's day. The first printed Bible in any modern European language was the German version from the press of Johann Mentelin of Strassburg in 1466, and that translation went back to the fourteenth century. In all, four Low German translations and fourteen High German had appeared in print before Luther ever began his work. Eight to ten thousand vernacular copies were on the market, each costing the equivalent of a town house or fourteen oxen.[16]

By paying such prices, German laity demonstrated how highly they prized their German Bibles. Within fifty years, the Strassburg German translation (1466) from the Latin Vulgate went through eighteen editions.

History's verdict in land after land and century after century is clear: A Bible in the language of the learned or the aristocracy does not become the people's Bible. Since the Word of God is for all people, it must be made available in the language of the people. Every Bible translator and each translation team must identify the level and style of the average person's language within their target group. A Bible translation in any other level or style steps backward toward the pre-Reformation tyranny of a professional priesthood. Translators tend to choose language type and language level in accord with their convictions regarding the authority of Scripture, the priesthood of every believer, the role of the church, and the universality of the gospel. Insistence upon a high language level and formal style reflect a practical denial of those tenets. Those who held these doctrines became the champions of common language translations in the Reformation. The Reformation witnessed a logical and happy congruence of theology and translation.

History's verdict in land after land and century after century is clear: A Bible in the language of the learned or the aristocracy does not become the people's Bible.

In every area of Christian endeavor, the labor of one individual is often multiplied many times over by those whom he or she has influenced. A seemingly endless chain of interrelated ministries grows into an overflowing river of blessing. In like fashion, Luther's Bible translation in the vernacular German spawned a number of Reformation Bibles:

- Low German translations based on Luther's High German
- A Dutch translation of Luther's New Testament (1523)
- A Danish New Testament (1524) heavily dependent on Luther's German translation
- A Swedish New Testament (1526) by a blacksmith's son who had attended Luther's lectures
- An Icelandic New Testament (1540) borrowed extensively from Luther
- A Finnish Bible translation (1548–52) begun by a Finn acquainted with Luther
- A Modern Greek Pentateuch (1547)
- The Gospels in Polish (1551–52)
- A Hebrew New Testament (by 1600) for missionary work among Jews.
- A Slovenian Bible (1584) published at Wittenberg
- A Croatian New Testament (1562–63) for Slavs
- Prior to 1555 the English translations of Tyndale and Coverdale were influenced by Luther's work.[17]

All of these translations had a common thread: they were translations for common people in the language of the people. Leaders of the Reformation believed that God never intended His Word to be the property solely of the clergy. The Bible confirms this truth: in the Old Testament, the Lord demanded obedience from the people, not just the priests; in the New Testament, Christ spoke His parables and taught His doctrine to the common people of Israel. He did not confine Himself to the temple in order to teach only the doctors of Mosaic Law. Since the target of Scripture's teaching has always been the common person, its language has always been the common person's language.

Obedience Proportionate to Understanding

Bible translation in the vernacular is rooted and grounded in the teachings of the Word of God itself. God purposes to communicate with mankind so that a person might know who God is and what He requires.

How does God convey that communication? He chooses to utilize hearing and reading. A person can neither believe nor understand what he or she has not heard or read.[18] In addition, merely hearing or reading without understanding cannot produce full obedience. God's Word in an understandable language stimulates the proper response. A seminary professor wrote, "In Bible translation, faithfulness to the original meaning of a text is important, but it is not enough. The other critical test is what it enables its readers to understand."[19]

The challenge of Bible translation, therefore, is to make the Word of God understandable. It is one of the greatest challenges to which the Christian exegete or expositor might respond.

The challenge of Bible translation, therefore, is to make the Word of God understandable. It is one of the greatest challenges to which the Christian exegete or expositor might respond. Understanding is the goal of all proclamation of Scripture (see Matt. 13:13–15, 19, 23). Without understanding the Scriptures, a person is unable to implement biblical instruction through obedience. Without obedience there is no divine blessing. The more accurate one's understanding, the more exactly and fully he or she will obey, and the fuller the resulting blessing.

One's own language—the language of his or her everyday existence—acts as the most efficient medium for understanding the Scriptures. When dire circumstances press upon us and we cry out to God for help, we do so in our own heart's language. We normally do not respond with some formalized and archaic liturgical language. In other words, we cry out, "Please, God, don't let this happen to me—not here, not now!" instead of "Our Father, Who art in heaven; hallowed be Thy name. . . . O God of heaven and earth, halt Thou this turmoil that hath engulfed me!" No matter how many languages we speak, we most readily pray and dream in our native tongue. That language must become the Bible translator's language—the common language of the common people in any one cultural setting. It might be Arabic or Zulu, Bengali or Yaqui, Chinese or Xhosa. It could be a major dialect or a small tribal tongue. No matter what its identity or linguistic behavior, it exists as the heart language of a people to whom the church should proclaim God's Word. They comprise a people, a language group, for whom Christ accomplished His redemptive work. He redeemed them "from every tribe *and tongue* and people and nation" (Rev. 5:9 NASB, emphasis added).

> ***Translating the Bible into the common language of common people is an uncommon challenge that produces an uncommon reward.***

Translating the Bible into the common language of common people is an uncommon challenge that produces an uncommon reward. Each individual has the joy of explaining some aspect of life to an eager young learner. It may be a subject as theologically profound as the Trinity or as down-to-earth simple as gravity. One person utilizes amazing plants like the Venus flytrap and the closing leaves of a mimosa to explain the marvels of creation. Another may enlist a clear plastic model of an automobile's combustion engine as a teaching tool. Whatever the occasion or whatever the subject matter, there is no greater reward than to witness a young person's glowing countenance when understanding comes. Likewise, beaming faces and shining eyes testify to the dawn of spiritual understanding when it comes through the instrumentality of an understandable translation of the Bible.

How Can They Understand?

In Bible college and seminary I fulfilled the obligatory translation assignments from both the Greek New Testament and the Hebrew Old Testament. My teachers awarded grades for accuracy, but the process was often purely academic. I possessed no deep sense of divine accountability for such assignments. My heart was not burdened by the potential of misleading a reader who depended upon my translation for knowing the will of God. However, when I became a Bible translator in Bangladesh, all of that changed. A professor's grade was not my goal. How individuals understood my translation might determine whether they might come before the Lord with an adequate or an accurate understanding of His demands for them. As a result of fifteen years of Bible translation experience in Bangladesh, I returned to the seminary classroom determined to help students look upon their translation assignments with a heightened sense of accountability. How might any reader understand or react to their translation? Yes, accuracy matters, but so do understandability and clarity.

> ***A spelling mistake might turn a serious text into a real laugher.***

Translation involves more than just getting the meaning right; it involves correct spelling, in order to avoid misunderstanding. Spelling in one's own language is difficult enough; spelling in a second language is sometimes a nightmare. In English, I had only one *d* and one *t* to remember and to employ accurately. Bengali presented me with four *d*'s and four *t*'s! Proper spelling is important when it comes to Bible translation. A spelling mistake might turn a serious text into a real laugher. Consider a translation of Genesis 37:34 that one of my seminary students submitted to me: "he put sack cloth around his waste." Confusion between two homonyms (similar sounding words: "waist" and "waste") results in a very different mental picture. Instead of Jacob wrapping himself with sackcloth as a symbol of his mourning, the reader pictures him bagging his trash (or worse). In this case, the error was harmlessly committed in an academic environment. What if such an error were to slip into a published translation of the Bible? How many might be misled? Unbelievers in Mongolia or Montana, India, or Indiana, who possess little familiarity with the Bible, will not always be able to filter out erroneous translations as they read. Attention to detail must be the hallmark of every Bible translator. Accuracy depends upon it. Right understanding depends upon it.

Misspelling a word is one kind of potential error. Let's consider what happens when translators ignore just one little word in the original languages of Scripture. English versions commonly translate the command of the Holy Spirit in Acts 13:2 as something like, "Set apart for Me Barnabas and Saul for the work to which I have called them" (NAS; compare NIV, KJV, NKJV, ESV, NRSV). All of these translations ignore the little two-letter word *dē* (pronounced like "day") following the imperative "set apart" in the Greek text. Translators often treat that little word as though it were nothing more than a marker of "relatively weak emphasis—'then, indeed' or frequently not translated but possibly reflected in the word order."[20] J. P. Louw and Eugene Nida suggest the translation, "set apart for me, then, Barnabas and Saul to do the work for which I have called them."[21] However, A. T. Robertson, a venerated Greek scholar, indicates that this Greek particle, though difficult to translate, remains strongly emphatic.[22] Combined with an imperative (as in Acts 13:2), it conveys a "note of urgency."[23] The nature of the particle is such that no translator should omit it from the rendering of the verse.[24] Therefore, translators should consider wording the Holy Spirit's command in such a way that it conveys the concept of "do it immediately." The premier Greek lexicon of H. G. Liddell and Robert Scott supports Robertson's view of the particle by indicating that it is "used to give greater *exactness*, to the word or words which it influences . . . *now, in truth, indeed, surely, really* . . . often with Superlatives, . . . *quite* the greatest, *confessedly* the best . . . ."[25] What difference does it make? Omitting the force of this one tiny Greek particle reduces the sense of urgency with which the Holy Spirit addresses the Antioch church's leadership. Those men who received the Spirit's instruction clearly understood the urgency, since they apparently commissioned Saul and Barnabas for missionary service immediately following the completion of their prayer and fasting. In the SBCL and MBCL Bible translations we employed the adverb "now" (Bengali, *ekhon*) to represent the Greek particle ("set them apart now"). The discussion of this particular Greek particle should not be taken as a claim that all particles should be translated. As D. A. Carson points out, "precisely because particles are subtle things, one can always find instances where any particular translation has it wrong."[26]

One verse's treatment in a Bible version does not necessarily characterize the overall translation philosophy and accuracy of that version.

How do these observations about Acts 13:2 affect an individual's understanding of the role of translation, the evaluation of translations, and the practical use of various Bible translations? Being aware of the potential for error in a translation should make each person aware of the fact that no translation of the Bible perfectly conveys every detail of the original languages in every passage. Also, one verse's treatment in a Bible version does not necessarily characterize the overall translation philosophy and accuracy of that version. We will pursue the topic of evaluating English Bible versions in chapter 8.

As a result of the matters we have discussed above, certain recommendations might be offered regarding the use of Bible translations.

- *Use a variety of versions in order to compare translations.* Through multiple translations, readers might become aware of details they sometimes miss in one translation as compared to another.
- *Refer to good commentaries based upon the original languages of Scripture.* By utilizing such tools, readers might discover which translation most closely represents the meaning of the original text.

Unfortunately, virtually every available English version provides incomplete or inaccurate translations of a few texts like Acts 13:2. However, the reader may rest assured that such situations are rare occurrences. Despite the variations one finds between popular English Bible translations, those versions testify to the faithful preservation of the God-given text with but rare exception. As a result, texts like Acts 13:2 and their less than accurate translation seldom affect major doctrinal teaching. But, having no major doctrinal implication need not eliminate the significance of each and every detail within the text. No Bible translator has the freedom to select certain elements of biblical content for preservation and to excise the remainder from the text. A translation must be fully accurate, not selective or partial in its translational integrity.

Despite the variations one finds between popular English Bible translations, those versions testify to the faithful preservation of the God-given text with but rare exception.

Ezra and the Books of Moses

When their exile in Babylon ends, the Jews return to Judah under the patronage of Cyrus, king of Persia. Back in the land out of which God had evicted them, they face external opposition from the Samaritans (Ezra 4–5; Neh. 4; 6). Their internal problems include the treatment of the poor (Neh. 5) and the divisiveness of intermarriage with Gentiles (Ezra 9–10). The latter problem creates a multilingual situation in Israelite homes (Neh. 13:23–24). That only intensifies the language problem the exiles bring with them from their captivity in Babylon, for most of them no longer speak Hebrew.

Yet, in the midst of all their problems, the people of Israel hunger for the Word of God. They desire divine direction so that God will not uproot them from their land again because of their disobedience to His teachings. The returned exiles express a desire to gather at the Water Gate in Jerusalem, and they request Ezra to read the Law of Moses to them (Neh. 8:1). The first day of the seventh month begins the civil New Year and the observance of the Feast of Trumpets (Lev. 23:23–25; Num. 29:1–6). Thus, the Israelites make some preparations for the occasion. Carpenters construct a platform of wood so that the gathered Israelites will be able to both see and hear Ezra (Neh. 8:4). Timing and arrangements are purposeful, but the eager attentiveness of the people is spontaneous (Neh. 8:3).

Ezra discerns that the people of Israel need spiritual revival. Indeed, he understands that obedience to the Scriptures will provide the catalyst for such a revival. He realizes, too, that obedience is predicated upon understanding. If the people cannot understand any particular instruction, they cannot obey fully—the more complete the understanding, the more complete the obedience. With this in mind, Ezra appoints men to help him in the task of proclamation, translation, and interpretation (Neh. 8:4, 7–8).

A threefold process takes place on the day of assembly. First, Ezra and some of the appointed men read aloud the text of the Law of Moses in the ancient Hebrew language in which it had been written: "They read from the book, from the law of God" (Neh. 8:8 NASB). Second, they translate the text into the language most returnees best understand after seventy years of Babylonian captivity. At the time, Aramaic, the language of Babylon, dominates as the language of the common Israelite. Interestingly, modern Hebrew script reveals just how much the Babylonian exile affected the people of Israel linguistically. What we call the "Hebrew" script today is actually an Aramaic script borrowed from Babylon.[27] The borrowing can be dated to the time of Ezra. Two different phrases in Nehemiah 8:8 may be interpreted as a reference to translation: "distinctly, and gave the sense" (KJV/NKJV)—compare ESV ("clearly, and they gave the sense"), NIV ("making it clear and giving the meaning"), and NASB ("translating to give the sense"). In other words, the best interpretation of the verse as a whole indicates that Ezra and his fellow teachers translated the reading of the Hebrew text into the more commonly understood Aramaic.

Third, Ezra and the leaders working with him cause the people "to understand." The words "understanding," "understand," and "understood" occur repeatedly in Nehemiah 8 (vv. 2, 3, 7, 8, 12, and 13). It is significant that the record of the events of that New Year's Day emphasizes understanding. The purpose of translating and interpreting is that people might understand (v. 8). The Israelites rejoice because they understand (v. 12). They even assemble again for that same purpose ("to understand," v. 13).

Hearing the Scriptures in their heart language, the people understand it so well that it produces a degree of obedience not seen in nearly one thousand years. They set about to observe the Feast of Booths in complete compliance with the Law of Moses. Not since the time of Joshua has there been such a complete and accurate observance of the Feast of Booths (v. 17). Out of such obedience even greater joy emerges (v. 18). What is more, one of Scripture's most beautiful prayers (Neh. 9) results from the experience of such understanding and obedience. All these things (the obedience, the joy, the prayer, and the ongoing desire to know more) arises out of understanding—an understanding rooted and grounded in the Aramaic vernacular translation, which they now understand better than they do the original Hebrew.

Vernacular Bible translation is an imperative, not an option.

For such a spiritual experience to occur in the present, ministers of God's Word must give equal attention to the production of an understandable translation of the Bible. Anything less results in the perpetuation of spiritual mediocrity—a mediocrity that could continue for more than a thousand years like it did in ancient Israel. Vernacular Bible translation is an imperative, not an option.

Jesus and the Parable of the Sower

Matthew 13:1–23 offers many enticing tidbits for the interested reader's study. Two significant statements occur in verses 19 and 23. Just like

Nehemiah 8, the key concept repeated in Matthew 13:1–23 is *understanding* (vv. 13, 14, 15, 19, and 23). In His interpretation of the parable of the sower (vv. 19–23), Jesus makes it clear that dissemination of God's Word depends upon understanding His words. If recipients of God's Word do not understand the words, Satan ("the wicked one") will be victorious (v. 19). On the other hand, if hearers and readers understand the Word, fruitfulness results and God will be victorious (v. 23).

Believers normally desire two spiritual products in their lives: joy and fruitfulness. Obedience to Scripture produces both. The more completely the believer understands Scripture, the more completely obedient he or she can be. Difficulty in understanding a Bible translation hinders the highest degree of obedience, thereby diminishing joy and fruit, or shutting down these two products completely. Translations difficult to understand tend to be unfruitful. If a Bible translation is too easily misunderstood, it can produce confusion, satanic interference, and spiritual starvation.

Lest we overstate the matter, it is true that a proper understanding of Scripture does not rest with translation alone. Translation does not eliminate the need for exposition and teaching. Nor does translation ignore the responsibility of the reader of God's Word to obey what they do understand. Adding too much to the text in the service of clarity can force a translation into the realm of inaccuracy and the insertion of too much subjective interpretation. As Sijbolt Noorda explains, "Ancient texts, and especially ancient religious texts, are not conspicuous by their clarity. We'd better be prepared in their case for some opacity, some obscurity. . . . We should practice restraint, avoiding excessive explanation and explication."[28] George Steiner simply states: "Bad translations communicate too much."[29] Translators too often face the temptation to overinterpret. Leland Ryken rightly complains about this very problem with many dynamic equivalence translations. In his words, "A translation that substitutes an interpretation for what the original actually says . . . removes the foundation on which to build a trustworthy interpretation of a text."[30]

Difficult as it might be, translators must allow the biblical text to force readers to think, rather than to be lazy in their approach to the text. Wisdom literature (as in Proverbs, Ecclesiastes, and some psalms in the Psalter) purposefully utilizes some ambiguity and incomplete statements to cause the hearers and readers to cogitate. God did not design Scripture to encourage lazy thinkers. Instead, He commands believers, "prepare your minds for action" (1 Peter 1:13 NASB; compare NKJV, "gird up the loins of your mind"—an apt cultural figure describing how a man in ancient times would tuck his long robe into his belt in order that his legs be unhindered in running or working). God desires that we use the minds He gave us. He demands we put them to work when we read His written Word.

With God's command in mind, how much interpretation should a translation reflect? What kind of interaction should exist between translation and exposition? Does the New Testament itself provide any direction concerning these matters? Its writers often translate Hebrew texts from the Old Testament and Aramaic statements from their own immediate environment into Greek. Should we follow their model? In order to answer that question, we now turn to a significant example in Acts 8.

Philip, the Ethiopian Eunuch, and Isaiah

When persecution came to the church in Jerusalem, a deacon named Philip (Acts 6:5) became an evangelist in Samaria (Acts 8:4, 5; 21:8). According to Acts 8, an angel from God directed Philip to "Go south to the road—the desert road—that goes down from Jerusalem to Gaza" (v. 26). Finding an Ethiopian eunuch in a chariot headed back to his home country, Philip hears him reading from a scroll the eunuch evidently had purchased before leaving Jerusalem. Philip asks, "Do you understand what you are reading?" (v. 30). This high official from the court of Queen Candace of Ethiopia appears to be a proselyte to the Jewish faith. A comparison of Acts 8:32–33 with Isaiah 53:7–8 reveals that he is reading the Greek Septuagint translation of the Old Testament. Greek is not his heart language, but it is the *lingua franca* (a convenient language for trading goods) of that day. Further investigation uncovers the fact that the Septuagint's translation of Isaiah 53:7–8 is "gravely deviant."[31] In spite of the handicaps, enough of the truth comes through with Philip's helpful guidance so that the eunuch comes to Christ by faith for salvation from his sins.

Until he clearly understands the Bible's message, the Ethiopian official cannot come to Christ. Theological realities (see John 8:43–44; 1 Cor. 2:14; Eph. 4:18) and language barriers both impair his understanding. Even though the Ethiopian has some proficiency in Greek, the poor quality of the translation hinders his understanding. Miraculously, the Holy Spirit intervenes to compensate for the deviant translation (Acts 8:29). In this situation the Spirit intervenes by sending Philip to provide a more accurate translation and explanation.

From this brief account in Acts 8 we learn several facts about Bible translations:

- *God can use a second language or even a deviant translation to bring people to Christ.* The Scripture in flawed Greek speaks to the Ethiopian's heart and stirs him to believe in Christ.
- *A translation may be so poor that by itself it cannot be the instrument of the Holy Spirit's work of regeneration.* The Septuagint Greek translation of Isaiah 53 is too flawed to bring the Ethiopian all the way to a complete saving knowledge of Christ without adequate instruction from someone like Philip.
- *Understandability is the key factor in regard to the efficacy of a Bible translation.* Only when the eunuch understands what Isaiah says does he believe in Christ and experience Holy Spirit regeneration.

The Holy Spirit normally operates by convicting the heart of the person who is reading God's Word in his native language.

We must realize that the understanding produced by the Word of God commences on the linguistic level, then moves to the spiritual. A missionary should not distribute Greek New Testaments to Americans, Mexicans, Ugandans, or Thais with the expectation that God will perform a miracle and allow the recipients to understand the Greek. The Holy Spirit normally operates by convicting the heart of the person who is reading God's Word in a language he or she understands—especially one's own language. Granted, believers, as well as unbelievers, will always find portions of the Scriptures difficult to fathom spiritually, even if the language itself is perfectly understandable. As Charles Taber points out,

> Understanding is never instantaneous nor is it "perfect or total. It can and does improve with time, and becomes sufficient for all practical purposes; and one can understand parts of M [the message] very well. But there is always room for growth and correction in our understandings. And yet through this humanly imperfect process, the marvel is that God speaks to

> us with power and clarity from the Scriptures, so that one can learn to know him, and to discern and do his will."[32]

But, that does not release the translator from the responsibility of rendering the Scriptures as clearly and accurately as possible. According to Peter, the epistles of the apostle Paul contain "some things hard to understand" (2 Peter 3:16 NKJV). Peter does not mean that Paul's vocabulary and grammar are too sophisticated, odd, foreign, or outdated. Spiritual concepts are the heart of the problem. Bible translation ministries must focus on the nuts and bolts of communication (and thus, of translation)—in other words, on language itself.

Some people, like the Ethiopian of old, read portions of the Bible in their second or even third language. No substitute exists, however, for reading God's Word in one's first language. Consider the testimony of a present-day "Ethiopian":

> Skip Firchow and David Akoitai (ah-KOY-tie) sat at the plywood desk translating Mark's Gospel into the Rotokas language. A cool breeze drifted through the open window, heralding the rain that fell every afternoon on this Papua New Guinean (PNG) island of Bougainville.
>
> Akoitai re-read the verse they'd just translated. He thought for a moment and then said to Skip, "When I read God's Word in my own language, it's much easier for me to understand than when I read it in English.
>
> "Trying to read the English Bible is like trying to drink out of a cup with a lid on it. I know there's water inside, but I can't get at it. When I read the Bible in Tok Pisin [PNG's main trade language], I understand it a little. It's like I can pry the lid partway off. I can sip some of the water.
>
> "But when I read the Bible in my own language, it's like drinking deeply from a full cup with no lid! My thirst is quenched. I understand completely."[33]

After nearly two thousand years of church history, one would think that at least the major languages of the world would possess understandable translations of the Bible. Even major languages, however, may have Bibles whose language the common person finds difficult to understand.

Bengali, the language of Bangladesh (formerly East Pakistan) and India's West Bengal, is one such language. According to the eighteenth edition of the Summer Institute of Linguistics's *Ethnologue* (SIL International, 2015), 245 million Bengali-speaking peoples comprise the world's tenth largest language group (surpassed in populations only by speakers of Mandarin Chinese, English, Spanish, Arabic, Hindi, Malay, Russian, French, and Portuguese—in that order). In 1966 the Association of Baptists for World Evangelism (ABWE) established a team of missionary and national translators to produce a new Bengali Bible in Bangladesh. Principles and practices learned in that translation project form a large part of my own experience in Bible translation and form a background for this book.

Since the first Greek translation of the Old Testament (the Septuagint) 2,300 years ago, Bible translation history chronicles the spread of God's Word to the farthest corners of the globe. A common language Bible for common people is that history's hallmark. The principle is rooted and grounded in the teachings of both Scripture Testaments. Ezra's public reading of the Law, Jesus Christ's parable of the sower, and the account in the book of Acts concerning the conversion of the Ethiopian all provide a powerful witness to the role of understanding how Scripture impacts people's lives.

The Reformation gave birth to a new eruption of Bible translations. In the past two centuries since William Carey's remarkable translation work in over forty Indian languages, Bible translation once again flourishes. The Bengali Common Language Bibles in the Muslim (MBCL) and the standard (SBCL) dialects serve as a recent example. Reading from the Gospel of Luke in the madrassa marked a seminal moment in my understanding of what effectively communicating the Word of God across linguistic and cultural boundaries involves. If Viggo Olsen[34] had not heeded God's leading into a ministry of Bible translation, that Muslim dialect Bengali New Testament would not have been available and I would not have had the experience of reading it in the mosque. Literally thousands of Muslims in Bangladesh have come to faith in Jesus Christ through that translation. Its language is their language, but its message is God's message. The language barrier has been shattered, now the Spirit of God is at work to tear down the spiritual barriers.

In the next chapter, we will examine common language translation more closely. How does one identify a so-called "common language"? What makes a particular Bible version a common language translation?

CHAPTER 2

COMMON LANGUAGE FOR COMMON PEOPLE

STANDING BEFORE A BIBLE CONFERENCE AUDIENCE in Čakovec, Croatia, I greeted the attendees with a brief and amateurish greeting in Croat. By the beaming faces, one would have thought that I had just given everyone a great gift. In fact, I had. By saying something in their heart language, I had shown respect for them and their native tongue. Everywhere I travel (perhaps with the exception of France, where people seem to take umbrage at amateurish pronunciations of their beloved language), I find the same response. The average person normally forgives mistaken pronunciations and basks in the glory of yet another speaker who recognizes, respects, and attempts to learn what he or she can of their language.

This should come as no surprise. First and foremost, people establish their social identity by means of their spoken language. Varieties of languages and dialects began at the tower of Babel (Gen. 11:1–9). From the time God divided the one original language into many, people have a distinct tendency to congregate by languages. Individuals who speak *with* one another normally speak *like* one another. Languages are not excessively monolithic—there are often a number of subgroups speaking a variety or dialect within a single language group. Bible translators must identify the common language of their target population. But, what exactly is the *common language* of any group of people?

The Same Vocabulary

Martha, give me the spider hanging on the wall. It's time to cook our dinner.

« « « » » »

American English spoken by Bostonians, southerners, Maineiacs, and Californians exhibits distinctly regional forms and vocabulary. In the coastal South of the United States and in parts of the North, "spider" is the term used for what people in the Midwest call a "skillet." The term commonly used by all regions is "frying pan."[35] Translating a kitchen manual from Portuguese to English requires that the translators first establish how widely they wish the manual's distribution to be. If they limit their target audience to the Midwestern United States, they might consider employing that region's common language equivalent, "skillet." However, if the target consists of the entire United States, authors will opt for "frying pan" as a common language translation extending throughout the whole country.

Common in this sense does not refer to any low, vulgar, or slang forms. It is the language dominating the public media—the language all American English speakers understand in common, regardless of regional dialect.

Major American television network newscasts attempt to employ only those forms and vocabulary common to all people in all regions of the United States. Common American English language is not gutter language—as much of a surprise as that might be in light of the marked increase in vulgar language on popular television programs. *Common* in this sense does not refer to any low, vulgar, or slang forms. It is the language dominating the public media—the language all American English speakers understand in common, regardless of regional dialect. Technically, therefore, a common language translation utilizes the commonly held language of a predetermined group of people. English is a major language group with a number of major dialects like British English, American English, Canadian English, Australian English, and New Zealand English—to name but a few of the major ones. While these five major dialects have much in common, there are also significant differences in both vocabulary and grammar. For example, in British English a teacher "*takes* an exam" while a student "*gives* an exam." In American English the teacher "*gives* an exam" while the student "*takes* an exam." The identical English phrase carries two totally different meanings in the two dialects.

Just as English is not the language of England alone, so Bengali is the language of Bangladesh, but not of Bangladesh alone. It exists as but one of the Indian subcontinent's major languages (others include such tongues as Hindi, Telugu, and Tamil). As the capital of West Bengal, Calcutta's vernacular is also Bengali. Before the partition of India in 1947 Bangladesh was known as East Bengal, West Bengal's neighboring Indian state. Decade after decade the ongoing development of the language of all Bengal perceptibly changes. Since the days of William Carey (1796–1834), who first translated the Bible into Bengali, the region's peoples recognize two distinct dialects of Bengali. According to J. S. M. Hooper (and W. J. Culshaw), Bengali

> was the first of the modern Indian languages to experience the full force of the wind of change at the beginning of the nineteenth century. . . . There are two distinct styles of literary expression: the first is known as *sadhu bhasha,* commonly translated "chaste language," a dignified style which adheres as closely as possible to Sanskrit in its vocabulary, having a somewhat rigid syntax. The other is known as the *chalti bhasha.* This is not quite the same as a colloquial style though it reflects to a great degree the speech of educated persons in Calcutta. It emphasizes modern usage more than rules and might be called the "contemporary style." This form of literary expression under the magic touch of Rabindranath Tagore became a powerful medium for the expression of ideas. One of the pioneers of prose writing in the *sadhu bhasha* was William Carey, whose most notable work of translation was that of the Bible into Bengali.[36]

These two Bengali dialects are class-oriented and socially driven. Carey's choice of the higher form of the language contributed to the demise of his Bengali Bible translation. While Carey's translation became a museum piece and a curiosity, the poems of Tagore capture the hearts of common Bengali-speaking people to this very day.

At first blush a common language might seem to be easy to reproduce in a Bible translation. After all, common language normally avoids technical vocabulary and highfaluting syntax. In actuality, however, it proves to be a difficult task. Leland Ryken rightly warns that

> the fact that God stooped to human understanding when he revealed his truth in human words does not itself settle the question of how simple or sophisticated, how transparent or complex, the Bible is. Human language encompasses an immense range of simplicity and difficulty. Nor does the fact that God accommodated himself to human understanding in itself say anything about the level of intelligence and artistic sophistication possessed by the writers and assumed audience of the Bible.[37]

When preaching or teaching in Bengali in Bangladesh, I often employ illustrations from their poet laureate, Rabindranath Tagore. What constantly amazes me is that even little children will stop their fussing and fidgeting as soon as they hear Tagore's words. It is almost scary—one can hear a proverbial pin drop. Tagore's language is simple, yet majestic. He did not choose the elevated language employed by William Yates's 1844 translation of Scripture, nor did he choose the lowest level of language that we tend at times to prefer as foreign speakers looking for simplicity and directness. True understanding does not negate high literary standards. Tagore was the Bengali wordsmith par excellence. His example is the best to follow. Just how does one go about doing that? It begins with the "ABC's" of spelling and extends through the employment of literary devices. Of all the SBCL Old Testament, I consider our Psalms translation to come the nearest to the standards reflected in Tagore's poems. Our core translation team, consisting of two missionaries (Dr. Lynn Silvernale and myself—during our absences Harold Ebersole worked with the team). These missionaries worked daily with two Bangladeshis (Mr. Polycarp Dores and Mrs. Basanti Das—during their absences Shamsul Alam Polash worked with the team). The entire team labored long hours to obtain the right reading and preserve accurately the exact meaning of the original Hebrew text of the Psalter. The literary skills Mr. Dores and Mrs. Das possessed served us well in that task. Mr. Dores had taught Bengali language and literature at the college level and Mrs. Das had taught in a girls' school and was an accomplished author. As native-born Bengali speakers their contribution to the translation project cannot be overstated.

In addition to historical and progressive changes in the development of the Bengali language, geographical or local variations in the language exist. Differences occur between the Bengali spoken in West Bengal (in India) and that spoken in East Bengal (Bangladesh). For example, "bread" in Calcutta is *roti* (pronounced *roh-tee*), but in Dhaka it is *ruti* (pronounced *roo-tee*). In addition, the two major regional dialects may be sub-divided within both countries into a number of local dialects. Chittagonian, Rangpuri, Sylheti, Bogran, and Comillan comprise just a few of the many subregional dialects in Bangladesh. Fortunately, a common standardized Bengali exists throughout all of Bangladesh's regions, making it possible to provide a Bible translation commonly understood by all Bengali-speaking people in the country regardless of their local dialect.

Dialects, like major languages, also fail to be monolithic. Great diversity can occur among sub-regional dialects. For example, in local dialects of Bengali there are many ways to express the English word "son" (meaning a male child or person in relation to his parents or parent):

- *chaowa* in Dinajpur
- *chaowal* in Pabna
- *shaowal* in Dhaka
- *showal* in Khulna
- *shal* in Jessore,
- *hola* in Noakhali
- *byata* in Bogra and Rangpur
- *put* or *pala* in Mymensingh
- *pua* in Sylhet
- *poa* in Chittagong

The high literary Bengali, or *sadhu bhasha,* is *putra* (pronounced *poo-troh*) while the common Bengali, or *chalti bhasha,* consists of *chele* (pronounced *cheh-lay*). Obviously, such a variety of possible ways to say "son" can cause problems for a Bible translation team attempting to provide a translation that means the same thing to all of its readers throughout the entire country. Translators must seek the Bengali term that everyone, no matter what his or her dialect, will understand clearly.

The SBCL Bible translation project in Bangladesh employs the common language of Bengali-speaking peoples. The translators adhere to the following principle:

- *Common language has priority over dialectal, literary, or technical language. Words and constructions understood by everyone take precedence over those known only to the highly educated or to those from but one region of the country.*

Therefore, the SBCL opts for *chele* as the translation of "son" when referring to human relationships. For the purpose of indicating a different relationship between God the Father and God the Son, however, we use the higher and more literary *putra* in all references to the Son of God. (Note that I used no capitalization with *putra*, even though referring to the Son of God. The Bengali language's Devanagari script does not use capitalization—just one of the challenges faced by Bible translators in many languages.) Throughout the translation process we sent drafts to various parts of the country for readers to send us feedback. These Bangladeshi checkers provided invaluable assistance in accomplishing the goal of a Bible translation that is understood across dialectal boundaries.

To aid the Bible translation team in its pursuit of the common Bengali language, the translators established the following guideline for vocabulary and forms to be employed in the SBCL Bible:

- *The language (especially vocabulary, as compared to grammar) of people in the 25–35 age group is to have priority over people older than 35 and younger than 25. This age group uses that which is today's accepted Bengali.*

Translators performed a linguistic survey in order to identify the group most accurately representative of the *chalti bhasha* ("common language") in Bangladesh. Since the under-25 age group represents over half of the population of Bangladesh, this group dominates the common language. The language of youth also dominates common American English, even though American youth are a much smaller segment of their country's population than the youth of Bangladesh. Around the globe television commercials employ youthful faces and bodies, youthful activities, and youthful vocabulary to sell everything from automobiles to zippers. Media molds the language of a people. Today's youth-speak affects tomorrow's language for good or ill.

> ***Around the globe television commercials employ youthful faces and bodies, youthful activities, and youthful vocabulary to sell everything from automobiles to zippers.***

Senior citizens in the United States may refer to a "stereo as a *hi-fi, record player, phonograph,* or *Victrola.* Similarly, the word *icebox* is still used by some people to refer to what younger generations call a *refrigerator*"[38] or just "fridge." And, of course, CD players, iPods, and smartphones have long since replaced the phonograph player. Large differences exist between the older generation's language and the newer generation's usage. Our grandchildren recently spoke of "excellent" things as "sick" things ("Wow! Jumping off a cliff into the water is sick") much in the same way their parents (our children) used "bad" for "good" ("That's a bad motorcycle!").

Languages continue to develop through the dynamic of age difference, because no language remains the same. All languages change. Historical and social developments within a language group determine the rate of change. Consider the simple fact that the older English versions' "meat offering" (e.g., Lev. 2:4 KJV) does not involve meat at all. Essentially, as the newer versions indicate, it was a "meal offering" (Exod. 40:29 NAS). This is not a typographical error switching a *t* for an *l*—in early English "meat" was a word often used of any food. It was often used of the grain fed to horses or cows.[39] Serious Bible translators should not utilize "meat offering" in English translations today. Translation decisions reverting to an older form of the receptor language (such as KJV English) tend to cause confusion and produce some very strange interpretations by readers who fail to note the changes in their own spoken language.

To become more aware of how language changes, it is helpful to read about the histories of various Bible translations. Such awareness has other benefits as well: it produces an appreciation for those who have labored in the field of Bible translation and it reveals that no *translation* is perfect, because no *translator* is perfect. The history of Tyndale's English Bible translation provides an excellent place to begin.

Tyndale's New English Translation

William Tyndale (1494–1536) published his English translation of the Bible in 1525. The earlier English of Wyclif's translations (1382–88) needed replacing because over "the course of two centuries the English language had undergone such great changes that his translation was no longer understood."[40] For his task, Tyndale possessed an unusual ability to translate Hebrew and Greek into an exceedingly pleasant and understandable form of English. (Blessed indeed is the Bible translation team that includes such a gifted speaker and writer of the receptor language.) Differences between Wyclif's translation and Tyndale's translation run far deeper than variation in the development of the language, however. David Daniell, Tyndale's modern biographer, points out that

> Tyndale's Genesis was something strikingly new. He was translating not the Latin, but the Hebrew. And he was writing recognisable English. Simply registering the changes in the English language from Chaucer's day to Tyndale's in no way explains the difference between 'Be made light; and made is light' and 'let there be light and there was light'.[41]

Today we would do well to follow Tyndale's insistence upon translating directly from the original biblical languages rather than from an extant translation—no matter how entrenched an authorized translation like the Vulgate or Old Bengali Bible or KJV (or in the future, the NIV or the ESV) has become. Over four hundred years of change in the English language (1611–today) has altered dramatically the meanings of biblical words and phrases like "gay clothing" (James 2:3 KJV; compare ESV, "fine clothing," and GNT, "well-dressed"). When translators base their translation upon another version in the same receptor language (e.g., the NIV or GNT), "it is in a double sense prone to the danger of inevitable distortions of the original text's meaning, or more positively, runs the risk of being twice removed from the source text's particular significance."[42] The same problem presents itself when revising an older translation. For example, although the New American Standard Update (1995, NASB) made nearly 20,000 changes in the NAS,[43] it still failed through the 2003 edition to correct an error in Psalm 14:4 where both NAS and NASB retained "Lord" for יהוה (*YHWH* = "Yahweh") instead of "Lord." Sometime after the 2003 reprint editors finally corrected that longstanding error.

Tyndale's prime directive was "to put nothing in the way of being understood."[44] As a result, his translation sounds more up-to-date today than the KJV, which was translated nearly one hundred years after Tyndale's.[45] Take for example, 1 Thessalonians 4:15 where the KJV has "shall not prevent," but Tyndale used "shall not come yerre"—"prevent" is easily misunderstood today, while "come yerre" (= "come before") carries a clearer meaning. Or, consider the example of Galatians 3:8, "And the scripture, foreseeing that God would justify the heathen through faith, preached before the gospel unto Abraham, *saying*, In thee shall all nations be blessed" (KJV) and "For the scripture sawe afore hande/that God wolde justifye the hethen thorow fayth/ & therfore shewed before hande glad tydynges unto Abrahā: In the shall all nacions be blessed" (Tyndale). The translation "glad tidings" of Tyndale avoids the interpretation that the "gospel" (KJV) here refers to the death and resurrection of Christ for forgiveness of sins by which one is saved. Tyndale used the word "gospel" in other texts, such as Mark 1:15 ("the tyme is come/and the kyngdō of God is at hande/repēt & beleve the Gospell") and Romans 15:20 ("So have I enforsed my selfe to preache the gospel/not wher Christ was named/least I shulde have bylt on another mannes foundacion"). Common language translations like Tyndale's usually possess a timeless quality. Ronald Knox, perhaps the greatest Roman Catholic Bible translator after Jerome himself, put it this way:

> The moral, surely, is that anybody who tries to do a new translation of the Bible in these days should aim at producing something which will not, in fifty or a hundred years' time, be "dated". In a word, what you want is neither sixteenth-century English nor twentieth-century English, but timeless English. Whether you can get it, is another question.[46]

No translator attains lasting understandability easily. One needs the artistic and linguistic touch of a Tyndale plus dogged persistence to try option after option until one rendering proves accurate, acceptable, and wonderfully pleasant to tongue and ear.

Translators must avoid what Workman calls "'stencil translation,' emphasizing the mechanical nature of the process."[47] An extreme example would be in the following retention of Hebrew word order in Psalm 19:1

in order to reproduce the chiasm[48] present in the original language. Note that the result is grammatically confusing in English, if read in the order of the Hebrew text's structure.

> The heavens
>   are declaring
>   the glory of God,
>   And the work of His hands
>   is making known
> the firmament.

A more frequent example of "stencil translation" occurs when translators in languages outside English attempt to employ a single term for theologically technical and exclusive terms like "propitiation," "reconciliation," "redemption," and "sanctification."[49] Such terms or their technical equivalents may not exist in another language. This is not true of theological terms alone. What about the variety of plants and animals in the Bible? Some languages are extremely restricted in certain realms of vocabulary. Steiner reports that "the gauchos of the Argentine know some 200 expressions for the colours of horses' hides, and such discrimination is obviously vital to their economy. But their normal speech finds room for only four plant names."[50] Therefore, in preparing a translation for the Argentine gauchos, hyssop or cedar or fig might have no equivalent terms.

Translators may become so casual in translating the Bible that they end up obscuring rather than clarifying.

Bible translators must make choices based upon their understanding of a particular text. Daniell cites the example of Tyndale's translation of John 14:1 ("Let not your hearts be troubled"). Tyndale may have chosen "heart" rather than "mind" because he felt that "a troubled heart is . . . a more sorrowful thing than having a troubled mind."[51] In an attempt to be more understandable, translators of the GNT utilized "Do not be worried and upset"—"as if the disciples were being told by Jesus to cheer up after having missed a bus."[52] As this example reveals, it is possible to go too far with common language translation. Translators may become so casual in translating the Bible that they end up obscuring rather than clarifying.

Interpreting the text in order to translate is not something only Tyndale did. According to Adele Berlin, the challenge of Bible translation from the original languages resides in the fact that it "is an abbreviated form of exegesis: exegesis that does not have the space to explain or justify itself."[53] The SBCL translation we produced in Bangladesh does not contain any interpretive notes. We had set a goal to express the text clearly without explanation. My Hebrew students find it somewhat exasperating when I require them to produce a translation without any footnotes explaining their choices. Pure translation is not an exercise for the lazy. The better translators labor to find the words and phrases that make no explanation necessary, but keep as close to the original text as possible.

Unfortunately, in the quest for a clear translation, some Bible translators rely upon paraphrastic expansions, rather than essentially literal renderings. This kind of excess prompted Ryken to write *The Word of God in English: Criteria for Excellence in Bible Translation*.[54] However, when he writes that "one cannot formulate a theology without theological vocabulary"[55] (words like "propitiation," "justification," and "redemption"), his argument focuses only on the English language and English Bibles. Many languages lack a theological vocabulary of the breadth and depth found in English. Some theologians might suggest that translators create new words to enrich the receptor language, but great care must be taken in inventing new words for a language. One of the reasons William Carey's Bengali Bible translation did not survive rests with his penchant for creating new terms from ancient Pali or Sanskrit that never caught on.[56]

Some languages await someone with Tyndale's talents for centuries. On the Asian subcontinent, Carey did not discover such a person for his Bengali Bible translation project. After Carey's death in 1834, his colleague William Yates spent ten years retranslating the Bengali Bible. Mainline churches in Bangladesh and India still use the Yates translation. Over fifteen revisions have been produced in an attempt to keep pace with developments in modern Bengali. However, even with the revisions, sections of the translation contain words no longer listed in Bengali dictionaries. The need for a common language translation became quite evident to missionaries and nationals alike. In much the same way, Tyndale produced a new translation of the Bible into English because of the changes in the English language since the time of Wyclif's translation.

God Created Male and Female

Rapidly changing language and the extinction of invented vocabulary played major roles in convincing the Association of Baptists for World Evangelism (ABWE) to produce a common language translation for Bangladesh. After much research and reflection, our team established the following guideline:

- *Bangladesh is a society publicly dominated by men. The men, therefore, are far more educated and socially aware than the women. A translation utilizing a male-dominated vocabulary would be over the heads of the women. Therefore, language used by the women of Bangladesh has priority over the language used by the men.*

Such a setting, therefore, requires the use of language that women understand if a translation is to reach all people. Even the learned Erasmus gave voice to this necessity in the preface to his Greek New Testament:

> I would wish even all women to read the gospel and the epistles of St Paul, and I wish that they were translated into all languages of all Christian people, that they might be read and known, not merely by the Scotch and the Irish, but even by the Turks and the Saracens. I wish that the husbandman may sing parts of them at his plow, that the weaver may warble them at his shuttle, that the traveler may with their narratives beguile the weariness of the way.[57]

Erasmus was "never far from William Tyndale's mind,"[58] so it is no surprise that he echoed Erasmus's wish in a response to a learned opponent of vernacular translation: "If God spare my life, ere many years I will cause a boy that driveth the plough shall know more of the Scripture than thou dost."[59] Rather than discussing the language and understanding of the plough boy, however, we will focus on the first group mentioned in Erasmus's wish: women.

The Bengali Bible translation does not seek so-called gender-neutral language. There is no need to avoid gender-specific vocabulary or grammar in Bengali. A number of difficulties, however, did present themselves to the translation team. For example, in Bangladesh the spoken language of women may change from village to village or even from one neighborhood of a city to another neighborhood of the same city. Linguists observe this characteristic in other regions of the world as well. Ann Cornelisen, archeologist turned anthropologist, describes an identical linguistic situation in southern Italy:

> Dipthongs tripped over diphthongs in what sounded like the spewings of an irate woman with a head cold. My first, full-dress encounter with the lingua franca of the peasants left me stunned. Dialects change from district to district and from town to town, and also, as I found out, in Torregreca from neighborhood to neighborhood.[60]

When societies limit women in their movements outside their own homes and families, those women develop their own speechways. Geographical and social factors may limit social interaction to a group of women living in close proximity to one another. Taboos about women initiating or carrying on conversation with men also produce linguistic isolation. Furthermore, pervasive poverty limits the number of televisions and radios to a few teashops and upper-class homes where only the men gather in the evenings. However, choosing women's language is not equivalent to selecting the least sophisticated forms of speech or literature. According to Steiner,

> In a few instances, and this is an extraordinarily suggestive point, the speech of women is somewhat more archaic than that of men. . . .
>
> The semantic contour, the total expressive means used by men and women differ. The view they take of the output and consumption of words is not the same. As it passes through verb tenses, time is bent into distinctive shapes and fictions. At a rough guess, women's speech is richer than men's in those shadings of desire and futurity known in Greek and Sanskrit as optative; women seem to verbalize a wider range of qualified resolve and masked promise. Feminine uses of the subjunctive in European languages give to material facts and relations a characteristic *vibrato*. I do not say they lie about the obtuse, resistant fabric of the world: they multiply the facets of reality, they strengthen the adjective to allow it an alternative nominal status, in a way which men often find unnerving.[61]

Students of Scripture will recognize that the language of women can prove to be an advantage in translating the Bible, since the Scriptures contain a number of monologues by and dialogues between women (e.g., 1 Sam. 1:15–2:10; Ruth 1:8–21; Luke 1:34–55).

For the Bengali Bible translation, the team gave priority to women's language over that of men only when a particular language preference is common to both men and women. If a translator were to opt for a woman's term or phrase that is in restricted use, the common language factor would be violated and a dialectal translation would result. Of course, upward trends in educating girls and women in Bangladesh over the last several decades increase both the number of women receiving a good education and their potential for equaling, if not surpassing, the level of Bengali language skills among men. Future revisions of the Bengali translations will need to take that into account to keep pace with the changes in language skills.

In addition to the guidelines for youth and women, the translation team composed yet another guideline regarding the level, style, and vocabulary of the Bengali translation:

- *The language utilized in the translation must be understood by non-Christians as well as Christians, if it is to be used in evangelism.*

Bible translations are not solely a provision for believers. If Christians are going to be obedient to the Scriptures (Matt. 28:19–20), they must involve themselves in spreading the message about Christ. The Scriptures themselves carry that message best. "Faith comes from hearing, and hearing by the word of Christ" (Rom. 10:17 NAS). Evangelization necessitates translating the Bible into the common language of common people. A significant corollary to this truth notes that churches must place a priority on the ministry of Bible translation for the world's mission fields. Since evangelism is a major purpose in the church's use of the Word of God, translators must give proper attention to the characteristics of the language unsaved persons understand. In Bangladesh, where less than 300,000 of the nation's 160 million people are "Christian," the need is for a translation that will aid in the evangelization of the nation.

Evangelization necessitates translating the Bible into the common language of common people. A significant corollary to this truth notes that churches must place a priority on the ministry of Bible translation for the world's mission fields.

The Same Forms

WHITE PAPER PUBLISHED BY ADMINISTRATION

« « « » » »

Thus reads the headline in an English-language newspaper. Some readers might find it amusing. After all, white paper is not published, it is produced so that someone might use it in publishing. Right? Actually, "white paper" in the diplomatic sense refers to a government declaration of an administration's position on a matter of national or international interest. That meaning, however, does not arise directly from the individual meanings of the two words themselves. The diplomatic usage differs from the ordinary sense of "white paper." (No wonder people think politicians do not speak plain English.) A government translator might face a problem translating "white paper" into another language—especially if he or she decides to translate it word-for-word.

"White paper" is an idiom. Technically an idiom is a word or group of words that has a special meaning not discernible from the parts comprising that word or group of words. Usually an idiom is an expression peculiar to a particular language and conveys a distinct meaning that may be contrary to the meanings of its component parts. Two different languages will rarely have the same idiomatic forms.[62]

Technically an idiom is a word or group of words that has a special meaning not discernible from the parts comprising that word or group of words.

Idiom, in a more general sense, may also refer to the syntactical, grammatical, or structural forms peculiar to a language. In discussions and debates about Bible translation, it is primarily this sense in which scholars use the phrase *idiomatic translation*. Idiomatic translation refers to the use of the forms (word order and syntax) of the receptor language. If translators maintain the same forms and the same vocabulary as in the original language, readers have difficulty understanding the meaning. In Bible translation, that can produce disastrous results. Readers and hearers must clearly and accurately understand God's revealed message, if they are to accurately apply it.

Translating the Bible into the Bengali language (or any other language) requires careful observation of grammatical and structural niceties in that language. Principles governing the SBCL team specify that naturalness of expression in proper Bengali receives priority over form. Guidelines for this aspect of the translation project include the following:

- *Reference to participants in a narrative should be made clear according to the proper Bengali pattern.*
- *Redundant expressions (such as* "saying said," "answering said," *or* "dreamed a dream"*) should be avoided. This kind of form in Bengali sounds as odd to the Bengali reader as* "he poeted a poem" *would sound to an English reader.*
- *The employment of emphasis must be in accord with proper Bengali usage. Hebrew, Aramaic, and Greek normally utilize changes in word order to indicate points of emphasis. In Bengali various particles (short words) or an inflection (an added vowel or syllable on the end of a word) are the common indicators of emphasis.*
- *Forms of addressing people which are uncommon or objectionable to Bengali should be avoided.*
- *The proper distinctions between the honorific and the familiar forms for pronouns and verbs must be accurately utilized in Bengali even though the biblical languages have no such form in their grammars.*

An example of this distinction in pronouns is the older English convention of capitalizing the pronouns referring to God: *He, You, Thou,* or *Thine.* Such conventions are foreign to Hebrew, Aramaic, and Greek. They actually represent an alteration of the original biblical forms so that the translation finds ready acceptance among the receiving audience. Bengali uses honorific pronominal forms when God is the antecedent, except in prayer. Bengali prayer utilizes the non-honorific second person pronoun *tumi* (pronounced *too-mee*) when addressing God, rather than the honorific pronoun *apni* (pronounced *ahp-nee*).

Bible translators must strike a delicate balance between being completely up-to-date and being fashionably classical in choosing idioms.

When certain phrases occur in the Scriptures the translator must ask, "What would an American have said?" or "What would a Bangalee have said?" or "What would a Swahili have said?" Biblical events and conversations took place many centuries ago. If the translator is too modern in his or her rendering of a phrase, it could appear to be making fun of the text. Listen to Ronald Knox:

> A Biblical phrase like "O King, live for ever!" has got to be changed; nobody ever talked like that in English. But you must not change it into "I hope that your Majesty's life may be spared indefinitely". You must get back to the language of a period when palace etiquette was more formal, "Long life to the King's majesty!"—something like that.[63]

Translating the Bible is like trying to take a picture of a bolt of lightning in mid-strike. Words and phrases can be exceedingly difficult to nail down. Idiomatic usage can be evasive and ephemeral. The pursuit of properly employed, understandable, and accurate idiom occupies the translator endlessly. The enormity of the task of Bible translation staggers the imagination and effectively humbles all who attempt it. Our team of translators in Bangladesh labored for thirty years to produce a common language translation of the Bible in Bengali. Such things are not accomplished overnight or even in a few brief years.

Translating the Bible is like trying to take a picture of a bolt of lightning in mid-strike. Words and phrases can be exceedingly difficult to nail down. Idiomatic usage can be evasive and ephemeral.

Common vocabulary and natural forms of expression bring the translator face-to-face with yet another major problem. What if translators cannot convey the correct meaning of the text without adding words or phrases which were not used in the original languages? Should such additions be considered legitimate when translating God's Word? This topic will occupy the next chapter.

CHAPTER 3

SEMANTICS AND CONTEXT IN BIBLE TRANSLATION

"My house is near the bank." The statement possesses an ambiguity. Which *bank* does the speaker intend? Is it the financial institution or the edge of a river? Grammatical rules alone do not govern the use of words and forms. Lexical semantics and context rule as the ultimate arbitrators. In the example with the English word "bank," the same vocabulary and the same form may display at least two very different meanings and are normally used in different contexts. Some languages, like Spanish, have two distinct vocabulary words for both meanings: *el banco* (the financial institution) and *la orilla* (the river's edge). How should translators deal with ambiguities? How should they handle cases where there does not seem to be any equivalent to a biblical word or concept in the receptor language?

Translational Additions

"Let their table become a snare before them: and *that which should have bene* for *their* welfare, *let it become* a trap" (Ps. 69:22 KJV, original 1611). The italicized words in the KJV are not for emphasis (a common misunderstanding). Italics indicate that the translators found it necessary to add words, in order to make the meaning of the original language clear in English. In this brief text consisting of six Hebrew words, the translators expanded them into a very different form utilizing twenty-two words (nine of which are additions not found in the Hebrew forms either lexically or grammatically). This particular example of expansion is paraphrastic. A paraphrase consists of "a restatement of a text or passage in another form or other words, often to clarify meaning."[64] There is an inherent danger in employing paraphrastic expansion in Bible translation. Robert Thomas explains the problem with paraphrases as follows:

> The more remote a translation is from the original, the less it reflects the precise meaning of the original and the more it reflects the interpretations of the translator(s). That remoteness entails a hindrance if one's purpose is to discover the meaning of the Bible. The translator's interpretations loom larger in the translation in proportion to the amount of freedom exercised in the translation technique. The reason for this is that the translator chooses his own ideas about the meaning of the text to replace the literal rendering of the text. A student of Scripture usually seeks the meaning of the text, not an interpretation of the translator. If he wants someone's interpretation, he will consult commentaries on the text. Free translations and paraphrases are especially harmful where the translator has erred in his interpretation. That misleads a student of the Bible as to what God actually said without the reader being aware that he is accepting someone's interpretation rather than what the original text says.[65]

As a longstanding practice Bible translators prepare an introduction to explain the basic translation philosophy they followed for their particular version. Before purchasing or using any Bible translation, first read the translators' introduction. It is vital to know how much the translators allow their interpretations to affect the text. Wooden word-for-word translations and paraphrases stand at the two extremes in translation practice. On the one end of the translation spectrum, readers find woodenly literal translations difficult to understand at times, as well as perhaps sounding archaic or outlandish. Aquila's Greek translation of Genesis 1:1, for example, reads (in the English translation of his Greek), "In beginning created God with the heavens and with the earth." Aquila's word "with" (Greek, *sun* pronounced like "soon") represents the occurrence of a direct object marker in the Hebrew text. Aquila chose that translation because, in some contexts, the same Hebrew word occurs as a preposition meaning "with." In order to represent every Hebrew word by the same Greek word, Aquila selected the Greek preposition *sun* ("with") to represent the word regardless of its meaning by context.

Commentaries and paraphrastic translations both have their place in the study of Scripture. The actual text of Scripture, however, supersedes both.

On the other end of the spectrum, it is the better part of wisdom to look upon clearly paraphrastic translations (such as The Living Bible, LB) as concise one-volume Bible commentaries. Readers need to compare a paraphrastic translation with more literal translations in order to recover more of what the original text actually says. Commentaries and paraphrastic translations both have their place in the study of Scripture. The actual text of Scripture, however, supersedes both.

How should the reader of Psalm 69:22 in the KJV evaluate that version's paraphrastic expansion? Compare the following translations:

Literal Hebrew	Let their table become a snare before them, and for wellbeing a trap.
KJV (1611)	Let their table become a snare before them: and *that which should have bene* for their welfare, *let it become* a trap.
NASB	May their own table before them become a snare; and when they are in peace, *may it become* a trap.
ESV	Let their own table before them become a snare; and when they are at peace, let it become a trap.
TEV	May their banquets cause their ruin; May their sacred feasts cause their downfall.

Obviously, when we strip away all the additions (whether or not translators italicized them to signal their addition), what remains is more difficult to understand. In such circumstances should translators do something to resolve the puzzle for the reader? The KJV translators believed that they should, and they did so—and so have many others after them. Were they wrong to expand the translation? In order to answer that question, we must discuss the nature of translation and the principles that govern accuracy in translation.

Sound translation principles require transferring the exact meaning of the original text into the receptor language while maintaining as much of the original wording as possible. Of course, the same spelling and pronunciation of a word in the original do not carry over into the second language, but rather a translation of that word (or in some cases, a transliteration—e.g., *Hallelujah* for "Praise the Lord"). What good is a translation which conveys no meaning—or worse yet, which conveys the wrong meaning? One Bible scholar explains the issue in the following fashion:

> Frequently one encounters the erroneous belief that a difference in *number* and *order* of words in the transference from the source language to the receptor language somehow equals a difference in *meaning* in the translation. Every translator, however, from the third-grade student who is studying French to the seasoned scholar who has years of translation experience, knows this is not true. Yet, among Bible translators and biblical language scholars there is very often a distrust of a translator who espouses the translation of meaning, or who casts Greek, Hebrew, and Aramaic idioms (especially dead metaphors) into idiomatic English. . . .
>
> If one were to ask someone "*Comment ça va?*" ("How are you?"), and he were to reply, "*Comme ci, comme ça*" ("So, so"), the translator has not distorted the message, nor has he added anything to the *meaning,* when he translates the French by the English "Not too good, not too bad," nor has he deleted anything if he translates "So, so." In the one case there are six words to the French four, and in the other case two, but the meaning is the same.[66]

Sound translation principles require transferring the exact meaning of the original text into the receptor language while maintaining as much of the original wording as possible.

The New Testament writer of the Greek Gospel of Mark (most likely Mark himself) followed a practice of adding words to clarify meaning in translating Jesus's Aramaic statements. Consider Mark 5:41, "And he tooke the damosell by the hand, and said vnto her, *Talitha cumi,* which is, being interpreted, Damosell (I say vnto thee) Arise" (original KJV[67]). In this case the italicized words indicate, not an addition, but the use of a foreign language. *Talitha cumi* is in Aramaic, the mother tongue of the Israelites of Jesus's day. The Gospel writer provides his readers with a translation of the phrase into Greek so that non-Aramaic speakers might understand what Jesus says to the young lady. In doing so, however, Mark adds the words "I say unto you" in order to provide the information necessary to make the meaning clear to his readers. Those four English words (two words in the original Greek) were not in the Aramaic statement made by Jesus. Observing this fact, the KJV translators placed those words in parentheses to indicate that this was an addition in the Greek.

Why was it necessary for Mark to add these words? The addition was necessary because the strict repetition of the form from Aramaic to Greek could not convey accurately and faithfully the meaning of the statement. By adding "I say unto you" to his translation, Mark was informing his readers that Jesus has not merely spoken, but has authoritatively commanded. One might claim that Mark's addition is interpretive. If so, he bases the interpretation upon the obvious intent of the Aramaic. However, what was possible to imply in Aramaic speech needs to be made explicit in Greek parlance in order for the readers to receive every intended (explicit as well as implicit) piece of information contained in the original Aramaic.

This brief examination of Mark 5:41 reveals that translating the Bible accurately requires accuracy in regard to both explicit and implicit meaning. Transferring the meaning of the original Hebrew or Greek into a totally different language with its own forms (an idiomatic translation) cannot be fulfilled by a simple transfer of vocabulary using a dictionary. Dictionary translations notoriously neglect the role of context for meaning.

> ***Translating the Bible accurately requires accuracy in regard to both explicit and implicit meaning.***

Words and Their Meanings

In the days before email, when the most common means of sending messages over a long distance involved a cable (i.e., an overseas telegram), the reception of an indecipherable message was commonplace. If a way existed by which someone might foul up a telegram, someone would

find it—especially international telegrams that pass from one language to another and then back to the former language. Originally one such cable sent to Russia declared, "Genevieve suspended for prank." But, the English back-translation for the Russian translation of that cable read, "Genevieve hanged for juvenile delinquency."[68] Dictionary translations can produce this kind of result.

No distinction should exist between accuracy and faithfulness in translation. An inaccurate meaning in a translation equals unfaithfulness to the text, even though the translator might have utilized the same number of words and the same forms. Languages often employ different structures to express identical meaning—and, to express different nuances of meaning that illustrate the old principle that similarity does not guarantee identity. The study of how languages structure meaning belongs to the study of semantics. Semantics is no modern development.[69] Varro, an ancient Roman grammarian, wrote a treatise in which he announced that he had discovered 228 distinct meanings for one Latin word for "good."[70] In some languages the term (or terms) for "good" would be impossible to use for all 228 of those meanings. How is it possible for a word to have so many different meanings? In one word: context. Context occupies the floor like an 800-pound gorilla. In real estate the mantra is "Location, location, location." In linguistics, semantics, and translation, "Context, context, context" dominates.

An inaccurate meaning in a translation equals unfaithfulness to the text, even though the translator might have utilized the same number of words and the same forms.

Each context in which a speaker or writer employs a word determines that word's meaning. In Bible translation, it is rarely possible to maintain one translation for all occurrences of the same Hebrew or Greek term. (Remember Aquila's attempt to use "with" for every occurrence of a single Hebrew word and the effect it had upon Genesis 1:1?) The variety of terms English Bible versions utilize to translate the Hebrew verb *qadash* with the meaning "be holy" or "sanctify" reveal how context changes meaning. In the KJV, eleven different English verbs translate this Hebrew verb. The NIV also uses eleven; the NAS and RSV each employ ten. Accurate conveyance of meaning necessitates such semantic variety in translation—there is no reasonable alternative. This is in total agreement with the translators of the KJV. In their "The Translators to the Reader" preface, they declared,

> An other thing we thinke good to admonish thee of (gentle Reader) that wee haue not tyed our selues to an vniformitie of phrasing, or to an identitie of words, as some peraduenture would wish that we had done, because they obserue, that some learned men some where, haue beene as exact as they could that way. Truly, that we might not varie from the sense of that which we had translated before, if the word signified the same thing in both places (for there bee some wordes that bee not of the same sense euery where) we were especially carefull, and made a conscience, according to our duetie. But, that we should expresse the same notion in the same particular word; as for example, if we translate the *Hebrew* or *Greeke* word once by *Purpose,* neuer to call it *Intent;* if one where *Iourneying,* neuer *Traueiling;* if one where *Thinke,* neuer *Suppose;* if one where *Paine,* neuer *Ache;* if one where *Ioy,* neuer *Gladnesse,* &c. Thus to minse the matter, wee thought to sauour more of curiositie then wisedome, and that rather it would breed scorne in the Atheist, then bring profite to the godly Reader. For is the kingdome of God become words or syllables? why should wee be in bondage to them if we may be free, vse one precisely when wee may vse another no lesse fit, as commodiously?[71]

An exact equivalent for certain Hebrew words in other languages defies context. For example, beginning Hebrew students tend to translate *nephesh* as "soul." However, *nephesh* has a much broader range of meanings in its 754 occurrences in the Hebrew Bible. It can mean "appetite" (Num. 11:6 NAS; Prov. 23:2 KJV), "breath" (Gen. 1:30 NRSV; Job 41:21 KJV), "life" (Gen. 19:17 KJV, NKJV), "himself" (1 Sam. 18:3 NAS, NIV) or even "me" (Ps. 6:4 [Heb. 5] NET), and "throat" (Job 24:12 NRSV; Isa. 5:14 NAS). A wide range of potential meanings characterizes many words in Hebrew, Aramaic, and Greek—all of the original biblical languages.

Bengali commonly uses the word *rag* (pronounced *rahg*) for "anger." Translators may use *rag* for equivalent Greek or Hebrew words as long as the term refers to human beings as the angry ones. If, however, the biblical text speaks of God's anger, a different term must be used since the Bengali term indicates uncontrolled anger (something never true of God). With this kind of situation in mind, the SBCL project follows the principle that *the meaning of the original text takes precedence over the form. Contextual consistency has priority over verbal consistency. A word in the Hebrew or Greek may have a different meaning in a different context—that difference should be carefully observed.* Guidelines for implementing this principle include the following.

- *No original language term (in Hebrew, Aramaic, or Greek) should be automatically translated by just one and the same Bengali term in all contexts.*
- *Figurative language and idioms may be replaced by parallel figures or idioms in Bengali only when it causes no historical or cultural difficulty and only when the new figure or idiom has the same meaning in Bengali.*
- *Retain the form whenever a literal translation produces an accurate, meaningful, and natural expression in Bengali. That form which is closest to the original text will be used if the exact form does not fit these criteria.*
- *Retain details of culture (customs, vocations, clothing, foods, and ceremonies), geography (places and features, climate and weather elements), and history (nations, empires, and events), even if they are not within the range of common knowledge for Bengali-speaking peoples. However, we may add classifiers or determinatives that make the terms identifiable in accordance with Bengali usage (for example, "Jordan* River," *"Bethany* village," *"Antioch* city," *or* "King *Hezekiah").*

All of these principles involve the matter of lexical equivalence across languages. Just as in English, Spanish, German, or Bengali, each of the Bible's Hebrew, Aramaic, or Greek terms includes its own associated form and function. Some terms parallel a corresponding term in the translator's language, others possess none. As an example in modern languages, consider the fact that German employs *die Uhr* in German for both wall clocks and for wristwatches. English, however, maintains a distinction. Anyone translating the German into English must make a choice governed by context. Of course, the translator might opt to retain the original *Uhr* as "clock," but add a qualifying prepositional phrase like "on the wrist," in order to make the meaning clear even though "on the wrist" does not appear in the German base. (We should note, however, that modern German has adopted *die Armband-uhr* for "wrist-watch.") Translators face the same kind of situations over and over again in the biblical languages (Hebrew, Aramaic, and Greek). In biblical Hebrew, *ben* is the only word available for "son" or "grandson" (or even "great-grandson"). It simply means "child" in some non-gender-specific contexts. In other contexts and specialized phrases, it acts as a classifier indicating something belonging to a certain class. English has separate terms for all of these meanings for which biblical Hebrew employs but one word.

Translators must exercise some restraint if they hope to produce an acceptable Bible translation within a single culture containing a variety of subgroups.

In an age when biblical literacy is plummeting to all time lows, translators should not assume that everyone understands that a simple phrase like "the children of Israel" does not refer either to infants alone or male offspring alone (as in KJV, NKJV, ASV, and JPS; or "the sons of Israel" as in NAS, NASB,[72] and YLT). Biblical writers most often use *beney-Yisrael* in the Hebrew Bible as an idiom meaning "Israelites" (thus correctly translated by NIV, NRSV, NLT, NJB, CSB, NET, and NJPS). The phrase refers to all Israelites, young and old, male and female. Therefore, the RSV and ESV utilize "people of Israel." In the right context the identical phrase refers to the literal sons of Israel/Jacob (see 1 Chron. 2:1–2). Technically, the same phrase might refer to the non-adult population (literal "children"). So, why not translate all the national references as "Israelites" rather than using the inaccurate and potentially misleading "children of Israel"? If translators were to remove the form in the interest of an accurate meaning, it could be especially discomforting for many of our African American brothers and sisters among whom "the children of Israel" is still a very meaningful phrase. It is biblical phraseology that has entered a people's vocabulary and includes cultural implications. With this difficulty in view, therefore, translators must exercise some restraint if they hope to produce an acceptable Bible translation within a single culture containing a variety of subgroups speaking the same language.

Depending upon the nature or characteristics of such subgroups, translators might need to produce more than one Bible translation. Our team in Bangladesh took that route to meet the needs of the Muslim community as compared to the Hindu and Buddhist communities. Muslims regularly use more loanwords from Arabic, Persian, and Urdu than their Hindu and Buddhist neighbors. However, Bangladeshi Christian leaders currently find that such Muslim dialectal differences are decreasing. Therefore, one of the former Bangladeshi members of the MBCL team has revised that version to conform more closely to the SBCL. The revision appears to be growing in popularity.

Words in one language having a corresponding term in another language might be equivalent in form but not in function or perhaps, in function but not in form. The translator must handle such situations with wisdom akin to that of Solomon. One veteran Bible translator wrote:

> Words are not coins, dead things whose value can be mathematically computed. You cannot quote an exact English equivalent for a French word, as you might quote an exact English equivalent for a French coin. Words are living things, full of shades of meaning, full of associations; and, what is more, they are apt to change their significance from one generation to the next. The translator who understands his job feels, constantly, like Alice in Wonderland trying to play croquet with flamingoes for mallets and hedgehogs for balls; words are for ever eluding his grasp.[73]

One approach to evaluating a Bible translation includes reading the Scriptures with careful attention to the words occurring in the text. In fact, the translator must also observe the terms that do *not* occur. Readers of the Old Testament in English translations find a surprising lack of certain words one would expect, given the various contexts presented within the text. Consider the absence of the word "danger" in English Bible translations. It never occurs in the KJV or NAS Old Testaments. In the NIV, RSV, and ESV it can be found a scant three times (1 Sam. 20:21; Prov. 22:3; 27:12; NRSV has these three plus 1 Sam. 30:6). In the TEV, however, "danger" appears thirty-seven times[74] in the Old Testament—a much more realistic frequency given the existence of at least five terms or phrases in biblical Hebrew for speaking of danger[75] and given the types of contexts in which English would normally use the word.

Knox's discussion of this phenomenon proves enlightening:

> It is a harder part of the translator's job to notice the negative effect produced by the absence of English mannerisms. Here is an interesting question you may

> put to an unsuspecting friend: 'Which is commoner in the Old Testament; the word *danger* or the word *peril*?' You will find that 'peril' has it; the concordance tells you that it occurs once in the Old Testament (Authorized Version), whereas 'danger' does not occur at all. 'Jeopardy' comes three times. Now, it is nonsense to suppose that the Hebrew mind has no such notion as danger; why is there no word for it? The answer can only be, that in Hebrew you express the same idea by a nearly-allied word which has to do duty, also, for slightly different ideas; a word like 'affliction', 'tribulation' or 'trouble'. That means that a good translation of the Old Testament will sometimes give you 'danger' or 'peril', where the stock translations give you 'fear' or 'terror'. The rendering which does not mention danger or peril jars imperceptibly on the mind.[76]

In an era of modern science, math, and computer technology, people have grown accustomed to the concept of equivalents. As one writer put it, "Wishful thinking and early training in arithmetic have convinced a majority of people that there are such things as equals in the world."[77] Therefore, people begin to think that an accurate and literal translation of the Bible must utilize an equivalent term. However, just as in the case of Hebrew *ben*, sometimes no English equivalent exists. English does not have a single word to do the same work and cover the same variety of meanings as the Hebrew *ben*.

Good translators take an interest in every aspect of life and culture. They are normally voracious readers inquisitive about everything from the Aaronic priesthood to zymurgy. Their vocabulary in the receptor language (whether English or Bengali or Japanese, et al.) must be expansive.

Generic words like "son" or "child" are not the only concerns. Bible translators must deal with details of architecture (as in the description of the temple in 1 Kings 6–7), zoological and botanical classification (as in the list of clean and unclean animals in Lev. 11 and the various plants mentioned in the Song of Songs), medicine (as in the description of skin disease in Lev. 13–14), gems (as in the description of the walls and gates of the New Jerusalem in Rev. 21:18–19), geography, astronomy, law, occult practice, and many other categories of knowledge. Good translators, therefore, take an interest in every aspect of life and culture. They are normally voracious readers inquisitive about everything from the Aaronic priesthood to zymurgy. Their vocabulary in the receptor language (whether English or Bengali or Japanese, et al.) must be expansive. Translators must examine every word of the text on both sides of the process (the source language and the receptor language). No Bible translator should ignore so-called "lesser words." Contexts must be scrutinized in order to understand every nuance with accuracy.

Let's consider an example from the New Testament. In Matthew 21:33, the householder plants a vineyard and builds a tower. The tower's purpose consists of providing a platform from which to watch for the approach of marauders who might plunder the vineyard or for the incursion of wild animals that might devour or spoil its fruits. It does not, however, serve as a refuge from human and animal marauders—it is merely a watch tower. The Aguaruna Indians of Peru also build towers, if they have enemies who might attack them. When the enemy approaches, the Aguaruna flee from their houses to the protection of the tower which gives them a strategic advantage over the enemy during the ensuing battle.[78] The form of the structure conforms basically to the biblical tower, but their functions are different. Translators going from Greek into the Aguarunas's dialect must consider the viability of using a footnote or modifying the word by specifying the function: "a tower *for a watchman*" or "a *guard* tower," if the language lacks an equivalent term identifying a tower from which people guard or watch over something.

Translators from Western cultures must constantly fight against their own misunderstanding of what they read in Scripture.

Even a word like "bread" can provide the translator with a challenge. For example, the Chontal of Mexico bake bread for special fiesta days only. The daily food belonging in the general category of bread is the tortilla. With this in mind, how should a translator treat Jesus's statement, "I am the bread of life" (John 6:35)? To a Christian in the United States, "I am the tortilla of life" would seem about as serious as "I am the pizza of life." At first blush the form seems different, even though the function is the same. Yet, a bit of research will yield the following observation:

> The large pone or thick, light loaf of the West is unknown in the East. The common oriental cake or loaf is proverbially thin. . . . It is still significantly customary at a Syrian meal to take a piece of such bread and, with the ease and skill of long habit, to fold it over at the end held in the hand so as to make a sort of spoon of it, which then is eaten along with whatever is lifted by it out of the common dish (cf. Mt 26 23).[79]

The tortilla better represents the shape, texture, method of cooking, and purpose of the kind of bread used in ancient Israel than modern loaves of bread with which we are most familiar in the United States. Therefore, "I am the tortilla of life" is not as outlandish as it first sounds to the non-Hispanic ear. In this particular case, therefore, what appears to be a cultural substitution is not. Western concepts result in the cultural substitution. Some years ago I picked up a bookmark for Bible reading with John 6:35 inscribed on it and a picture of a plate of sliced bread. Thus, the bookmark inaccurately depicted the biblical reality.

Translators from Western cultures must constantly fight against their own misunderstanding of what they read in Scripture (like their visualization of a loaf of sliced bread for "bread" in the Bible). They also must be on guard against erroneous teachings they receive from teachers who ignore or improperly interpret the Scriptures. An example of this second kind of error involves Matthew 19:24, "it is easier for a camel to go through the eye of a needle than for a rich person to enter the kingdom of God" (ESV). A popular explanation attributes the picture to the existence of a small gate within the usual city gate in ancient Near Eastern cities.[80] Such a small gate would permit a person to enter, but not a camel—especially one fully laden. However, that explanation finds little support and commentators largely reject it because it misses the main point Jesus made: salvation is *impossible* for human beings to attain.[81] Translators should avoid using an explanatory translation like that of William MacDonald: "Again, I assure you it is easier for a camel to pass through a needle's eye [a slender door within a city gate] than for a wealthy person to get into God's kingdom" (Matt. 19:24 MIT).

An Oriental culture exhibits greater correspondences to biblical culture than Western cultures. Thus, in countries like Bangladesh, Bible readers hold an advantage over readers in the United States because their culture possesses greater affinity to everyday life in ancient biblical cultures. Even in the West, less advanced or Third World cultures in many respects more closely approximate biblical cultures than more advanced industrial cultures.

Anachronisms provide yet another kind of intrusion to which Bible translators must be alert. Anachronistic errors occur any time translators wrongly associate a postbiblical entity with a biblical entity. For example, "kerosene" does not make a viable equivalent for "olive oil." Such a correspondence fails to maintain fidelity to the original historical and cultural setting. "Kerosene" would be as jarring as substituting armored tanks for chariots in Old Testament battle scenes. Such cultural dynamic equivalents might make good illustrations for sermons or Sunday school lessons, but have no place in the biblical text. Translators must preserve the cultural integrity of the biblical text.

One of our translators for the Bengali Bible project frequently suggested equivalents for "rain" implying that ancient Israel possessed the same climate as subtropical, monsoonal Bangladesh with its torrential downpours of one hundred to two hundred inches of rain per year. Such monsoonal rains produce the jungles and mangrove swamps of Bangladesh that were unknown in biblical Israel. Our colleague reasoned that the reader of the translation would be better able to understand a climate similar to his or her own. When asked if it would be acceptable for a translator in the western United States to translate the poems of Rabindranath Tagore, the Bengali poet laureate, by representing the torrential rains of Bengal as an occasional cloudburst causing a flashflood in a dry gulch and by describing the monsoon winds' effect as producing "dust devils" rather than causing the tops of trees to bow to the ground, he was rightly appalled by such substitutions. As he put it, "If you remove the Bengal monsoon from Tagore, you take the heart out of his poems." After it was explained to him that obscuring the desert environment of much of Israel also misrepresents the biblical setting and literature, he ceased suggesting such substitutions. He came to understand the need to preserve the integrity of the text in its own particular setting.

> ***Anachronistic errors occur any time translators wrongly associate a postbiblical entity with a biblical entity.***

Cultural substitutions need not be limited to gastronomic and climatological elements. Translators encounter a similar issue in translating the names of animal species. In ancient Israel the wolf was a peril to sheep (cf. John 10:12). Tropical areas around the world may not have wolves; instead, tigers, leopards, and jackals commonly prey upon domesticated animals in tropical and subtropical regions. Should the translator make a cultural substitution? If the truth being taught necessitates the form, the translator must not substitute another culture's entity (or form). What if the form is not significant? What if translators might preserve the same meaning and the same truth with another form? Then the problem becomes more sticky. We must consider not only the problem of historical fidelity, but of symbolic fidelity in the total context of Scripture. The SBCL translation composed a guideline covering theological symbolism: *Retain words having symbolic value within the theological framework of the Bible (such as the "Lamb of God," "blood," and "cross").*

As D. A. Carson forcefully argues, one altered word not only violates the symbolic and prophetic consistency and the historical context of the Scripture, it might also require a large number of attendant changes.

> Suppose, for instance, a tribe has a long tradition of sacrificing pigs, but has never so much as heard of sheep. Is it in that case justifiable to render John 1:29, "Look, the swine of God, who takes away the sin of the world!"? I would argue strongly in the negative, not only because of the importance of historical particularity . . . but because of the plethora of rich allusions preserved in Scripture across the sweep of salvation history. In what sense does Jesus "fulfill" the Old Testament sacrificial system if that system sacrificed lambs on the Day of Atonement and at Passover, whereas Jesus is portrayed as a swine? How then will John 1:29 relate to Isa. 52:13–53:12, the fourth servant song, or to images of the warrior lamb in the Apocalypse (e.g. Revelation 5:6)? Shall we change *all* such references to "pigs" ("All we like swine have gone astray . . . ")? And if so, do we then

> make the biblical pig-references clean, and designate some other animal unclean? No; it is surely simpler to preserve "lamb" in the first instance. If this involves inventing a new word, so be it: a brief note could explain that the word refers to an animal frequently sacrificed by the people of the Bible, along with a succinct description of the animal's characteristics.[82]

Accurate communication of a message from one culture (that of the ancient Near East) to another culture (such as that of modern-day Bangladesh or Britain or Botswana) faces many difficulties. The two cultures do have some things in common, but many things are very different. One of the differences involves the very way people perceive or think about common actions or events.

Cultural or Theological Confusion

By reason of its ancient Near Eastern setting, the Bible presents an exercise in cross-cultural communication. Translators must transform linguistic information in order to communicate accurately with the translation's receptors in another cultural setting. Transformation, however, does not include the freedom to alter the cultural realities of the biblical text. Transformation of linguistic forms (as in "*give* an exam" for "*take* an exam"; see chapter 2) is not the same as transformation of strictly cultural forms (as in "pig" for "lamb"). Translators misinform and misdirect their readers by replacing Israel's geographical realities (such as rocky cliffs, sandy deserts, and dry streambeds), climatic realities (such as snow), or vocational realities (such as potters, shepherds, and camel drivers) with another culture's geographical, climatic, or vocational realities. Bangladesh possesses no deserts and no snow, but, for the sake of both accuracy and faithfulness, translators must not convert snow to rain or deserts to jungles. The Bible's cultural, geographical, and historical details must be left intact. Only then does the translation enable readers to gain an accurate picture of the cultural, geographical, and historical contexts of Scripture. Without those contexts, interpretations run rampant over the text, foisting one's own culture upon the ancient biblical cultures.

For example, the seemingly harmless replacement of "recline at food" or "recline at table" with "sit down to eat" may produce confusion for readers. As Carson points out, "We are going to have a tough job imagining how John managed to get his head on Jesus's breast. Preservation of descriptions of what is to us an alien custom, reclining at tables, makes it possible to understand a later action, John placing his head on Jesus's breast."[83]

For the sake of both accuracy and faithfulness, translators must not convert snow to rain or deserts to jungles. The Bible's cultural, geographical, and historical details must be left intact.

This problem of cultural, historical, geographical, and climatic elements in the translation of the Scriptures reveals how idiomatic translation can take a perverse turn. The common usage of the term *idiomatic translation* often refers to free translation involving cultural substitutions. Idiomatic translations might substitute "pig" for "lamb" in a cultural setting where sheep are unknown but pigs are familiar. Our Bengali Bible translation team in Bangladesh produced principles standing at odds with a loose kind of idiomatic translation. Beyond the local ancient Near Eastern setting, translators must not alter transcultural or universal truths in Scripture in either form or meaning.

How can the Bible translator insure that the recipients of the translation understand it? Is it possible to produce a reasonably faithful and accurate translation, but fail to connect with the minds and hearts of the readers? What does Scripture itself reveal concerning simplicity and clarity in Bible translation? In the next chapter we will take up this very matter.

CHAPTER 4

SIMPLICITY AND CLARITY IN BIBLE TRANSLATION

PASSING THROUGH THE CROWDED STREETS of Chittagong to arrive at my Bible translation office for the first time, I had already charted every hour of my day. After all, I had committed myself to but three years as a short-term missionary. Every minute must count. I affixed my daily schedule to the side of a metal file cabinet adjacent to my desk. It took but a few months for me to learn that nothing moves according to plan in a place like Bangladesh. *Interruptibility* and *flexibility* became key words relating to missionary service—even as a Bible translator. Three years turned into fifteen—that's part of the reality of maintaining a big picture, rather than going into isolation, cut off from the people for whom you hope to produce a good Bible translation. As a missionary of the gospel of Jesus Christ, I had to be available when inquirers came. Without believers to read the translation, of what use could it possibly be? We learned that some Bangladeshis had used Bible pages for rolling cigarettes and for making paper bags—but those were not the uses for which we worked and prayed.

Every Bangladeshi with whom I conversed taught me more and more about the Bengali language and the Bangalee people themselves. When our translation team sent a draft of a Bible portion out to the selected translation checkers scattered throughout the country, we anxiously awaited their comments, knowing that an acceptable Bible translation must be an understandable translation. Would those checkers understand what we had produced—regardless of which region of the country they lived in? Did we make the text clear enough? Did the draft meet our established translation standards? Would the translation impact the checkers' lives, even as they looked over the translation with a critical eye to linguistic accuracy and consistency?

Every Bible translator fears that he or she might have followed all the principles of translation correctly and yet the reader might miss the intended meaning. Technical accuracy does not ensure understandability. Grammatical and lexical accuracy do not guarantee that the reader will understand the translation. How can understandability be obtained?

Every Bible translator fears that he or she might have followed all the principles of translation correctly and yet the reader might miss the intended meaning. Technical accuracy does not ensure understandability.

Same Statement, Different Styles

William F. Buckley Jr. and his wife Pat had been blissfully married for years when their marital success became a topic in a journalist's interview. Bill waxed eloquent on the "psychic consummation of marriage." Pat, however, merely said, "I guess we just like each other." That is plain speech—plain and simple. We often adjust the language we speak to fit the situation or to fit specific individuals within a particular setting. Both speaker and listener influence the language choices a speaker makes. We adjust our speech in accord with age, gender, education, socioeconomic class, vocation, ethnic background, and many other factors. Technically, the varieties of language which speakers and writers use in different settings are called *registers*. Commonly, registers are referred to as styles. Linguistically, a register consists of the language variety a speaker chooses for a particular purpose—which might be determined by the social setting. Formal English, as one example, avoids dropping the *-g* off *-ing* words such as "talking" (not "talkin'") and "flying" (not "flyin'"). The choice of "child" or "kid" might also be affected by formal speech choices (the latter word being more befitting an informal or family setting).

What registers or styles of biblical Hebrew, Aramaic, and Greek did the writers of Scripture speak and write? Were the original languages of the Bible technical, highly literary, or sophisticated? Were they specially devised languages invented by the Holy Spirit, rather than extant languages utilized by ancient Near Eastern peoples? Who spoke them and understood them? The answers to these questions, when possible to determine, provide translators with valuable information. Surely, the language style and level chosen by God for His written revelation should be an acceptable pattern for modern translations to replicate.

School children's exercises, letters between friends and family members, and household shopping lists predating (and postdating) the New Testament demonstrate that New Testament Greek was the common language of the common people.

Discoveries of substantial amounts of everyday written materials in first-century Greek confirm that God did not specially invent it so that it might be used as the language of the New Testament. School children's exercises, letters between friends and family members, and household shopping lists predating (and postdating) the New Testament demonstrate that New Testament Greek was the common language of the common people.[84] The language of the courts in Athens and of the schools in Corinth do not dominate the Greek New Testament. There are some isolated exceptions. As in any setting, the vocabulary and grammar varies with the speakers and their audiences. As one New Testament scholar observes, "It is not true, as some have maintained, that all the Acts speakers speak alike, for the various types of speeches are admirably suited to their respective audiences, the Areopagitica in Acts xvii. 22ff. furnishing a conspicuous example."[85] Although Luke's language appears at times to be a little higher style, it is just a register of the common Greek. Claims of medical language in Luke's writings, however, have been overstated.[86] Common folk spoke New Testament Greek (or Koine Greek) in the marketplaces of Corinth, Ephesus, Antioch,

Jerusalem, and Alexandria. Marketplaces, by the way, served as the equivalent of modern public media sources—they were the news centers of that era, the Facebook of that time.

Greek was not the native language of the inhabitants of Israel, but rather their second or even third language. Ancient Israelites living after the return from the Babylonian exile spoke Aramaic as their mother tongue. In the temple and in the court of the Jewish Sanhedrin, men conducted worship and law in Hebrew. Latin, however, functioned as the language of the Roman courts of Israel, as well as throughout the Roman Empire.

Like modern missionaries working in a second language, the people of Israel generally were not versed in the sophistications of Greece's mother tongue. Attic Greek existed as a highly sophisticated and literary language beyond the grasp of common non-Greek citizens living in the countries around the ancient Mediterranean Sea. Instead, the common folk used a very simple and modified form of Greek suited to their communication needs. It was known as Koine (pronounced *koy-NAY*) Greek. *Koinē* means "common."[87] The Holy Spirit chose to employ this common language for communicating God's most recent revelation to the people of the first century and, by extension, to all peoples of planet Earth.

Common Idea, Different Words

Imagine that you are a time traveler visiting the Greek-speaking world of the first century. You watch as people browse through tiny shops in the ancient Mediterranean cities' narrow streets. A shopper chooses to stop at a pottery shop. The interior of the shop has only ambient light. It is too dark to be certain of purchasing good ceramic ware, so the potential buyer takes a piece into the sunlight outside the shop's doorway in order to get a good look at it before settling on a price. Holding the ceramic vessel up to the sun, dark spots (or sometimes, extra light spots) in the ceramic indicate flaws. Having assessed the vessel's quality, she returns to the interior to haggle with the shopkeeper over the price.

From this common practice, Greek speakers combined the words for "sunlight" (*heilē*) and "to judge" (*krinein*) to say that the pottery was "unmixed, pure" (*eilikrinēs* as the adjective and the noun *eilikrineia*). Speakers coined the words in the context of the marketplace and the New Testament writers employed them (see 1 Cor. 5:8; 2 Cor. 1:12 and 2:17; Phil. 1:10; and 2 Peter 3:1). Some English translations use the word "sincere" for this Greek adjective. "Sincere" itself possesses a similar origin in the ancient Roman marketplace. Its Latin root means "without wax." Potters frequently used wax in an attempt to hide flaws in their pottery. This word picture comprises but one example of the lexical wealth of common Greek and common Latin.

Koine Greek functioned as a simplified Greek—in both forms and style. Do not make the mistake, however, of concluding that Koine Greek served as a debased form of Greek. It was a beautiful, flexible language, though generally unsophisticated.

Scholars cannot so neatly categorize the two languages of the Old Testament (Hebrew and Aramaic). No one has yet discovered any extensive collection of extrabiblical literature written in the Hebrew of the Old Testament (Classical Hebrew). Hebraists observe changes in the language from the earlier books (such as Job and the books of Moses) to the later books (Esther, Zechariah, Haggai, Nehemiah, and Malachi) within the Old Testament itself. However, historical narratives (Numbers and Joshua, for example), legal materials (Leviticus), prophetic materials (Isaiah), poetic materials (Psalms), and dramatic materials (Job) all utilize the same basic vocabulary and grammar. Biblical Hebrew, though adaptable to a number of styles and topics over a wide range of history, does not display a technical, sophisticated, or highly literary form. Undoubtedly it was nearly identical to the commonly spoken language of the average individual. The Old Testament's recorded conversations (like that between Joseph and his brothers, between Boaz and Ruth, or between David and Jonathan) prove that common folk spoke the language.

Aramaic is a different matter. The Aramaic sections of Daniel (2:46–7:28) and Ezra (4:8–6:18 and 7:12–26) are in a language often classified as "royal Aramaic" or "official Aramaic." The similarity of biblical Aramaic to the Aramaic of the official documents found in extrabiblical source materials (legal contracts, royal decrees, and international treaties) provides evidence for its classification. The commonly used Aramaic of personal letters and other such nonofficial documents does not appear to be that of biblical Aramaic. Neither is it the same Aramaic as that spoken in the time of Christ by the common people of Israel. This should not surprise us. Ezra and Daniel served as government officials and they addressed their Aramaic writings primarily to, or recorded the actions and words of, kings and government officials in the Babylonian and Persian Empires.[88]

A careful study of the original languages of the Scriptures proves the common language style of both Old and New Testaments. J. Harold Greenlee concludes, "The style of the Greek NT has implications for translations into other languages. If the original was written in the language of common speech, then a translation into English or any other language should likewise be in the language of common speech."[89] Thus, a Bible translation, like the one our team produced in Bangladesh using common Bengali, carries on the divinely initiated pattern of common language Scriptures.

> ***Even when biblical writers record an act of sin or blasphemy, they convey it in a fashion proper to divine revelation instructing readers in godly living.***

Common language translation does not ignore the varieties of Hebrew, Aramaic, and Greek found in the Bible. The SBCL team adhered to the principle that *every effort should be made to reflect the different styles of language found in different parts of Scripture*. This does not mean, however, that the recorded conversations of prostitutes and corrupt public officials should be handled in a vulgar style. *In general, the level of language should be neither too formal nor too casual or slangy.* Such a principle harmonizes with the general tone adopted by the original languages of Scripture. Even when biblical writers record an act of sin or blasphemy, they usually convey it in a fashion proper to divine revelation instructing readers in godly living.

Having made that point for a less than vulgar tone in Bible translation, we cannot ignore the fact that the biblical writers occasionally used blunt language which we often avoid in most social settings—and especially in the pulpit. The KJV's "any that pisseth against the wall" (1 Sam. 25:22) might come to mind first. Nearly every recent translation takes the phrase as descriptive of a male human being, so use "male" (e.g., NIV, NRSV, ESV). The CEB, however, went with "one single one who urinates on a wall." Another example arises in Paul's diatribe against the Judaizers in Galatians 5:12, "I wish those who unsettle you would castrate themselves!" (NRSV; cf. ESV, NIV, NET, HCSB). Paul's somewhat shocking statement fails to come across the same with the DRA's "I would they were even cut off, who trouble you." Such a declaration might sound coarse and unchristian. However, the apostle, rather than being ill-tempered or vulgar, expressed concern for the gospel. He instructs legalists to go the whole distance to fulfill human endeavor to save oneself—even to the extent of the pagan practice among priests of the mother goddess Cybele to make themselves eunuchs.[90]

The following selected translations for familiar Bible passages illustrate common, idiomatic, simple, and clear translation in keeping with the principles highlighted thus far. In other words, English language Bible versions on the whole normally exhibit consistency with the literal meaning of the original text and attempt to preserve English suitable to a common person's speech. Keeping in mind that the Elizabethan English of the KJV was common English in its own time, we find that the more recent translations use English nearer to our own forms of spoken English. The list below provides the year for each translation to produce a chronological order for the thirty-seven selected English versions.[91]

- Wyclif Bible = WYC (1382–85)
- Tyndale New Testament = TNT (1534)
- Bishop's New Testament = PNT (1595)
- Geneva Bible = GNV (1599)
- King James Version = KJV (1611/1769)
- English Revised Version = ERV (1885)
- English Darby Bible = DBY (1884/1890)
- Young's Literal Translation = YLT (1882/1898)
- Douay-Rheims American = DRA (1899)
- American Standard Version = ASV (1901)
- Weymouth New Testament in Modern Speech = WEY (1903)
- Jewish Publication Society Bible = JPS (1917)
- New English Bible = NEB (1970)
- Revised Standard Version = RSV (1952/1971)
- New American Standard Bible = NAS (1960/1986)
- New King James Version = NKJV (1982)
- New Jewish Publication Society Bible = NJPS or TNK (1985)
- New Jerusalem Bible = NJB (1985)
- Revised English Bible = REB (1989)
- New Revised Standard Version = NRSV (1989)
- Good News Bible = GNT (1966/1992)
- New American Standard Update = NASB (1995)
- God's Word Translation = GWT (1995)
- New International Reader's Version = NIRV (1995/1998)
- Complete Jewish Bible = CJB (1998)

- International Standard Version, New Testament = ISV (2000)
- New Century Version = NCV (2005)
- New English Translation or NET Bible = NET (1996–2006)
- New Living Translation = NLT (1996/2007)
- MacDonald Idiomatic Translation, New Testament = MIT (2008)
- Holman Christian Standard Bible = HCSB (1999/2009)
- New American Bible (Revised) = NAB (1970/2010)
- New International Version = NIV (1973/2011)
- New International Version (UK) = NIVUK (1979/2011)
- Common English Bible = CEB (2011)
- English Standard Version = ESV (2001/2016)
- Christian Standard Bible = CSB (2017)

In order to illustrate the types of language change observable in English versions over the years, we will examine one representative familiar passage from each testament. The selections do not avoid translation problems nor do they favor any particular translation style (literal, essentially literal, dynamic, or paraphrastic).[92]

Genesis 1:27

Translation differences among English language versions of the Bible show up in the very first word of this verse. Biblical Hebrew uses a conjunction attached to a sequential verb form. Translators must determine the meaning of the conjunction by examining the context. The conjunction possesses a wide range of potential meanings ("and," "but," "so," "thus," "therefore," "then," "even," etc.). Sometimes the conjunction serves no translatable purpose and the context allows for its omission in translation—especially when the receiving language prefers not to use one due to unnecessary repetition. Translators make their choice after evaluating the flow of the context. They ask the following questions:

- Is the relationship a mere connection as in a list or in a series of coordinated events?: *and*
- Is the relationship a contrast with what precedes?: *but*
- Is the relationship temporal, depicting a chronological event in a sequence?: *then*
- Is the relationship more of a logical matter showing result, summary, or consequence?: *so, thus, therefore*

- Is the relationship explanatory?: *even*
- Does the flow of the context not really require the conjunction in any form in the English?: Omit.

Although there are small differences in meaning, most English versions understand a logical, rather than temporal, relationship for Genesis 1:27.

Thus: "Thus God created the man in his image: in the image of God created he him: he created them male and female."—GNV (1599)

So: "So God created man in his *own* image, in the image of God created he him; male and female created he them."—KJV (1611/1769); cf. NEB (1970), RSV (1952/1971), NKJV (1982), NAS (1960/1986), NRSV (1989), GNT (1966/1992), GWT (1995), NIRV (1995/1998), CJB (1998), NCV (2005), NLT (1996/2007), HCSB (1999/2009), NIV (1973/2011), NIVUK (1979/2011), ESV (2001/2016), CSB (2017)

And: "And God made of nouȝt man to the ymage and his lickenes; to the ymage of God he made hym; maal and femaal he made hem of nouȝt."—WYC (1382–85); cf. ERV (1885), DBY (1884/1890), YLT (1882/1898), DRA (1899), ASV (1901), JPS (1917), NJPS (1985), NAS (1960/1986)

Omit: "God created man in the image of himself, in the image of God he created him, male and female he created them."— NJB (1985); cf. REB (1989), NASB (1995), NET (1996–2006), NAB (1970/2010), CEB (2011)

The next area of variation in the wording replaces "created" with "made of nought": "And God made of nouȝt man to the ymage and his lickenes; to the ymage of God he made hym; maal and femaal he made hem of nouȝt" (WYC, 1382–85). Wyclif believed that "create" meant to "make out of nothing." However, the first man was not made of nothing, but of the dust of the ground (Gen. 2:7)—and, the woman was made out of the material God removed from Adam's side (Gen. 2:21–22). The Hebrew verb "create" may only be said to imply "out of nothing" with the original creation in Genesis 1:1, but that concept is never a legitimate semantic element inherent to that verb. Instead, the verb implies divine action, since God is the only subject the verb "create" takes in the

Hebrew Bible. YLT reveals an unusual and also inaccurate translation of "created" by the verb "prepared": "And God prepareth the man in His image; in the image of God He prepared him, a male and a female He prepared them." The English translations overwhelmingly, and rightly, have chosen "created" as the verb in Genesis 1:27.

Given the current sensitivity to gender in translation, it is no surprise that we can identify a change through time in translating "man" in this verse:

the man:	"Thus God created the man in his image: in the image of God created he him: he created them male and female."—GNV (1599); cf. YLT (1882/1898)
man:	"And God made of nouȝt man to the ymage and his lickenes; to the ymage of God he made hym; maal and femaal he made hem of nouȝt."—WYC (1382–1385); cf. KJV (1611/1769), ERV (1885), DBY (1884/1890), DRA (1899), ASV (1901), JPS (1917), NEB (1970), RSV (1952/1971), NKJV (1982), NJB (1985), NJPS (1985), NAS (1960/1986), NASB (1995), NIRV (1995/1998), HCSB (1999/2009), ESV (2001/2016), CSB (2017)
mankind:	"God created mankind in his image; in the image of God he created them; male and female he created them."—NAB (1970/2010); cf. NIV (1973/2011), NIVUK (1979/2011)
humankind:	"So God created humankind in his image, in the image of God he created them; male and female he created them."—NRSV (1989); cf. CJB (1998), NET (1996–2006)
humanity:	"God created humanity in God's own image, in the divine image God created them, male and female God created them."—CEB (2011)
human beings:	"God created human beings in his own image; in the image of God he created them; male and female he created them."—REB (1989); cf. GNT (1966/1992), NCV (2005), NLT (1996/2007)

humans: "So God created humans in his image. In the image of God he created them. He created them male and female."—GWT (1995)

However, the context and the pattern within this verse indicate that Moses first refers to the creation of the first man, Adam, making the older translation more accurate.

Another unusual translation appears fairly early with "to" rather than "in": "And God made of nouȝt man to the ymage and his lickenes; to the ymage of God he made hym; maal and femaal he made hem of nouȝt" (WYC, 1382–85); and, "And God created man to his own image: to the image of God he created him: male and female he created them" (DRA, 1899). The choice grates on the ear and did not catch on—partly because the Hebrew preposition better represents "in" than "to."

Next, we come to the addition of "own" to "His/his image" to stress the identity with God Himself. Through time it appears that translators decided that the double statement ("in His image" and "in the image of God") provides adequate emphasis. In other words, clarity dominated most translators' choice while fewer opted for simplicity.

own: "So God created man in his *own* image, in the image of God created he him; male and female created he them."—KJV (1611/1769); cf. ERV (1885), DRA (1899), ASV (1901), JPS (1917), NEB (1970), RSV (1952/1971), NKJV (1982), NAS (1960/1986), REB (1989), NASB (1995), NIRV (1995/1998), CJB (1998), NET (1996–2006), NLT (1996/2007), HCSB (1999/2009), NIV (1973/2011), NIVUK (1979/2011), CEB (2011), ESV (2001/2016), CSB (2017)

omit: "And God made of nouȝt man to the ymage and his lickenes; to the ymage of God he made hym; maal and femaal he made hem of nouȝt."—WYC (1382–85); cf. GNV (1599), DBY (1884/1890), YLT (1882/1898), NJPS (1985), NRSV (1989), GWT (1995), NCV (2005), NAB (1970/2010); note the variation "in the image of himself" (NJB, 1985)

One translation chose to insert "God's own" to clarify "His," then followed it with "in the divine image" (CEB, 2011). Two versions chose to avoid "image" altogether:

> "So God created human beings, making them to be like himself. He created them male and female."—GNT (1966/1992)

> "So God created man in his own likeness. He created him in the likeness of God. He created them as male and female."—NIRV (1995/1998)

Wyclif added "and his lickenes [likeness]" to the first occurrence of "image," perhaps thinking back to the previous verse: "Then God said, 'Let Us make man in Our image, according to Our likeness; and let them rule over the fish of the sea and over the birds of the sky and over the cattle and over all the earth, and over every creeping thing that creeps on the earth'" (NASB).

The final matter to observe among the selected English versions involves "He created him; male and female He created them" (NASB). Note how the versions have handled the pronoun "him" (whose antecedent is "the man" in the Hebrew text):

him: "And God made of nouȝt man to the ymage and his lickenes; to the ymage of God he made hym; maal and femaal he made hem of nouȝt."—WYC (1382–85); cf. GNV (1599), KJV (1611/1769), ERV (1885), DBY (1884/1890), YLT (1882/1898), DRA (1899), ASV (1901), JPS (1917), NEB (1970), RSV (1952/1971), NKJV (1982), NJB (1985), NJPS (1985), NAS (1960/1986), NASB (1995), CJB (1998), NIRV (1995/1998), HCSB (1999/2009), ESV (2001/2016), CSB (2017)

them: "God created human beings in his own image; in the image of God he created them; male and female he created them."—REB (1989); cf. NRSV (1989), GNT (1966/1992), GWT (1995), NCV (2005), NET (1996–2006), NLT (1996/2007), NAB (1970/2010), NIV (1973/2011), NIVUK (1979/2011), CEB (2011)

Many of the English versions retain "him" in keeping with the Hebrew pronoun. The antecedent for "him" is "man," which some take as a singular collective equivalent to "mankind" as a whole. Thus the translations with "him" do not necessarily refer to "the man" as an individual (Adam). It appears that only GNV (1599) and YLT (1882/1898) unambiguously specify an individual here ("the man").[93]

Summary: Translators behind these selected English versions from John Wyclif to the team of translators working on the CSB have earnestly attempted to provide a translation of Genesis 1:27 that is understandable. They sought to use clear and simple English to convey the original Hebrew text accurately. Those differences that might appear large to the reader (e.g., "the man" vs. "mankind") rest upon good exegetical reasons for making the choices. Good exegesis does not always mean that the interpreters always reach the identical conclusion. That's part of the difficulty of dealing with any language—and, especially a language spoken 3,500 years ago. That's where commentaries enter the picture—to explain translation choices.

1 John 1:9

Few New Testament verses (other than John 3:16) find as much favor with Christians as 1 John 1:9. Most Scripture memorization plans include it, so it becomes one of the first to be stored in the memory of new believers. Analyzing the English versions' treatment of this beloved text reveals some changes throughout the history of the English Bible.

The start of 1 John 1:9 depends upon how the translators understand the relationship to the previous verse: "If we say we have no sin, we deceive ourselves, and the truth is not in us" (1 John 1:8 ESV). A few translations change the word order so that the conditional sentence comes second.

if:	"If we knowlechen oure synnes, he is feithful and iust, that he forȝiue to us oure synnes, and clense us fro al wickidnesse."—WYC (1382–85); cf. TNT (1534), PNT (1595), GNV (1599), KJV (1611/1769), ERV (1885), DBY (1884/1890), YLT (1882/1898), DRA (1899), ASV (1901), WEY (1903), NEB (1970), RSV (1952/1971), NKJV (1982), NJB (1985), NAS (1960/1986), NRSV (1989), REB (1989), NASB (1995), NIRV (1995/1998), CJB (1998), ISV (2000), NCV (2005), NET (1996–2006), NLT (1996/2007), MIT (2008), HCSB (1999/2009), NAB (1970/2010), NIV (1973/2011), NIVUK (1979/2011), ESV (2001/2016), CSB (2017); see change of order below for GWT (1995)
But if:	"But if we confess our sins to God, he will keep his promise and do what is right: he will forgive us our sins and purify us from all our wrongdoing."—GNT (1966/1992); cf. CEB (2011); see change of order below for NIRV (1995/1998)

Change order: "God is faithful and reliable. If we confess our sins, he forgives them and cleanses us from everything we've done wrong."—GWT (1995); "But God is faithful and fair. If we admit that we have sinned, he will forgive us our sins. He will forgive every wrong thing we have done. He will make us pure."—NIRV (1995/1998)

Changing the order of the original text does not necessarily skew the text or treat it inaccurately. Normal clause order in English often differs from biblical Hebrew and Greek. The two versions that change the clause order (GWT and NIRV) switched the order of the "if" (protasis) and "then" (apodosis) clauses. They appear to have done so to (1) highlight the character of God and (2) enable a closer connection of the confession with the result God brings about.

The next variation occurs with regard to the word "confess":

knowledge/acknowledge: "If we knowlechen oure synnes, he is feithful and iust, that he forȝiue to us oure synnes, and clense us fro al wickidnesse."—WYC (1382–85); cf. TNT (1534), PNT (1595); GNV (1599), NJB (1985), CJB (1998), NAB (1970/2010)

admit: "But God is faithful and fair. If we admit that we have sinned, he will forgive us our sins. He will forgive every wrong thing we have done. He will make us pure."—NIRV (1995/1998)

confess: "If we confess our sins, he is faithful and just to forgive us *our* sins, and to cleanse us from all unrighteousness."—KJV (1611/1769); all remaining selected translations

Readers would be hard-pressed to make any meaningful distinctions between "acknowledge," "admit," and "confess." Anyone seeking to create some significant theological differences would be stretching English semantics. English Bible versions use all three English words for the same Greek verb. The following list offers just a few such examples.

acknowledge:	**Matthew 10:32** (WEY, NEB, REB, RSV, ESV CSB); **John 12:42** (NEB, REB); **Hebrews 11:13** (WEY, RSV, REB, ESV); **13:15** (NEB, RSV, REB, ESV)
admit:	**John 12:42** (NIRV); **Acts 24:14** (NEB, REB, RSV, GNT, NASB, CSB); **Hebrews 11:13** (GNT)
confess:	**Matthew 10:32** (GNV, KJV, ERV, DBY, YLT, DRA, NASB); **John 12:42** (GNV, KJV, ERV, DBY, YLT, DRA, RSV, NASB, ESV, CSB); **Acts 24:14** (GNV, KJV, ERV, YLT, DRA, WEY, ESV); **Romans 10:9** (GNV, KJV, ERV, DBY, YLT, DRA, WEY, NEB, REB, RSV, GNT, NASB, ESV, CSB); **Hebrews 11:13** (GNV, KJV, ERV, DBY, YLT, DRA, NEB, NASB, CSB); **13:15** (GNV, ERV, DBY, DRA, GNT, CSB)
avow:	**John 12:42** (WEY); **Acts 24:14** (DBY)
give thanks:	**Hebrews 13:15** (KJV, YLT, WEY, NASB)
declare publicly:	**Matthew 10:32** (GNT)
say:	**Matthew 10:32** (NIRV); **Romans 10:9** (NIRV)
openly said:	**Hebrews 11:13** (NIRV)
talk about it openly:	**John 12:42** (GNT)
say they believe:	**Hebrews 13:15** (NIRV)
it is true:	**John 12:42** (NIRV)

The next phrase, "our sins," appears to have been translated differently only by NIRV: "that we have sinned." The meaning is essentially the same, so this particular example could be termed "essentially literal," even though the phrasing has switched from a possessive pronoun modifying a noun to a plural pronoun as subject of a verb. The form is different, but the meaning is the same. Such variation does produce a side effect for serious

Bible students: if anyone desires to identify all occurrences of "our sins" in the Bible, this verse would be missing, if they stick solely to the NIRV.

"He is faithful and just" comprises the fourth component of the verse.

faithful and just:	WYC (1382–85), TNT (1534), PNT (1595), GNV (1599), KJV (1611/1769), DRA (1899), WEY (1903), RSV (1952 / 1971), NKJV (1982), NRSV (1989), NLT (1996/2007), NAB (1970/2010), NIV (1973/2011), NIVUK (1979/2011), CEB (2011), ESV (2001/2016)
faithful and righteous:	ERV (1885), DBY (1884/1890), ASV (1901), NAS (1960/1986), NASB (1995), ISV (2000), NET (1996–2006), MIT (2008), HCSB (1999/2009), CSB (2017)
faithful and reliable:	GWT (1995)
faithful and fair:	NIRV (1995/1998)
stedfast He is and righteous:	YLT (1882/1898)
just, and may be trusted:	NEB (1970), REB (1989)
trustworthy and upright:	NJB (1985)
trustworthy and just:	CJB (1998)
because we can trust God to do what is right:	NCV (2005)

All of these English versions focus on the concept of God's faithfulness, justice, or righteousness. It all boils down to God being trustworthy or reliable. As the NCV puts it, "we can trust God to do what is right." GNT's "he will keep his promise and do what is right" offers a slight paraphrastic expansion to help readers understand. The GWT actually stands outside all other translations, because it effectually eliminates "righteous/just/fair/upright/right" and uses "reliable" to duplicate the basic idea of "faithful." Therefore, one could argue that its translation actually departs from what appears to have been the author's intent in using two words with mainly different semantic ranges.

God's action of forgiving comprises the subsequent element of the verse.

that he forgive to us/that He may forgive us:	WYC (1382–85), YLT (1882/1898), WEY (1903)
so that he will forgive:	NJB (1985)
to forgive us:	TNT (1534), PNT (1595), GNV (1599), KJV (1611/1769), ERV (1885), DBY (1884/1890), DRA (1899), ASV (1901), NKJV (1982), NAS (1960/1986), NASB (1995), ISV (2000), NLT (1996/2007), HCSB (1999/2009), CEB (2011), ESV (2001/2016), CSB (2017)
to forgive:	NEB (1970), REB (1989)
will forgive us:	NRSV (1989), GNT (1966/1992), NIRV (1995/1998)
will forgive:	NCV (2005)
and will forgive us:	NIV (1973/2011)
and will forgive:	RSV (1952/1971), CJB (1998), NAB (1970/2010)
forgiving us:	NET (1996–2006)
he forgives:	GWT (1995)
to handle that by forgiving:	MIT (2008)

Every one of these English translations choose "forgive" as the most accurate representation of the Greek word. The Greek particle *hina* starts the compound clause expressing both a purpose ("in order to forgive") and result ("so that he cleanses"). Four of the versions (WYC, YLT, WEY, and

NJB) attempt to translate *hina* directly ("that" and "so that"). Most versions employ an infinitive ("to forgive"), thereby omitting a more specific use of "in order that" or "so that," making the English translation read more simply and smoothly. The English infinitive also allows for both the purpose and result concepts for the two parts connected by "and."

Since the verb is an active form, most versions since 1989 employ "will forgive" or "forgives" leaving the purpose or result to the reader's understanding or contextual interpretation. Two translations (NET and MIT) choose a participle ("forgiving") as an equally acceptable means of treating the verb in its context. The MIT adds "to handle that by" in order to fill out the English ellipsis to clarify the meaning of the clause and its relationship to God's character qualities.

The presence of "us" in most versions results from a literal translation of the Greek text. A number of translations omit "us" as seemingly redundant when accompanied by "our sins." That brings us to observations about the English versions' handling of the objects of "forgive."

to us our sins:	WYC (1382–1385)
us our sins:	TNT (1534), PNT (1595), GNV (1599), KJV (1611/1769), ERV (1885), DBY (1884/1890), DRA (1899), ASV (1901), WEY (1903), NKJV (1982), NAS (1960/1986), NRSV (1989), GNT (1966/1992), NASB (1995), NIRV (1995/1998), NET (1996–2006), NLT (1996/2007), HCSB (1999/2009), NIV (1973/2011), CEB (2011), ESV (2001/2016), CSB (2017)
us the sins:	YLT (1882/1898)
us those sins:	ISV (2000)
our sins:	NEB (1970), RSV (1952/1971), NJB (1985), REB (1989), MIT (2008), NAB (1970/2010)
them:	GWT (1995), CJB (1998)

The overwhelming majority of English versions preserve the personal pronoun "us" (a dative in the Greek, which could be taken as "to us"—the indirect object grammatically). Then they add "our" to "sins" (the direct object in the clause) to conform to the earlier "confess our sins." That backward glance in the flow of the verse leads the ISV to use "those sins." Both the GWT and CJB decide against repeating "sins," so they use "them." The YLT's "the sins" seeks to be as literal as possible—which fits the claims of the translator and his version's title.

One might argue that English versions omitting "us" obscure the personal aspect of divine forgiveness. God forgives those who confess. His act involves more than just pardoning sin itself—the sinners themselves gain relief from the guilt of their sin—they personally and individually experience the divine pardon. However, the omission of "us" in any of the versions does not in any way deny that truth nor did the translators seek to remove or avoid that truth.

Since the Greek does use the definite article "the" with "sins," the force of the grammar refers back to the previous "sins" confessed by the sinner. In other words, only those confessed sins receive God's pardon or forgiveness. The ISV, GWT, and CJB succeed best in making that connection crystal clear.

"And" introduces the second portion (the result) of the compound clause, connecting it to the previous portion (the purpose).

that . . . and cleanse us:	WYC (1382–85), YLT (1882/1898)
that . . . and cleanses us:	WEY (1903)
and to cleanse us:	TNT (1534), PNT (1595), GNV (1599), KJV (1611/1769), ERV (1885), DRA (1899), ASV (1901), NKJV (1982), NAS (1960/1986), NASB (1995), NLT (1996/2007), HCSB (1999/2009), ESV (2001/2016), CSB (2017)
and cleanse(s) us:	DBY (1884/1890), NEB (1970), RSV (1952/1971), REB (1989), NRSV (1989), GWT (1995), ISV (2000), NAB (1970/2010), CEB (2011)
and will cleanse us:	NJB (1985)
and cleansing us:	NET (1996–2006)
He will cleanse us:	NCV (2005)

and purify us:	GNT (1966/1992), CJB (1998), NIV (1973/2011)
and purifying us:	MIT (2008)
He will make us pure:	NIRV (1995/1998)

No significant distinction exists with regard to "cleanse" vs. "purify," so the versions display no real disagreement in the meaning of the verb. Likewise, all identify the object as "us." Variation appears only in the means of expressing the relationship between the first half of the compound purpose-result clause and the second half. The oldest English versions employ "that" for the purpose of repeating the key particle with which the clause is introduced. "And" represents a literal translation of the conjunction. The two that omit any particle or conjunction (NCV and NIRV) do so because they reconstruct the word order and simplify the structure. No essential meaning is lost, nor does any version skew the meaning.

The final element of the verse exhibits some variety in the noun "unrighteousness" (the majority) and its adjective ("all" or "every").

from all wickedness:	WYC (1382–85), NLT (1996/2007)
from all unrighteousness:	TNT (1534), PNT (1595), GNV (1599), KJV (1611/1769), ERV (1885), DBY (1884/1890), ASV (1901), WEY (1903), RSV (1952/1971), NKJV (1982), NAS (1960/1986), NRSV (1989), NASB (1995), ISV (2000), NET (1996–2006), HCSB (1999/2009), NIV (1973/2011), ESV (2001/2016), CSB (2017)
from every unrighteousness:	YLT (1882/1898)
from all iniquity:	DRA (1899)
from all wrongdoing:	CJB (1998), MIT (2008)
from all our wrongdoing:	GNT (1966/1992)

from all the wrongs we have done:	NCV (2005)
from every wrongdoing:	NAB (1970/2010)
from every kind of wrong/wrongdoing:	NEB (1970), REB (1989)
from everything we've done wrong:	GWT (1995), CEB (2011)
He will forgive every wrong thing we have done. He will make us pure.:	NIRV (1995/1998)
from all evil:	NJB (1985)

The noun in the Greek (*adikia*) represents the negative of the second adjective for the character of God earlier in the verse (*dikaios*, "just" or "righteous"). The *a*- prefix behaves just like the *a*- on some English words: atheist, amoral, ahistorical, asynchronous, and asymmetrical. The English versions above use "wickedness," "unrighteousness," "iniquity," "wrong" or "wrongdoing," and "evil." According to the Greek dictionaries, *adikia* can carry the sense of "an act that violates standards of right conduct, *wrongdoing*" or "the quality of injustice, *unrighteousness, wickedness, injustice*."[94]

Three translations appear to be different: "wickedness" (WYC and NLT), "evil" (NJB), and "iniquity" (DRA). However, all three fall within the semantic range, as demonstrated by the following English versions' renditions of *adikia* elsewhere in the New Testament:

ASV: **iniquity/iniquities** (Luke 13:27; Acts 1:18; 8:23; Heb. 8:12; James 3:6), **unrighteous** (Luke 16:8), **unrighteousness** (Luke 16:9; John 7:18; Rom. 1:18 *2x*, 29; 2:8; 3:5; 6:13; 9:14; 1 Cor. 13:6; 2 Thess. 2:10, 12, 19; 1 John 1:9; 5:17), **unrighteous** (Luke 18:6), **wrong** (2 Cor. 12:13), **wrong-doing** (2 Peter 2:13, 15)

NASB: **evildoers** (Luke 13:27), **unrighteous** (Luke 16:8; 18:6), **unrighteousness** (Luke 16:9; John 7:18; Rom. 1:18 *2x*, 29; 2:8; 3:5; 6:13; 1 Cor. 13:6; 2 Peter 2:15; 1 John 1:9; 5:17), **wickedness** (Acts 1:18; 2 Thess. 2:10, 12, 19), **iniquity/iniquities** (Acts 8:23; Heb. 8:12;

James 3:6), **injustice** (Rom. 9:14), **wrong** (2 Cor. 12:13), **doing wrong** (2 Peter 2:13)

NET: **evildoers** (Luke 13:27), **dishonest** (Luke 16:8), **worldly** (Luke 16:9), **unrighteous** (Luke 18:6), **unrighteousness** (John 7:18; Rom. 1:18 *2x*, 29; 2:8; 3:5; 6:13; 2 Peter 2:15; 1 John 1:9; 5:17), **unjust** (Acts 1:18), **sin** (Acts 8:23), **injustice** (Rom. 9:14; 1 Cor. 13:6; 2 Cor. 12:13), **evil** (2 Thess. 2:10, 12, 19), **evil deeds** (Heb. 8:12), **wrongdoing** (James 3:6), **harmful ways** (2 Peter 2:13)

NIV: **evildoers** (Luke 13:27), **dishonest** (Luke 16:8), **worldly** (Luke 16:9), **unjust** (Luke 18:6; Rom. 9:14), **false** (John 7:18), **wickedness** (Acts 1:18; Rom. 1:18 *2x*, 29; 6:13; 2 Thess. 2:10, 12, 19; Heb. 8:12; 2 Peter 2:15), **sin** (Acts 8:23), **evil** (Rom. 2:8; 1 Cor. 13:6; James 3:6), **unrighteousness** (Rom. 3:5; 1 John 1:9), **wrong** (2 Cor. 12:13), **harm** (2 Peter 2:13), **wrongdoing** (1 John 5:17)

ESV: **workers of evil** (Luke 13:27), **dishonest** (Luke 16:8), **unrighteous** (Luke 16:9; 18:6), **falsehood** (John 7:18), **wickedness** (Acts 1:18), **iniquity/iniquities** (Acts 8:23; 2 Thess. 2:19; Heb. 8:12), **unrighteousness** (Rom. 1:18 *2x*, 29; 2:8; 3:5; 6:13; 2 Thess. 2:12; James 3:6; 1 John 1:9), **injustice** (Rom. 9:14), **wrongdoing** (1 Cor. 13:6; 2 Peter 2:13, 15; 1 John 5:17), **wrong** (2 Cor. 12:13), **wicked** (2 Thess. 2:10)

The range of meaning used by each of these versions draws attention to the diversity of individual biblical contexts with which the translators wrestle. Sometimes it appears that some translators have chosen a particular translation for *adikia* to remain consistent within a particular New Testament book (e.g., Romans). Other explanations for the variety between the biblical books include different translators or teams of translators working with different biblical books or sections, or translators purposefully preserving a very popular and well-known translation (e.g., 1 John 1:9—all five of the selected versions retain "unrighteousness" in this text regardless of the spread of meanings elsewhere in the New Testament within the same versions).

As for the difference between "all" and "every," the translators work with the ambiguity of biblical Greek to determine whether the context seems to indicate either a global or universal ("all"), or a distributive ("every") meaning.[95] Regardless of choice, no confessed sin is omitted—whether looked at together or individually (each and every one).

Summary: As with the previous discussion of the English versions' treatment of Genesis 1:27, the differences between the versions remain mostly within the realm of good exegetical practices. Each version's translator or translation team aims to provide readers with an accurate and understandable translation remaining faithful to the original Greek text of 1 John 1:9. Immediate context within 1 John, the broader biblical context, and the normal vocabulary and speech patterns of the receiving audience (the version's intended readers) determine the translators' choices. The potential exists that the popularity of such a well-known verse might have influenced the majority of English versions in the twentieth and twenty-first centuries to preserve "unrighteousness" in the wording ("cleanse from all unrighteousness"). Yet, through all the variations, each version displays the desire to set clarity and simplicity as goals for each translation.

Concluding Thoughts

Our examination of Genesis 1:27 and 1 John 1:9 in thirty-seven different English Bible versions discovered many similarities and very few differences (at least not differences of any significance to meaning or to doctrine). Such similarities do not change the fact that some verses in some versions do contain significant differences with regard to both meaning and doctrine. However, such examples are few and far between. In his own survey of a variety of English versions, Dave Brunn identified twenty-six similarities between them. Below are a select few of those twenty-six.

- Every version translates thought for thought rather than word for word in many contexts.
- Every version gives priority to meaning over form.
- Every version gives priority to the meaning of idioms and figures of speech over the actual words.
- Every version allows the context to dictate many of its renderings.
- Every version steps away from the original form in order to be grammatically correct in English.
- Every version translates some Hebrew or Greek words many different ways.
- Every version leaves some Hebrew and Greek words untranslated.
- Every version paraphrases in some contexts.[96]

In other words, his survey covering many more texts (though looking at fewer versions) basically confirms our results. Most English versions handle the biblical text with reasonable care, giving attention to simplicity and clarity in translation without losing accuracy and faithfulness to the original language.

Most English versions handle the biblical text with reasonable care, giving attention to simplicity and clarity in translation without losing accuracy and faithfulness to the original language.

Proverbial Brevity

Simplicity and clarity become more challenging when translators work with poetic wisdom texts, as in the book of Proverbs. Some Bible translators argue eloquently for more of a super-literal, word-for-word rendering of Hebrew proverbs.[97] Such translations seem to preserve the punch of the proverb more than the smoothed-out translations employed by the vast majority of even literal English versions from the earlier KJV to the more recent CSB. The original Hebrew deliberately displays verbal density. Compare the following two renderings of Proverbs 16:18.

Literal: Before breaking, pride; and before stumbling, height of spirit.

KJV: Pride *goeth* before destruction, and an haughty spirit before a fall.

The second translation is unarguably smoother, but the addition of "goeth" and the change in word order obscure the Hebrew text's perfect parallelism. The more difficult and dense literal rendering causes the reader to stop and consider what the meaning might be. The readers must supply the smoothing of the translation for themselves. That accomplishes the purpose of Hebrew proverbs: to challenge the readers to consider the saying and mull it over in their mind. Just consider some English proverbs in comparison: "Easy come, easy go" and "Pretty is as pretty does." Therefore, Proverbs 25:13 ("As the cold of snow in the time of harvest, *so is* a faithful messenger to them that send him," KJV) in English proverbial style might read something like "faithful messenger, harvest snow."[98]

Perhaps this kind of translation for Hebrew proverbs would fit more appropriately in a commentary rather than in a Bible translation.[99] A commentary allows discussion of the possible meanings and potential translations of a proverb while presenting support for the meaning chosen by the commentator. Perhaps all commentaries might benefit from this type of inclusion. Such a commentary's format might include both the literal rendering and a parallel smooth rendering at the head of the interpretive comments. Meanwhile, translators continue to wrestle with the best way in which they might translate the proverbs with both clarity and simplicity.

Translators must maintain theological integrity as much as cultural integrity. In the next chapter, we will explore the frequently stormy relationship between theology and translation. At times theology depends heavily on the Bible translation theologians employ as their basic reference work.

CHAPTER 5

THEOLOGY AND BIBLE TRANSLATION

THOUGHT INFLUENCES LANGUAGE AND LANGUAGE influences thought. Howard Rheingold asks an interesting question: "If you have no words for green, for example, is it more difficult to discriminate between a green card and a blue one?"[100] In Bangladesh we found that Bangladeshis had difficulty distinguishing between green and blue. My wife asked a Bangladeshi employee to purchase one color and he returned with the other. To him it made no difference. In spite of the fact that the Bengali language of Bangladesh possesses distinguishing words—*nil* (pronounced *neel*) for blue and *shobuj* (*show-booj*) for green—Bangladeshis regularly fail to recognize the distinction in practice. Throughout Bangladesh we noted the same occurrence. It could not be explained by color blindness nor by a lack of distinct terminology. Perhaps the reason lies deep in the culture.

The question finds application in the realm of biblical theology. If a culture does not possess words for *propitiation* or *atonement*, does that culture have knowledge of the concepts? Can its native speakers understand the basic idea involved in each of these theological terms? Why are certain concepts (including theological ones) apparently absent in certain languages? Can a people adequately comprehend a loan-word from another language? A Bible-based theology has no choice but to be wedded to Bible translation. Therefore, one's theology heavily depends upon one's understanding of Scripture in translation, whether of one's own making or a published version in some language. On the other side of the coin, Bible translation inextricably depends on theology, since the translators' doctrinal position can influence their translation. As evangelicals we tend to guard ourselves with the dictate that the Scriptures in their original languages form the final authority in all matters of faith and practice. In reality, however, pastors or theology teachers must communicate with their congregation or students via some form of translation. Congregations and students alike will interact with theological teaching on the basis of the translations with which they are most familiar.

A Bible-based theology has no choice but to be wedded to Bible translation. Therefore, one's theology heavily depends upon one's understanding of Scripture in translation, whether of one's own making or a published version in some language.

Translators of Scripture seek to elucidate the whole truth (and nothing but the truth) embedded in the ancient text. The very nature of the daunting task of Bible translation limits translators. They must immerse themselves as deeply as possible into each biblical text, mindful that a specific cultural and historical context in the ancient Hebrew, Aramaic, or Greek produced that text. The problems inherent in recreating these components stagger the imagination of the knowledgeable, not just the unknowing. Authorial intentions sometimes quite alien to those of the present day produced the biblical text. The linguistic features, literary traditions, and cultural contexts have vastly changed and either lack current vitality or are poorly understood—sometimes both.[101]

We cannot discuss Bible translation without touching upon the linguistic distance between the ancient and modern languages. Classical Hebrew, biblical Aramaic, and Koine Greek are very different from modern American English, Mexican Spanish, or Bangladeshi Bengali. That vexes the literalist tendencies we possess as evangelicals. In the attempt to close the gap between the ancient text and the present reader, some translations convert the modern receptor language into Hebraistic, Aramaic, or Hellenistic English or Hebraistic, Aramaic, or Hellenistic Spanish. However, that approach does not really resolve the distance problem. The resultant translation might end up misrepresenting the original author's meaning and tone. Why is it that, in the vast majority of Bible translations into English, the entire text tends to be identical in style and manner of expression? It certainly should not be due to the single language factor—namely, that it was penned in biblical Hebrew, Aramaic, or Greek.[102] If significant differences exist between the English styles of Walter Kaiser, Eugene Merrill, and Edwin Yamauchi in their respective histories of the Old Testament, certainly differences emerge between the Hebrew narrative styles of, for example, Moses and the Chronicler. Likewise, distinct differences become noticeable between the styles of Paul's letters as compared with John's letters. The reader of the Pentateuch and 1 and 2 Chronicles or Ephesians and 1 John in translation ought to be able to see those differences. Moses did not write or speak like David. John did not write or speak like Paul. Ruth did not sound like Boaz, and Ezekiel did not write or speak like Joshua.

To be sure, an overly idiomatic translation might produce insuperable difficulties by disrupting the intricate unity of Scripture. Such translation could result in an equally idiomatic theology freely altering elements of biblical theology to fit a modern culture. Thus, in a society dominated by a particular sinful activity, one might reason that the Bible's condemnation of that sin was solely a cultural matter—perhaps the activity was simply unacceptable to the majority at that time and place. Now, however, things have changed with the times. Does Scripture embody absolute truth (transcultural or universal truths) which translators ought to preserve in either form or meaning? A translation must conserve such truths if it is to maintain theological as well as linguistic and cultural integrity.[103]

On the other hand, an overly literal translation might tend to obscure the meaning to such an extent that the reader either does not understand what it says or comes away with an erroneous concept of the text's meaning. Another look at an example from chapter 3 might illustrate this point. *Beney-Yisrael* ("the sons of Israel") in Genesis 42:5 has quite a different meaning than it does in 32:33. The first refers to literal sons (male offspring), while the second refers to a national or ethnic group. The older translations, by employing "the children of Israel," add a third potential meaning: male and female offspring. The reader who is unfamiliar with the peculiarities of traditional biblical English might misunderstand some of the more vague references in a literal translation. Translating the national or ethnic references as "Israelites" clarifies and accurately preserves the meaning intended by the Hebrew author. Obviously, a single translation of the phrase undermines a translator's commitment to accuracy of meaning as opposed to mere replication of form. As in the case of Aquila's Greek translation of the Old Testament, adherence to a single form might indicate more clearly the translation's base, but would prove useful only to those who have an extensive knowledge of classical Hebrew and significant exposure to the technicalities of textual criticism. It is more than foolish to foist such literalism upon the average reader. It smacks of both elitism as well as rebellion against the divine intent that the Scriptures be understood and obeyed (see Neh. 8; Matt. 13:18–23).

In a worst-case scenario, a translation might even obscure the truth, thereby limiting or hindering the development of a consistent theology—consistent, that is, with the original text. An examination of various translations of select texts in the book of Genesis reveals the dynamic interaction of translation and theology. For the sake of convenience, the texts will be discussed in their canonical order.

In a worst-case scenario, a translation might even obscure the truth, thereby limiting or hindering the development of a consistent theology—consistent, that is, with the original text.

Who Blesses Whom? (Gen. 12:3)

The Mosaic record of Yahweh's pronouncement of blessing through Abram consists of a text whose translation possesses significant theological implications. Depending on the Bible translation one reads, this text might imply a kind of double predestination. Double predestination teaches a dual election: an election to salvation and an election to damnation. Millard Erickson writes the following about this doctrine:

> Calvin called this a "horrible decree," but nevertheless held it because he found it in the Bible. Others say that God actively chooses those who are

> to receive eternal life, and passes by all the others, leaving them in their self-chosen sins. The effect is the same in both cases, but the latter view assigns the lostness of the nonelect to their own choice of sin rather than to the active decision of God, or to God's choice by omission rather than commission.[104]

In addition to this particular theological issue, a translation of Genesis 12:3 might refer either directly or indirectly to divinely bestowed blessing upon all peoples. Both double predestination and universal blessing can affect one's theological summary of the contents and implications of the Abrahamic covenant. Patrick Miller declares,

> The critical theological place of Gen. xii 1–4a in the book of Genesis and more particularly in the Yahwistic form of the patriarchal narratives has understandably prompted a considerable amount of analysis and interpretation. Much attention has been given to explaining the syntax of the whole, especially the relation of vs. 3b to the preceding verses. The issues in understanding the syntax are not merely superficial, for the meaning of the text is to a large degree uncovered by a careful understanding of the relation of the clauses to each other.[105]

Consider the following translations of verse 3:

NJB: "I shall bless those who bless you, and shall curse those who curse you, and all clans on earth will bless themselves by you."

NJPS: "I will bless those who bless you
And curse him that curses you;
"And all the families of the earth
Shall bless themselves by you."

REB: "those who bless you, I shall bless;
those who curse you, I shall curse.
All the peoples on earth
will wish to be blessed as you are blessed."

KJV: "And I will bless them that bless thee, and curse him that curseth thee: and in thee shall all families of the earth be blessed."

NIV: "I will bless those who bless you,
and whoever curses you I will curse;
and all peoples on earth
will be blessed through you."

NLT: "I will bless those who bless you and curse those who treat you with contempt. All the families of the earth will be blessed through you."

The same translation problem occurs again in Genesis 18:18 and 28:14 with the various translations seeking to be consistent in all references. Thus, this example helps to illustrate the fact that a translation in one passage might affect the translation of related passages. In this case, it also might affect the translation of the New Testament's quotation of Genesis 12:3 in Acts 3:25 and Galatians 3:8.

Interpreting the verse involves Hebrew word order, syntax, and vocabulary. The word order of the first half of the verse displays a chiasm in which each word or phrase is mirrored by an equivalent word or phrase in inverted order:

A *I will bless*
B *those blessing you*
B' *the one disdaining you*
A' *I will curse*

Moses employed chiasm in order to emphasize the central members of the inverted structure. In this particular case, the chiasm highlights the blessing or cursing of Abraham and his descendants by all people. That leads naturally into the last part of the verse where emphasis again falls on people: "all the families/clans of the earth." It is noteworthy that the first **B** element is plural while the second one (**B'**) is singular. This difference in number could imply that "more people will bless Abraham than will maltreat him, and that God desires to bless many and curse few."[106] The chiastic structure might also provide a convenient and natural means of breaking the chain of four verbs expressing determination ("I will make you," "I will bless you," "I will magnify," "I will bless") and one imperative ("let it be") following the initial imperative ("go") of verse 1. According to Miller, the contrasting clause ("but the one disdaining you I will curse") serves to make this concept distinct, "so that there can be no confusion between the form and the function of the clause . . . and the preceding clauses."[107] This results in the curse being made to appear as though it were not a part of Yahweh's intention: "God commands Abraham to go out in order to receive a blessing and bring about a stream of blessing in the world. But Yahweh does not command Abraham to go out in order to bring about curse."[108] Miller applies this interpretation of the Hebrew syntax to a description of God's purpose in blessing Abram and, through him, the nations: "When Yahweh sent Abram out, it was to bring about blessing, not curse. That is the good report which the Bible transmits to each generation."[109] Having thus related the text to a denial of the doctrine of double predestination, he then suggests a translation that would be conducive to the reader reaching the same conclusion:

> 1 And Yahweh said to Abram:
> "Go from your land, from your kindred, and from your father's house to the land which I will show you,
> 2 that I may make you a great nation, and bless you, and make your name great that you may effect blessing,
> 3 and that I may bless the ones blessing you—and should there be one who regards you with contempt I will curse him.
> So, then, all the families of the earth can gain a blessing in you."[110]

Another aspect of the text involves the use of two different Hebrew words for "curse" (translated in the chiastic diagram above as "disdaining" and "curse"). Genesis commentator Gordon Wenham observes that "Traditional English translations fail to bring out the difference between these words, usually translating both 'curse.'"[111] The point of the text seems to be that even if an individual treats Abram lightly, treats him with contempt, or despises him, the judicial curse of God will fall upon him.[112]

One element in the last half of verse 3 accounts for the most serious variation in translation—the verb translated by the NIV as "will be blessed" (also employed in 18:18 and 28:14). This verb's Hebrew form[113] might be passive, reflexive, reciprocal, or middle in its grammatical voice.[114] In all four the subject of the verb also acts as the object of the verb (the recipient of the verb's action). The passive voice of the verb implies an outside agent ("they will be blessed *by someone*"); the reflexive voice makes the subject the agent ("they will bless themselves");[115] the reciprocal voice consists of a plural subject that normally participates in mutual action ("they will bless each other"); and, the middle voice presents the subject as affected in some way by the action ("they will acquire blessing for themselves").

The middle voice may be somewhat ambiguous because it might speak of either an outside agent (as in the passive) or the subject as agent (as in the reflexive). The question is not a minor one. According to Hebraist Steven Boyd, it is a crucial interpretational issue: "Significant theological conclusions follow from the interpretation of these passages [Gen 12:3; 18:18; 28:14]."[116] How can the translator know which usage is involved? Normally the context reveals the usage.

Frankly, this particular context provides little help in resolving the issue. This situation occurs from time to time in Scripture just as it does in normal human communication. Observing this impasse, translators normally fall back on their knowledge of the rest of Scripture as well as their own theological backgrounds. Daniel Arichea cites the example of a missionary translator who rejects the reflexive solely on the basis that he believes that it might support the doctrine of universalism (that everyone will eventually receive salvation and forgiveness of his or her sins).[117] Some interpreters appeal to the alternate form of the concept stated in 22:18 and 26:4. These two verses employ a different form of the Hebrew verb for "bless."[118] The form of the verb in those two verses normally expresses a reflexive, so the expected translation might be "all the nations of the earth will bless themselves through your seed/offspring." Hebrew grammarians point out that this form "historically tends to take on the passive functions"[119] of the form that is found in 12:3. In other words, both forms may express the passive sense.[120] However, both forms might also express the reflexive sense.[121] Yet, strong arguments can be presented supporting the middle voice instead of either the passive or reflexive voices.[122] Ultimately, as Michael Brown explains, "grammatical arguments are not decisive."[123]

Does the voice translators attribute to the verb in this case make any difference? According to Claus Westermann, it makes no difference at all—the Abrahamic blessing still reaches all of earth's peoples.[124] On the other hand, Victor Hamilton ("this is not a point of esoteric grammar"[125]), Ephraim Speiser ("it is of great consequence theologically"[126]), and Walter Kaiser[127] all stress that the voice carries theological significance. As Brown observes, "In point of fact, it is one thing to receive blessing through Abraham's seed (passive or middle sense); it is another thing to desire to be like Abraham's seed (based on the reflexive sense)."[128] Kaiser carefully specifies the theological distinction between the reflexive and passive as follows:

> It would not be a matter of the nations looking over the fence to see what Israel had done and then, in copy-cat fashion, blessing themselves. It would be only by grace, by a gift of God—not by works. This would be the basis for God's blessing humanity in personal salvation.[129]

Ancient versions like the Samaritan Pentateuch, the Aramaic Targums, the Greek Septuagint, the Latin Vulgate, and the Syriac Peshitta, as well as the New Testament (cf. Acts 3:25 and Gal. 3:8)[130] all employ a passive/middle voice to translate the Hebrew verb in this passage.

When biblical authors suddenly alter a reoccurring word or phrase in any way, the interpreter or translator must seek a reason for the change.

Why would Genesis 22:18 and 26:4 employ a different form of the verb "bless"? Does this distinction in forms possess any exegetical significance? When biblical authors suddenly alter a reoccurring word or phrase in any way, the interpreter or translator must seek a reason for the change. Grammar alone may not determine which voice (passive, middle, reflexive, or reciprocal) the translator ought to use in translating these five occurrences of "bless." But, grammar might very well provide an answer for the question regarding the variation between the two forms. Hebrew intensive verb forms[131] possess the potential for referring to repeated actions.[132] Roots like the Hebrew verb for "bury" (*qabar*) maintain a non-repetitive meaning in the simple verb forms,[133] especially with singular subjects. For example, "Abraham buried his wife Sarah" (Gen. 23:19) is the simple verb form, because Abraham is burying only one person.[134] But, in 25:10 where the text reads, "Abraham and his wife Sarah were buried," the intensive-pluralative verb form occurs, since two people are being buried.[135]

Interestingly, the verb forms of "bless" in Genesis 12:3, 18:18, and 28:14 consist of simple forms all followed by "in you [singular]" in 12:3 and 28:14,[136] and "in him" in 18:18.[137] Moses modifies the forms in 22:18 and 26:4, however, by "in your seed/offspring."[138] It appears, therefore, that the plurality of "offspring" offers a viable explanation for variation in the verbs.[139] When the blessing emphasizes the agency of Abraham, the verb is a simple form but, when the agents are the descendants of Abraham, the verb is an intensive form implying the repetitive nature of the blessing generation after generation. This explanation might negate, to a certain degree, the argument claiming that the use of the intensive form of "bless" in 22:18 and 26:4 is driven by its reflexive meaning (which is then imposed upon the simple form in 12:3, 18:18, and 28:14).[140] As Michael Grisanti aptly concludes, no translational distinction between the simple and intensive "constructions naturally rises from the text. Consequently, they should all be translated in the same fashion."[141]

Proposed translation:

I will bless those who bless you, [Abram]—
But, should any treat you with contempt, I will curse him.
[In conclusion,] all of earth's peoples will be blessed through you.

Where the Fathers Are (Gen. 15:15)

First occurrences of a phrase's translation tend to set the tone for all subsequent appearances of the phrase or of any other phrases similar to it. However, translators might find that the interpretation guiding them in the phrase's first occurrence does not hold up under scrutiny in other contexts. For example, Yahweh's declaration to Abram in Genesis 15:15 consists of a parallelism that would seem to be synonymous:[142]

NASB: "As for you, you shall go to your fathers in peace; you will be buried at a good old age."

NJPS: "As for you,
You shall go to your fathers in peace;
You shall be buried at a ripe old age."

NRSV: "As for yourself, you shall go to your ancestors in peace; you shall be buried in a good old age."

REB: "You yourself will join your forefathers in peace and be buried at a ripe old age."

NLT: "(As for you, you will die in peace and be buried at a ripe old age.)"

The concept involved in the phrase "you shall go to your fathers" occurs also in the phrase "be gathered to his people" (cf. Gen. 25:8, 17; 35:29; 49:29–33; Num. 20:24, 26; 27:13; 31:2; Deut. 31:16; 32:50). Translators often treat each phrase as an idiom or as a mere "euphemism for death without clear theological import."[143] There are three different views concerning these phrases: (1) they indicate a belief in immortality,[144] (2) they are mere euphemisms,[145] or (3) they indicate the practice of multiple burial.[146]

Out of the translations quoted above, only NLT employs a rendering that would indicate a euphemistic interpretation ("you will die"). A number of arguments may be made for the immortality view:

(1) Abraham had no *fathers* (Gen. 15:15) in his grave—only his wife, Sarah (25:8–10). That there is no evidence that Abraham's "fathers" were believers (cf. Josh. 24:2) provides a counterargument. However, such an argument is invalid since Luke 16:19–31 seems to teach that the unbelieving dead and the believing dead (among whom Abraham is specifically mentioned) were both in the realm of departed spirits, not a family tomb. They were in view of each other and could also communicate.

(2) Jacob had no people in Egypt with whom to be buried and had no tomb, yet he "breathed his last, and was gathered to his people" (49:33; cf. v. 29).

(3) Aaron was buried alone on Mount Hor near the Edomite border, yet Yahweh said, "Aaron shall be gathered to his people" (Num. 20:24).

(4) Yahweh also told Moses that he would "be gathered" to his people (Num. 27:13), but he was buried at an unidentifiable site (Deut. 34:6). His body was also a matter of dispute between Satan and Michael (Jude 9).

(5) The patriarchs did possess a concept of immortality and a belief that God could resurrect them from the dead (cf. Job 19:25–27; Heb. 11:17–19).

The immortality viewpoint is consistent with God referring to Himself as the "God of Abraham, Isaac, and Jacob" (cf. Exod. 3:6; Mark 12:18–27).[147]

Regardless of the Bible translator's interpretation of such phraseology, it would be the better part of wisdom to avoid employing the NLT's reduction of the phrase ("you will die"). With so many evangelical scholars defending the literality of the phrase and the implications for the Old Testament doctrine of life after death, it would be better to translate the text literally and leave the debate to the commentators and theologians. Perhaps this is one example to which Daniel Arichea's warning might apply: "One should guard against some rather particularistic views, that is, views held only by one or two scholars. Often such views present the eccentricities of scholars rather than serious contributions to the interpretation of a text."[148] Leaving the text as it is does no damage to any of the various interpretive views. The NLT's translation purposefully (but perhaps not wisely) excludes other views, including the majority evangelical interpretation.

With so many evangelical scholars defending the literality of the phrase and the implications for the Old Testament doctrine of life after death, it would be better to translate the text literally and leave the debate to the commentators and theologians.

Proposed translation:

> But as for you, you will go to your ancestors in peace; you will be buried at a ripe old age.

More Than One (Gen. 19:24)

Unfortunately, translation can obscure theological details. An example of that kind of problem occurs in Genesis 19:24. A literal translation of the Hebrew text reads as follows: "Then Yahweh rained upon Sodom and upon Gomorrah sulfurous fire from Yahweh, from the heavens." By placing "Yahweh" at the head of the clause, the author emphasizes Yahweh's role in the event. As Allen Ross puts it, "The text . . . simply emphasizes that, whatever means were used, it was the Lord who rained this judgment on them."[149] While this is an accurate observation, it is only one part of the overall meaning of the clause. A second occurrence of "Yahweh" appears later in the verse: "from Yahweh." Is it a redundant expression in order to extend the emphasis of the first word? Or, is it the result of Moses's careful attention to theological detail? Notice what some translations have done with this second reference to Yahweh:

NJPS: "the LORD rained upon Sodom and Gomorrah sulfurous fire from the LORD out of heaven"

NIV: "Then the LORD rained down burning sulfur on Sodom and Gomorrah—from the LORD out of the heavens."

KJV: "Then the LORD rained upon Sodom and upon Gomorrah brimstone and fire from the LORD out of heaven."

REB: "and the LORD rained down fire and brimstone from the skies on Sodom and Gomorrah"

NLT: "Then the LORD rained down fire and burning sulfur from the sky on Sodom and Gomorrah."

NJB: "Then Yahweh rained down on Sodom and Gomorrah brimstone and fire of his own sending."

There are three variations among these versions:

(1) "brimstone and fire" / "fire and brimstone" / "fire and burning sulfur" / "burning sulfur" / "sulfurous fire"
(2) "heavens" / "heaven" / "skies"
(3) "from the LORD out of heaven" / "from the heavens" / "of his own sending"

In the first of these variations, the KJV's and NJB's "brimstone and fire" present a very literal rendering. REB's "fire and brimstone" reorders the two terms to match the normal English idiom. The NLT also reorders the terms, but avoids depicting chunks of sulfur falling from the skies by saying that it is "burning sulfur." A similar concept is conveyed by NIV's use of only "burning sulfur" in an attempt to translate the two nouns as a nominal hendiadys wherein the first noun of a pair "modifies the second, so that their translation often sounds like a noun with an adjective."[150] However, such a translation does not accord well with the principle of Hebrew grammar by which the first term of a hendiadys describes the second term, not the reverse. Therefore, the translation of NJPS ("sulfurous fire") preserves the most faithful treatment of the two nouns as a hendiadys.[151]

The second set of variations reveals the interpretive decision translators make regarding the meaning of "heavens." The NIV and REB opt to translate the Hebrew form very literally and leave the determination of the actual meaning to the readers themselves. "Heavens" in biblical Hebrew might mean either the sky, the celestial bodies, or the abode of God. The REB decides to specify that Moses intends only the "skies." Both the NJPS and KJV choose to use "heaven" as a way of indicating their preference for the interpretation that Yahweh sent the judgment from His own residence. Walther Eichrodt appeals to passages like Genesis 19:24 as proof of an early belief that God's dwelling-place is in heaven.[152] The NJB's translation might also imply that the text refers to the divine residence since it takes "heavens" as representative of the Lord Himself.

The third variation in this text provides the primary purpose for examining the impact of translation on theology. The REB, NLT, and NJB eliminate the second reference to Yahweh, treating it as a redundant expression. In his commentary on Genesis, Wenham accepts a similar conclusion, but for different reasons. He believes that by the repetition the "narrator stresses that 'it was from the LORD.'"[153] Therefore, Wenham translates the verse as follows: "and the LORD rained brimstone and fire on Sodom and Gomorrah: it was from the LORD from the sky."[154] This is a legitimate attempt to translate the text as it stands. It takes into account the Masoretic accents dividing the verse. However, the treatment of this final portion of the verse as a noun clause (viz., "it was") lacks convincing grammatical evidence. Instead, it would be more natural grammatically to take these last two phrases as adverbial prepositional phrases modifying the main verb, "rained."

However, these versions might very well obscure the presence of two different persons of the Godhead. If the expression were an intentional redundancy, one would expect to see such repetition of "Yahweh" employed elsewhere in the Old Testament. However, it does not occur elsewhere. This is a unique expression clarified by later revelation. The Old Testament reveals that in a number of cases the "Angel" or "Messenger of the LORD" is the immediate agent of judgment (cf. 2 Sam. 24:16–17; 2 Kings 19:35; Ps. 35:6–7).[155] Therefore, it is no surprise to the theologically minded that the same arrangement for judgment might apply in the matter of Sodom and Gomorrah.

Such a verse as Genesis 19:24 hits at the heart of aberrant theology propagated by groups like the Jehovah's Witnesses. This text speaks of two persons with the title of Yahweh—one in heaven above and one with a presence nearer to or upon the earth. A number of theologians adhere to this view of the verse. Augustus Hopkins Strong places this text alongside Hosea 1:7 and 2 Timothy 1:18 as examples of passages in which "Jehovah distinguishes himself from Jehovah."[156] James Borland points to the same distinction of persons in Genesis 19:24.[157] Victor Hamilton, on the other hand, argues that the phraseology is not to be "dismissed as a doublet or a gloss."[158] However, in so doing, he stops short of mentioning any distinction between divine persons in the passage.

Does this mean that the translators of the REB, NLT, and NJB are anti-Trinitarian? Absolutely not. A theologically insensitive translation does not tell the reader anything about the theological position of the translators. The translation merely indicates that the translators did not believe this specific passage advocates that particular theological concept. When evaluating a particular Bible translation, it is irresponsible to stigmatize the translators with a particular theological error or heresy on the basis of a single passage's translation. For example, the RSV's translation of Isaiah 7:14 ("a young woman") does not mean that the translators took a theological position denying the virgin conception of Jesus Christ. They merely rejected explicit prophetic revelation of the virgin birth in Isaiah 7:14. Likewise, the ASV's "every scripture inspired of God" in 2 Timothy 3:16 offers no proof the translators claim only some of the Scriptures are inspired.

A theologically insensitive translation does not tell the reader anything about the theological position of the translators.

Do such translations weaken the evidence supporting a particular doctrine? Yes, but that is not the same as denial of that doctrine. A number of passages throughout the Bible usually support those doctrines to which we ought to adhere. Any doctrine that relies upon a single text of Scripture probably does not qualify as a cardinal doctrine of the Christian faith. If that one text is problematic, it is unwise to base a doctrine or practice upon it (e.g., snake handling on the basis of the disputed final verses of the Gospel of Mark).

Proposed translation:

> Then Yahweh rained sulfurous fire upon Sodom and Gomorrah from Yahweh in heaven.

or

> Then Yahweh rained sulfurous fire upon Sodom and Gomorrah from Yahweh—from heaven itself.

Conclusion

Bible translators must approach every passage of Scripture with reverence and careful attention to detail. The text must not be made to say something the original author did not intend for it to mean. Translators must not add meaning, nor must they subtract any of the meaning. The goal should be to accurately and fully translate the text into its receptor language. Since the Scriptures ought to be the sole source of theology, translation is vitally wedded to theologizing. Translation affects theology just as much as theology can affect translation. The translator must be keenly aware of the interaction of the two disciplines.[159]

Since the Scriptures ought to be the sole source of theology, translation is vitally wedded to theologizing. Translation affects theology just as much as theology can affect translation.

The example of Genesis 12:3 reveals how no translation fully exposes the Hebrew text's theological implications. Some translators seem to have pursued their task unaware of the significance of the text. However, some commentators, linguists, and theologians recognize one or two of the issues, but none appear to deal with all of the issues. Translators dependent upon such commentaries find no help in their difficult task due to the absence of full discussion for such theologically laden passages. This text also demonstrates how important Hebrew syntax is to exegesis, theology, and translation of the Hebrew Bible. Bible translators need to pursue a high degree of facility in the biblical languages as well as a full study of theology (biblical, systematic, and historical).

The second text, Genesis 15:15, presents an opportunity to observe the interaction of archaeology with interpretation—multiple burials in family tombs cause some to turn an ancient phrase into an old euphemism. However, when one takes into account the context of some of the passages using the phraseology, as well as New Testament testimony, the cautious translator cannot settle the matter so easily. Perhaps the translator of such a debated text should avoid locking the translation into a minority viewpoint. No theologian should base any doctrine upon a hotly debated text. Likewise, the translator of a debated text should not employ a questionable translation to push a minority theological agenda. On the other hand, a situation might exist requiring the translator to violate such a general rule in order to protect the integrity of the biblical text and its teachings. Such a move, however, must proceed on the foundation of much exegesis, thought, counsel, and prayer.

The final passage, Genesis 19:24, illustrates the way in which translations can obscure key theological details. It provides a useful springboard to discuss the pitfall of impugning the translators' theological position by appealing to what some scholars might consider a translational error or translational indiscretion. One translation decision in one text does not a heretic make.

How we understand and translate the text determines our beliefs. Our translation's intelligibility buttresses our theology's lucidity and coherence.

Our examination of this handful of texts in Genesis reveals the necessity of paying attention to every detail of the original Hebrew. The accuracy of one's theology must rest upon the original text. How we understand and translate the text determines our beliefs. Our translation's intelligibility buttresses our theology's lucidity and coherence.

The next chapter examines the wide variety of translation methodology from excessively literal to extremely free. Psalm 23:1, a very popular Old Testament text, provides the illustrations. Differences in translation methodologies offers both positive benefits and negative results. Perhaps it proves the old adage, "Nothing is good for nothing—it can always serve as a bad example."

CHAPTER 6

TRANSLATING THE SHEPHERD PSALM'S FIRST VERSE

COMPARING DIFFERENT TRANSLATIONS OF EVEN a single verse offers a very instructive exercise. Great benefit might accrue from assessing various versions of a very familiar passage of Scripture. In this chapter we will consider a variety of translations for the familiar and beloved first verse of Psalm 23. The most literal of the versions will be discussed first and the most freely translated versions will be considered last. Those in between will gradually run the gamut from the literal to the free in the range of versions.

Unmodified Literal Translation of the Hebrew

"YHWH my-shepherding-one, not do-I-lack."[160]

Maintaining the order and relationships of the Hebrew as literally as possible, the helping verb "is" (normally supplied in translation after Yahweh) has been omitted in this representative word-for-word translation. The original Hebrew uses a mere four words: *YHWH ro'iy lo' 'echsar.*[161] In the translation example, all words that relate to the same Hebrew word form are linked by hyphens. For example, "my-shepherding-one" (or "my-shepherd") indicates that "my" is a pronominal suffix on the Hebrew word for "shepherding-one." "Shepherding-one" treats the Hebrew participle as a verbal adjective; "shepherd" looks at the word as a participle used as a noun (in other words, a substantival participle). No English Bible version known to this author contains this translation retaining the participle as a verbal adjective. It is too literal for even the most literal-minded translators. I use "YHWH" here to represent the special divine title by means of its four consonants (thus its common moniker, "the Tetragrammaton") in a form acceptable to both Christian and Jew. Most English versions use "LORD"—note the purposeful utilization of an initial capital letter followed by small capital letters in contrast to "Lord" (only the initial capital letter). "Lord" translates the Hebrew *'Adonay*. See below, under "A Capital Matter," for a more detailed explanation of the origin of this use of LORD/Lord in Bible translations.

Literal English Translation

JB: "Yahweh is my shepherd, I lack nothing."

In seven English words, the JB provides a highly literal translation. Significantly the translators chose the present tense for both verbs. Translations of this verse typically fluctuate between the present tense and the future tense. In Hebrew, however, context determines the tense or time of a verb more than the verb form itself. Therefore, in contexts like Psalm 23:1, different translators might understand the time element differently. Such non-specificity in biblical Hebrew requires that the translator approach the text with all the caution and attention to detail with which a commentator might approach the text.

The nature of translating Hebrew verbs remains complex to this day despite the immense amount of energetic study and analysis which many world-class Hebraists have produced. Such a state of affairs exists in Hebrew verb syntax that Waltke and O'Connor make the observation, "Most translators, we think it fair to say, fly by the seat of their pants in interpreting the Hebrew conjugations."[162] In the end, the translator must make a choice, since multiple-choice translations (either in the body of the translation or in footnotes or marginal notes) do not gain the readers' confidence. Readers should realize that many a translator has agonized deeply over having to make such decisions in difficult passages. The problem of translation is further compounded by the brevity and complexity of Hebrew poetic style.

Readers should realize that many a translator has agonized deeply over having to make such decisions in difficult passages.

THE JB translators chose what is called a gnomic present. A gnomic present indicates a general truth or represents a characteristic action or state. Support for this decision can be derived from the tenor of the entire context since the psalmist appears to speak of current experience in his life. It is not that YHWH would *become* his shepherd or that He already had been so in the past—YHWH *is* his shepherd at the moment of penning or singing this psalm. Likewise, the psalmist does not indicate that he is claiming a promise not to suffer any lack or sufficiency in the future. He indicates that he *is* adequately provisioned with life's necessities at that very moment and that such a state characterizes his situation for the foreseeable future. God's care for him *is* ever-present—not just a past experience that has ended, nor a future hope that has not yet begun.

Therefore, as surprising as it might be to many Christians who have prejudged the JB, the version presents a very laudable literal translation of Psalm 23:1. Its rendering not only conforms to the actual Hebrew text, but provides a sound foundation for devotional thought and exposition.

Literal with Modified Divine Title

Moffatt: "The Eternal shepherds me, I lack for nothing."
Segond (French): *L'Éternel est mon berger: je ne manquerai de rien.*
("The Eternal is my shepherd: I do not lack anything.")

SBCL:[163] *Shodaprobhu amar rakhal, amar abhab nei.*
("*Shodaprobhu* [is] my shepherd, I have no lack.")

Eight English words, ten French words, and six Bengali words compose these translation examples. They do not differ greatly from that of the JB, but they exhibit one significant variation: all three represent the divine title by an educated translational guess regarding the meaning of *YHWH*. The Bengali *Shodaprobhu* (presented here in transliterated script—the language uses Devanagari script, an entirely different alphabet) is roughly equivalent to "Eternal Lord." The translators chose it because it has been the translation for *YHWH* since the first Bengali Bible version produced by William Carey in the late 1700s through the early 1800s. Whereas English Bibles characteristically employ "LORD" for *YHWH* and "Lord" for *'Adonay*, Bengali versions normally translate *'Adonay* with *Probhu*, thus providing distinct translations for the two titles. *Shodaprobhu*, like "the Eternal" and *L'Éternel*, is a translation, not a transliteration. Such treatment of a name would be similar to translating "William" as "Hard-headed" since the name is generally considered as originating with the German *Wilhelm* which means "helmet of resolution." All of us named William might be offended if someone were to address us with that translation rather than speaking our given name. Such translations are not even very accurate—at best they are only educated guesses. Basically, these three translations could have achieved approximately the same effect by translating the verse as "God is my shepherd, I lack nothing."

Modified Literal (Divine Title and Verb Tense)

> KJV/NAS/RSV: The LORD is my shepherd; I shall not want.
> NIV: The LORD is my shepherd, I shall not be in want.
> NEB: The LORD is my shepherd; I shall want nothing.
> OBB: "*Shodaprobhu* [is] my shepherd, my lack shall not be."

The Old Bengali Bible (OBB) version is the fifteenth edition of William Yates's 1844 translation, which replaced the translation of William Carey. A transliteration of the Bengali text would be *Shodaprobhu amar palok*. Most Bengali transliterations would use *Shadaprobhu*, but I purposefully substituted an *o* for the first *a*, since that is the way Bengali speakers pronounce the divine title. Too often inexperienced Bengali speakers (like new missionaries) pronounce it as transliterated with the *a*, but that actually means "white lord." Best then to avoid the problem by changing the transliteration.

The six versions above still remain on the literal side of the range of translation methodologies, but they modify both the divine title in the first half of the verse and the verb tense in the second half. Although a future tense appears for the second verb, the translators' intended meaning should not be taken as being radically different from those translations employing the present tense. The future can be used to express confidence and certainty, rather than simple futurity. Especially in the older English translations, "shall" could indicate determination or promise, though most often with the second person (you) or third person (he, she, it, they), rather than first person (I, we).[164] The Coverdale (1535) translation of Amos 9:11 ("I shal repayre it") is an example of a first person promise, however. In modern English, "shall" is widely neglected and "will" occurs most often in both simple futurity and emphatic futurity.[165] In Psalm 23:1, the meaning is obviously not one of promise or determination, but it could be understood legitimately as personal confidence or certainty. As in all passages, however, the question must be: What did the original writer intend? or What did the divine Author intend? Context supplies the best indicator. Those versions using a future tense in the second verb of verse 1, set it in a context of present tense verbs (v. 1: "is"; v. 2: "makes," "leads"; v. 3: "restores," "leads"). We will examine this issue of present vs. future time in Psalm 23 in an analysis of the entire psalm in chapter 8.

> ***Although a future tense appears for the second verb, the translators' intended meaning should not be taken as being radically different from those translations that employ the present tense.***

Modified Literal (Divine Title, Participle as Verb, and Verb Tense)

Septuagint (LXX): *Kurios poimainei me, kai ouden me usterēsei.*
("[The] Lord shepherds me, and nothing shall be lacking [for] me.")

Syriac Peshitta: "Mariah tends me and nothing at all shall be lacking for me."

Syriac is even more closely related to Aramaic than to Hebrew and is written in a script similar to Arabic and Persian. Transliterations of the Hebrew and Syriac texts of Psalm 23:1 demonstrate the similarities:

Hebrew:	*YHWH*	*r'y*	*l' 'hsr*
Syriac:	*mry'*	*nr'yny*	*wmdm l' nhsr ly*

In these versions a third modification emerges: they treat the participle (the actual Hebrew form for the vocational noun "shepherd") as a present tense verb. The rendering "God is shepherding me; I will have no lack," could also be proposed for this classification. The choice of the present tense verb might be intended as a means of fleshing out the characteristic activity of a shepherd—lending the proposition greater vividness. Such versions are still fairly literal translations. However, there is an increasingly subjective interpretive element drawing the translation toward paraphrase. Neither example cited above is an English version. To accurately measure the degree of subjectivity in the translations cited above, one would need to be sufficiently fluent in Septuagintal Greek and the Syriac of the Peshitta. Do these languages commonly employ participles as nouns? Would a Greek or Syriac participle fulfill the same role as the Hebrew participle in such a context? Is it normal for the Septuagint translators to employ a present tense verb in their translation of Hebrew participles? Was the choice a literary choice or a linguistic choice?

Modified Literal (Divine Title, Participle as Verb, Idiomatic Verb)

Latin from Greek: *Dominus reget me et nihil mihi deerit.*
("The Lord will lead me and nothing is lost to me [*or* I lack nothing].")

Latin from Hebrew: *Dominus pascit me nihil mihi deerit.*
("The Lord leads me to pasture [*or* feeds me], nothing is lost to me [*or* I lack nothing].")

The Latin Vulgate of Jerome stands as a stupendous effort to draw the drifting Latin and Greek translations of Scripture back to the original Hebrew text of the Old Testament. He produced his first translation of the Psalms in A.D. 384 while he was in Rome at the court of Pope Damasus (who died in December, A.D. 384). Damasus probably instigated Jerome's pursuit of a new Latin translation of the Bible. Jerome revised the existing Latin text of Psalms with the Greek Septuagint translation as his base. He completed this first translation prior to his awakening to the necessity of returning to the original Hebrew text. Unfortunately, his first translation of Psalms may have been lost irretrievably.[166]

The Latin Vulgate of Jerome stands as a stupendous effort to draw the drifting Latin and Greek translations of Scripture back to the original Hebrew text of the Old Testament.

Jerome based his second translation of Psalms upon the Greek Septuagint as corrected by Origen. Since it was first introduced into Gaul, it has come to be known as the Gallican Psalter. Centuries later it succeeded in replacing his later translation of Psalms based upon the Hebrew. It was not superseded in the Roman Catholic church until the New Latin Psalter in 1945.[167] At least in his translation of Psalms, Jerome "was sometimes prepared to prefer a reading consecrated by tradition and church usage to the one required by the Hebrew."[168] We have already observed this type of translation choice in our examination of the word "righteousness" in 1 John 1:9 in chapter 4.

Jerome's commentaries and his translations "implied a two-fold breach: with the official version of the Church, that of the Septuagint, and with the traditional method of exegesis, allegory and spiritual applications."[169] Of Jerome's translation of Isaiah, Jean Steinmann writes,

> There are moments when he tones down the Hebrew, strays from it, makes mistranslations and mistakes. But what faithfulness he displays in transcribing the proper names, rendering the alliterations of the Hebrew, echoing its rhythm, and above all, using a Latin which fits Isaias's Hebrew like a glove, in a translation which is no servile transcription but which recreates the thrill of the original, its ample rhythm and its nobility, and its very music. The great visions . . . are presented in an impassioned and lyrical Latin, at once melodious and majestic, which is a delight to the ear. It is obvious that Jerome is himself a poet. His readers ought to have acclaimed the work a miracle. Thanks to him, Isaias was for the first time speaking the language of Virgil.[170]

Other manuscripts of the Latin Vulgate have *regit* (present tense) rather than *reget* (future tense). Of the two readings, the former generally is preferred. It is consistent with the Vaticanus Codex's Greek reading (*poimainei*, present tense), as compared with the reading of Codex Alexandrinus and Codex Sinaiticus (both have *poimanei*, future tense). Also, it is consistent with Jerome's translation from Hebrew (*pascit* is present tense) and with his translation of the second verb in the verse (*deerit* is present tense—even though the Greek of the Septuagint is a future tense).

Semi-literal with Negative Restructured as Positive

TEV: "The LORD is my shepherd; I have everything I need."

This classification moves into a new region of translation methodology. The first half of the verse preserves what we have observed in the literal categories, but the second half of the verse utilizes a restructuring of the original grammar. The translators of TEV convert a negative declaration ("I have no lack") into a positive statement. Another possible translation might be, "The LORD is my shepherd; there is sufficient supply for me." Although it could be argued that the meaning does not differ greatly, the tone of the translation has changed and the potential for misunderstanding has been increased. "I have everything I need" could be taken as boasting (whether good or bad), since the statement occurs as a common expression of self-sufficiency in modern American English. Although Christians familiar with Psalm 23 and the scriptural context might be less likely to interpret the phraseology in such a manner, biblically illiterate non-Christians might very well take the phrase in its more negative implication. That means that the translation has lost some of its punch and clarity. The translators could have been driven by a misguided concept that it is always better to say something positively rather than negatively. Does that imply that God does not know how to communicate well? After all, He has employed an abundance of negative statements and prohibitions in Scripture—take the Ten Commandments as just one example (only two out of the ten are stated in the positive; Exod. 20:1–17).

Restructured Free Translation

LB: "Because the Lord is my shepherd, I have everything I need!"

The use of "because" to commence the verse is based upon what the translator perceived to be the implied relationship between the two halves of the verse. The writer, King David, very well might have intended such a relationship, although he may have chosen to omit any Hebrew word for "because" in order to maintain certain poetic standards for a psalm. Translators, however, must choose to either objectively render the text as it stands, or subjectively translate it according to some interpretative inclination that cannot be proven. The LB's translator opted for the latter. Therefore, the verse has been restructured into a less than literal translation—one freer with the structure of the original text. However, this approach does no essential harm to this particular verse and the original is still discernible. But, it obscures the original more than in the modified literal and semi-literal translation groups.

Translators, however, must choose to either objectively render the text as it stands, or subjectively translate it according to some interpretative inclination that cannot be proven.

It is interesting that the revision of the LB, the NLT, chooses to revert to a more literal translation of Psalm 23:1, "The LORD is my shepherd; I have everything I need." Evidently the revisers also believed that the restructuring by the older translation had been too free. Of course, it is very difficult to determine what other subjective factors may have influenced the translators of either version.

In the case of Psalm 23, its traditional popularity in the KJV means the average reader will treat any alterations (even legitimate ones) with a certain degree of suspicion. Translators, therefore, in order not to diminish their translation's marketability, often will avoid touching such sacred cows, even if the original language indicates that the traditional translation is not as accurate as it could be.

Free Translation with Cultural Substitution

"God is my swineherd. He sees to it that I have all I need."
"My God is my undertaker. He provides all my needs."

Both of these imaginary translations take dynamic equivalence to an extreme by adapting the text to a specific, limited group of readers. The first might seek to connect with people living in a culture without any knowledge of sheep. The second targets people who make their living by being morticians. These two hypothetical translations help make a point about cultural or social substitutions in the process of Bible translation. (For a fuller discussion of this particular matter, see the last section of chapter 3 above.)

Free Translation = Expanded Paraphrase

"The Lord [or Yahweh], the covenant God of Israel, is continuously leading, feeding, and caring for me; there is not anything that I need which I do not have supplied to me by Him."

Free translation methodologies may go two different directions: (1) expansion or (2) contraction. The hypothetical translation above represents the former. The translator, in this process, seeks to include every potential element of meaning that can be milked from the original text and inserts all such elements directly into the translation.

Free Translation = Shortened Paraphrase

"God provides everything I need."
"My God takes care of me."

Here we have the second type of free translation (also hypothetical), the kind that contracts the wording down to a minimum in order to express the concept expressed in the original text. Such minimalistic translation resorts to a newspaper headline kind of summation. These summations might clarify a theme or identify a topic, but they do not represent the actual wording of the text itself. God never intended His words to be reduced to such an extent that what He actually said is no longer preserved.

These sample translations of Psalm 23:1 illustrate several features of language (especially English) we too often take for granted. The characteristics of spoken languages include their sophistication as well as their flexibility. More than one way to say the same thing always exists in a language. However, the differences in how something is said can also lead to different emphases and even totally different meanings. In addition, we too often assume that other languages have the same features (primarily grammar and vocabulary) we find in English. But, every language is different.

One Word Makes a Difference

These translations of Psalm 23:1 reveal a wide range of approaches to the Hebrew text. With the exception of the Syriac translation, all the versions used a different form or structure than that found in the original Hebrew. The Hebrew form has "YHWH my-shepherding-one" but English form requires "YHWH *is* my shepherd." The connecting verb is unnecessary in Hebrew. "YHWH my-shepherd" is a grammatically perfect and complete sentence in Hebrew.

What would English be like without "is," "was," and "am"? Some languages do not use those little helpers. Bengali, like the Hebrew, does not need "is." The English translation's use of the helping verb does not comprise nonliteral translation. "YHWH *is* my shepherd" in English and "YHWH my-shepherd" in Hebrew are linguistic equivalents.

The choice of translation, therefore, will depend upon the terms available in the receptor language that are appropriate and faithful to the context.

In the first clause of Psalm 23, a variety of translations were used for the Hebrew participle (normally an -ing word in English). Translations choosing "shepherd" interpreted the participle as a noun in its usage. Those opting for "shepherding" to translate the same Hebrew term emphasized the verbal element in the participle. Both are equally accurate as long as the translation conveys the concept that the word involves a continual or characteristic activity. No indication exists in the Hebrew to determine whether one of these elements (continual and characteristic) should be preferred over the other. Other vocabulary words could be used for the same Hebrew word: "feeding/feeder," "pasturing/pastor," "shepherding/shepherd," "leading/leader," "tending/tender," and "caring for/caretaker" all offer possible translations. All indicate meanings contained in the Hebrew verb root and consistent with the context of Psalm 23. The choice of translation, therefore, will depend upon the terms available in the receptor language that are appropriate and faithful to the context.

The psalmist did not use any particular Hebrew idiom in Psalm 23:1. The meaning of each of the terms used in the Hebrew can be understood individually. The verse possesses nothing like the diplomatic "white paper." In a sense, however, all of the above translations are idiomatic—they utilize the idiom (generally speaking) of the language receiving the translation. Only two of the translations would fall outside the category of common language translation for this one verse: the old Bengali and the expanded paraphrase.

It is well to keep in mind that one verse is not necessarily indicative of the kind of translation employed throughout an entire Bible translation. As a matter of fact, most translations exhibit a number of different types of translation in various passages. The LB is not consistently a paraphrase, nor is the KJV consistently literal. In isolated passages, the LB is literal and the KJV is paraphrastic. Whenever different individuals or different teams translate different passages, this phenomenon occurs even more frequently. The Old Bengali Bible utilized a high form of the verb in the second half of the verse. Such verb forms are not common to Bengali usage in conversation or in the public media of Bangladesh (especially TV and radio). The expanded paraphrase mentions "the covenant God of Israel." Most readers would have no idea why "covenant" would be specified, what it means, or where the concept comes from in the text. It was derived from the use of *YHWH* in the Old Testament as the name of God when the text stresses His relationship to His covenant people, Israel.

This final comment concerning the use of *YHWH* requires a more detailed explanation. Why is *YHWH* often translated "LORD" in our English versions?

A Capital Matter

Evidence from the Lachish Letters (c. 586 B.C.) indicates, at least until that time, the Jewish people pronounced the Tetragrammaton with its own vowels. However, within three centuries the translators of the Greek

Old Testament (the Septuagint, c. 250 B.C.) came under the influence of a religious custom observed by the Jews of that time. The modern reader must understand that the Jews in Egypt in those days were not necessarily orthodox in their beliefs. Indeed, if anything, the Jews in Egypt were exceedingly syncretistic in their faith—mixing many pagan idolatrous concepts with the religion of the Old Testament. Yehezkel Kaufmann gives the following description of the beliefs of Jews living at Elephantine, an island in the Nile River, from about 525 B.C. onward:

> The religion of the Jewish garrison of Elephantine as reflected in the Elephantine papyri is an interesting phenomenon in its own right; it must not, however, be viewed as representative of the ancient popular religion of Israel. The garrison was founded before the Persian conquest of Egypt in 525; the Jews of Elephantine had spent over a century isolated in an alien environment by the time of the papyri. No Israelite writing was found among them, although the pagan Ahikar romance was. They had become assimilated linguistically and intermarried with their neighbors. Whatever "idolatry" they brought with them from their native land cannot but have been heightened in these circumstances. In contrast to the Babylonian colony of exiles they had no prophets among them, though they did have priests. Their religion can therefore be used only in a most qualified way to reconstruct the popular religion of Israel in Palestine.
>
> Despite the various pagan god names in the Jewish onomasticon none of the "gods of the nations" after whom biblical Israel strayed (Baal, Ashtoreth, Chemosh, etc.) are worshiped by the Elephantine Jews. The peculiar divine names found in the papyri (Herembethel, Anathbethel, Anathiahu, Ashambethel) are never found in these forms in the Bible. If they were originally Israelite divinities—and this is by no means certain—they can at most have been akin to the satyrs of the popular religion that had no recognized, public cult in Palestine. How they were conceived of in Elephantine we do not know. Only YHWH is described: he is the "Lord" or "God" of heaven. Only he has a temple and festivals. Ashambethel and Anathbethel have a treasury in the temple of YHWH, but only YHWH is represented as a universal God. The minor deities (if so they be) are given a place in his temple apparently as members of his entourage.[171]

Thus, it would seem to be theologically dangerous to adopt the practices of Jews in Egypt with regard to the pronunciation of the divine name.

The Jews refused to pronounce the divine title Yahweh because of a misunderstanding of the third commandment (Exod. 20:7).

The Jews in Egypt refused to pronounce the divine title *Yahweh* because of a misunderstanding of the third commandment (Exod. 20:7). The custom at that time was to substitute the Hebrew word *ʾAdonai* ("Lord") for *YHWH* (the four consonants in the Hebrew text for *Yahweh*). In the Greek, *Kurios* ("Lord") substitutes for *YHWH*. This departure from the actual Hebrew text made the translation acceptable to the target audience including the Jews in Alexandria, Egypt, the heretical Jews at Elephantine, and the polytheistic Egyptian culture in which they resided. However, R. Laird Harris points out an unexpected consequence of not pronouncing the divine title:

> The result seems really to have been a profanation of a different kind. Not to use the name of God seems to profane it just as the coarse use of the Name would have done. But the facts are plain. The ancient Hebrews, naturally, pronounced and wrote the name of God.[172]

This Jewish custom from the third century before Christ caused confusion since two different Hebrew names of God (*Yahweh* and *ʾAdonai*) were being translated identically—by the Greek *Kurios* ("Lord"). Later, the Syriac Peshitta and the Latin Vulgate followed suit. Readers of these three ancient versions were unable to distinguish between these two significant names of God. Our English translations continued the practice with one helpful modification: "LORD" (the last three letters set in small capitals) represents *Yahweh,* while "Lord" represents *ʾAdonai*. In the public reading of the Scriptures, however, the listener cannot distinguish between "Lord" and "LORD" since the pronunciations are identical. Modern Jews get around the problem by reading *Hashshem* ("the Name") for *YHWH* when they come upon that name in the text of the Old Testament.

Translations representing *Yahweh* by "LORD" resort to a cultural substitution. "LORD" could be termed a dynamic equivalent because it represents an attempt to produce in the reader an identical response to that of a third century B.C. Jewish reader. In this case the response consists of reverential fear to speak what is considered to be a holy name (*Yahweh*). The ultimate question should be, "Did Abraham, Moses, David, Isaiah, and other Old Testament saints likewise refuse to pronounce the divine name of *Yahweh*?" It appears that the later Jews unnecessarily modified the biblical text based upon their misunderstanding of the third commandment. Louis Hartman, in the *Encyclopaedia Judaica* (bearing the imprimatur of the Chief Rabbi of Israel), says,

> The true pronunciation of the name YHWH was never lost. Several early Greek writers of the Christian Church testify that the name was pronounced "Yahweh." This is confirmed, at least for the vowel of the first syllable of the name, by the shorter form Yah, which is sometimes used in poetry (e.g., Ex. 15:2) and the *-yahu* or *-yah* that serves as the final syllable in very many Hebrew names.[173]

The popular hybrid "Jehovah" derives from a later Christian misunderstanding of the intended purpose of the Masoretic pointing. Copiers of the Hebrew Bible intended *Y^ehwah* to represent the vowels for *'Adonai*, signaling that readers should substitute *'Adonai* in place of *Y^ehwah*. However, Christians began to pronounce it *Y^ehowah*, supplying the missing *o*-vowel with the first *h* since they had heard it in the Jewish pronunciation, *'Adonai*. That practice led the Spanish of the Reina-Valera 1960 Revised Version to use *Jehová*. Even though it might not meet the standards of some Hebraists, it at least has the advantage of not confusing *Yahweh* and *'Adonai*. Even in public reading the proper divine title is clear with this Spanish version.

The SBCL Old Testament consistently uses *Shodaprobhu* (the name used in the older Bengali Bible) for *YHWH*. For *'Adonai* the SBCL uses *Probhu* ("Lord"). Since the Devanagari script of Bengali has no capital letters, it would be impossible for the translators to use a convention like that observed in most English translations.

The names for God are one kind of translation problem. Among a number of other issues, the identification and translation of time elements for verbs presents a major problem. The difficulty is twofold: (1) there is the problem of time in the Hebrew verb system; and (2) there is the problem of time in the verbs of the receptor language(s).

Was That Tomorrow or Yesterday?

Bengali time references can be confusing to a rookie missionary. When a Bangladeshi is asked when he will complete a task he might respond, "*Kalke*" (pronounced *kahl-kay*). *Kalke* can mean either "yesterday" or "tomorrow." Only the context or further conversation clarifies which meaning is intended. When a Bengali speaker uses the verb *chollam* (pronounced *chohl-lahm*), the context has to be carefully observed to determine whether it means "I am about to go," "I went," or "I am going." The same Bengali word serves to express all three meanings.

Each language has its own ways of expressing past, present, and future action in its verbs. The second clause of Psalm 23:1 presents the translator with the problem of the Hebrew verb's expression of time. Many English translations have chosen to interpret the tense of the verb as future: "I shall/will not want." The Hebrew verb forms, however, do not contain any inherent indicator for time—the forms might provide a hint, but they are not absolute. Context acts as the most consistent determiner of the time element for Hebrew verbs, rather than the verb forms themselves. The context of Psalm 23:1 and the tone of the entire psalm seem best understood as in the psalmist's present experience. It is a psalm about one's daily living in the presence of *YHWH*. *YHWH* Himself continually cares, leads, and protects. Translating the verb with a future tense can misdirect the readers and expositors. Any translation base using the future tense would also prove inappropriate for translating the psalm into a third language.

> ***All translations need to be checked against the Hebrew Old Testament and Greek New Testament texts.***

This type of error in translation occurs often enough that it is perilous to trust to an English (or any other language) base. All translations need to be checked against the Hebrew Old Testament and Greek New Testament texts. To do this, the missionary translator needs to be capable in Hebrew, Aramaic, and Greek, as well as the receptor language. Ideally, of course, national translators should be trained in the biblical languages so that they can do the checking. The catch to this is that nationals often need to be taught the biblical languages through the medium of their own language.

This might offer an even greater challenge for the missionary translator. Either way, it behooves missionary translators to be reasonably fluent in both the receptor language and the biblical languages.

The SBCL guidelines for translation specify that *the original languages must be consulted at all times and have priority over any translation in any other language.* Having accepted this operating principle, the choice of the editions of the Hebrew and Greek texts becomes a vital issue. A translation is only as accurate as its source text. The text used for the SBCL Old Testament is the Hebrew Masoretic text represented in *Biblia Hebraica Stuttgartensia*. Our principles specified that we follow the Masoretic text without emendation (alteration).[174]

Our text for the SBCL New Testament was the United Bible Societies (UBS) Greek New Testament. The translation team, however, chose to depart from that text in a number of places—mainly by rejecting any suggested change that had less than a "B" (= moderate certainty, "almost certain")[175] rating in the UBS Greek New Testament. The new Bengali translation is closer to the Greek text published by Zane Hodges and Donald Farstad[176] than to any other Greek edition of the New Testament. Treatments of the Greek text that rely too heavily on just one or two manuscripts (Sinaiticus and Vaticanus, for example) or on just one family of manuscripts (Byzantine, for example) are not compatible with the principles followed by the SBCL translation project.

From the analysis of potential translations for Psalm 23:1 we discovered a variety of translation methods or philosophies. Translators can approach a text very differently. Sometimes the method depends upon the differences between the original language (known as the target language) and the receptor language. However, as with the very significant name of God, *YHWH*, the approaches can arise out of theological presuppositions. Each Bible translator (or Bible translation team) seeks to make the text understandable to a target audience. Chapter 7 will look in more detail at how translation methods and philosophies succeed (or fail) in making the text of God's Word understandable.

CHAPTER 7

THE ULTIMATE CHALLENGE OF BIBLE TRANSLATION

If a translation of the Bible is not understandable, it cannot have its divinely intended effect upon the hearer or reader. That is the key challenge for Bible translators. How can the Word of God be conveyed with both accuracy and clarity? From time to time it will be necessary for the translator to wrestle with different ways of expressing the meaning of the text. Ephraim Speiser observed that the "main task of a translator is to keep faith with two different masters, one at the source and the other at the receiving end."[177] One characteristic of good Bible translators consists in their intense preoccupation with the matter of accuracy. Too often, however, translators believe they know better than the biblical writers and proceed to restate the text. "As one gentle critic put it, with tongue in cheek," Speiser notes, "translations are so much more enjoyable than originals, because they contain many things that the originals leave out."[178] Bible translators, however, must avoid such expansions, revisions, and skewing of the text.

The following examination of Proverbs 8:1–11 with regard to the process of translation serves as an example of the process translators might follow while seeking to faithfully preserve the exact meaning of the original language with both accuracy and clarity. This verse-by-verse discussion reveals the complexity and sophistication of Hebrew poetry and how that might impact the final version in a receptor language.

> ***The "main task of a translator is to keep faith with two different masters, one at the source and the other at the receiving end."***
>
> **—E. A. Speiser**

Translational Examination of Proverbs 8:1–11

[1] Does not Wisdom call *to us*
And Understanding cry out?[179]

The first clue encountered in the Hebrew text consists of the interrogative particle attached to the first word, the negative adverb. Translators immediately think of something like "Is not . . . ?" or "Does not . . . ?" depending upon where the rest of the sentence takes them. The second word in the Hebrew is a noun meaning "wisdom" (*hokmah*). By context the word appears to be a title for personified wisdom, therefore translators may capitalize the word as a proper name, "Wisdom." The verb stands last in this first part of the compound sentence. Context leads translators to the conclusion that the verbs in verse 1 act as characteristic present tense verbs (also known as gnomic presents[180]). This results in the first line being, "Does not Wisdom call . . . ?"

In some languages two other options might need to be considered by translators. (1) The rhetorical question implies a positive answer. If this is not clear to the readers in the receptor language, translators might wish to convert the form to provide that information: for example, "Indeed, Wisdom calls out . . ." (2) Some languages might require the specification of an object (or indirect object) for the verb. Thus, translators might consider adding "for us" or "to us."[181] This added phrase could be italicized to indicate that it is an addition—a traditional practice in English versions. Or, the addition could be placed within square brackets: "[for us]" or "[to us]"—the more academic practice.

Before we proceed farther in the text, we need to note that the rhetorical question acts as an introduction to the following poetic discourse on wisdom. As we move through these eleven verses, we will also observe the poem dividing itself into four-line stanzas (= two-verse stanzas, since each verse possesses two poetic lines) except for verse 1, which serves as the introduction to the poem. Such discoveries contribute to how we might format the finished translation for the readers.

The second half of verse 1 forms a poetic parallel line to the first line—a type of repetition in order to expand upon the concept and to give the readers/hearers an opportunity to acquire the meaning. The Hebrew conjunction leads the way ("and") with the parallel noun, "Understanding" (a synonym for "Wisdom"). Translators may capitalize this noun also, since its use parallels the noun in the first line of the verse. Expecting the verb to behave like the first verb, we may assume that it should be translated as a characteristic present tense, "give." This verb, however, has a direct object, "her voice." The pronominal suffix on "voice" agrees with the grammatical number and gender of the noun "Understanding" (feminine singular). The personification seems to be what we might refer to as "Lady Wisdom" or "Lady Understanding." If translators desire to make the gender of these nouns explicit in their translation, they might choose to add "Lady"—the text does not contain the word itself, but the gender certainly presents a good case for the concept being implicitly present. For languages without capitalization, other means (perhaps the addition of "Lady"?) might serve to identify "Wisdom" and "Understanding" as names. Proverbs 7 speaks of the adulteress woman who leads naïve young men to a disastrous end. Therefore, the preceding context sets up the contrasting woman, "Lady Wisdom."

For languages without capitalization, other means (perhaps the addition of "Lady"?) might serve to identify "Wisdom" and "Understanding" as names.

The meaning of "gives her voice" refers to raising the voice, speaking out, or crying out—providing translators with several possible selections that might depend upon how people in the receptor language might most naturally say it. Being parallel and equivalent to "call," "cry out" seems the best option, at least in English.

[2] On the hilltops, beside[182] the way,
At the crossways she stands;[183]

[3] Beside[184] the gates in front of the town,
At the entrance to the doors she shouts:[185]

Having observed a four-line structure for each stanza in the poem (with the exception of v. 1), we will continue our examination stanza by stanza (two verses at a time). Following this procedure will allow translators to determine whether such a division of stanzas really matches the realities of the text. If the observation proves untenable, they may always change the format in the final version.

Literally, the Hebrew of verse 2 reads, "on head of heights." First of all, English demands the use of the definite article for smooth grammar. In Hebrew poetry, the definite article occurs much less frequently than in prose. However, nouns without a definite article can be definite either by context or by the requirements of the receptor language. "Head" just means the "top" of something. "Heights" might seem ambiguous and insufficiently specific in this context. Hebrew usage normally refers to a natural high point (like hills and heavens), so translations associating these "heights" with tall buildings or city walls can mislead the readers. [186]A translation like "mountains" does not fit the city setting of this stanza, since the "heights" involve elevated places within the city. Thus, "on the hilltops" (cf. NKJV, NLT) appears to be a good translation—or "at the highest point" (NIV). Translators will also avoid the use of "high places" (KJV), since that might imply pagan shrines or altars.

"Beside the way" modifies the previous phrase adverbially. The accents in the Hebrew text associate the prepositional phrase with the first poetic line, not the second. The phrase can also be translated "on the side of the road" or "along the road" (NLT).

"*At*" in italics indicates that the second line lacks a preposition—just like the second line of verse 1. Hebrew poetry often leaves out the preposition, because the readers/hearers will understand the meaning, or the preposition at the start of the verse might be considered implied for the second line.

The first two Hebrew words in the second poetic line of verse 2 read literally, "house of paths." This idiomatic expression refers to the crossing of paths or roads—"crossroads" (NJB). The line closes with a verb conveying a characteristic present tense by context (cf. the verbs in v. 1). The specific form of the verb can be translated with a reflexive voice: "stations herself" or "takes a stand."

Hebrew poetry often uses multiple idioms to express the same concept in the same immediate context—perhaps to avoid redundancy.

Verse 3 continues the description of Wisdom's geographical location in the poet's figurative composition. Hebrew poetry often uses multiple idioms to express the same basic concept in the same immediate context—perhaps to avoid redundancy. Here is yet another idiom for "beside." Literally the text reads, "to the hand of the gates" or "at the hand of the gates." This means "beside the gates." A second prepositional phrase occurs in the first poetic line of this verse: "in front of the town" (literally, "to the mouth of the town"). The meaning could be either "entrance" or "in front of." Since "entrance" occurs in the very next line, using the same translation would make it appear as though the Hebrew words are identical. Therefore, translators should choose the alternative.

The second poetic line of verse 3 continues the variety of idioms to describe Wisdom's position at the city gates where the main activities of commerce and government take place—as well as socializing. "Entrance of openings" needs the same type of expansion the second line of verse 2 required: "*At* the entrance to the doors." Translators face the challenge of trying to find multiple ways to say "beside" or "at" or "in front of the town" in the receptor language. Of course, ancient Israelite cities were different from most modern cities and that difference needs to be preserved for historical and cultural integrity. The importance of the gateway to ancient cities should not be ignored or omitted from the text.

As in verse 2, the main verb of verse 3 comes at the end of the Hebrew structure. This same grammatical structuring might need to be avoided in some languages, and translators need to preserve the naturalness of expression in the receptor language(s).[187] The Hebrew verb root here refers to a ringing cry or loud shout. It often indicates the exultant cry of victory, but in this context no such meaning occurs. Instead, the concept is that of loudly hailing or calling to someone. As the third such verb (see v. 1, "call" and "cry out") to refer to this particular action, the text stretches the capacity of translators to identify legitimate and natural synonyms for their translations.

Of course, ancient Israelite cities were different from most modern cities and that difference needs to be preserved for historical and cultural integrity.

[4] "To you, O men, I call,
And my cry is to humankind.[188]

[5] "O naïve, understand prudence;
And fools, understand the heart.[189]

As we arrive at verse 4, we must pay close attention to any required punctuation for speech in the receptor language(s). The quotation marks in the translation above indicate the commencement of direct discourse—the words spoken by Lady Wisdom. Note that, in English usage, each verse begins with quotation marks to show that each verse is included. The closing quotation marks come at the end of either the translated portion, or the end of the discourse. Some Bible translations (e.g., KJV and ASV in English and Reina-Valera 1960 in Spanish) omit quotation marks, making readers determine the beginning and end of direct discourse.

"Unto you" uses a second person masculine plural pronominal suffix in the Hebrew text. That signals the direct address, which is then followed by the vocative of address, "O men." The address could be understood as gender specific—just as the situation described in Proverbs 7 was gender specific. Lady Wisdom could be addressing men, not women, in this figurative depiction. However, the greater context makes it clear that "men" ultimately represent all human beings, since the address of Lady Wisdom will actually prove to apply to both male and female.

"Call" at the end of the first poetic line uses the same Hebrew word as "call" in the first line of verse 1. Therefore, translators should use the same translation for both occurrences—especially since two other synonyms have already occurred in the text. Then, in the second line "cry" represents the translation of one of the two Hebrew words used in verse 1 for "cry out" (literally, "gives her voice") appears here in verse 4 as just the noun ("my voice"). No verb occurs in the second line. The verbless grammar commonly demands the stative verb "is" for the English translation.

In this second line, the Hebrew idiom "sons of man" (or "sons of Adam": *b^e^ney-'adam*) takes "humankind" as the referent. As with "men" in the first line, "humankind" possesses a vocative role in the sentence—the ones being addressed by Lady Wisdom. The phrase clarifies the identification of "men" as more than just males (see also the phrase's use in Gen. 11:5; Deut. 32:8; 2 Sam. 7:14; 1 Kings 8:39; Pss. 12:1; 14:2; etc.). These two poetic lines demonstrate that what scholars have identified as synonymous parallelism might rather reveal a second line defining or explaining the first line.

What scholars have identified as synonymous parallelism might rather reveal a second line defining or explaining the first line.

Verse 5 continues Wisdom's speech. The vocative of address consists of the second Hebrew word in the verse: "naïve." Fourteen of its eighteen occurrences in the Hebrew Bible come in the book of Proverbs (Pss. 19:8 [Eng. 7]; 116:6; 119:130; and Ezek. 45:20 are the four remaining occurrences). It refers to those who are young, inexperienced, needing guidance, gullible, or easily seduced. Wisdom calls upon the naïve to gain understanding of cunning and cleverness—or more positively, "prudence" or "good sense." Some English versions have chosen to associate such cunning or cleverness with "shrewdness" (NJPS) or "subtility" (DRA). In Joshua 9:4 the same word ("craftily" NASB) occurs in describing the actions of the Gibeonites who pretended to come from a far country. The Septuagint translated the Hebrew word with the Greek *panourgia*. The same Greek word identifies the "cunning" (2 Cor. 11:3 ESV) of the serpent in deceiving Eve in the Garden of Eden.

The second line of verse 5 introduces the fourth descriptor of those whom Lady Wisdom addresses: the "foolish," or the insensitive, dull, stupid, or insolent. Such people lack common sense or wisdom. Therefore, Wisdom admonishes them to "understand heart"—an idiom meaning either "put some sense in your heart"[190] or "pay attention" (RSV; cf. "take this to heart"[191]

CEB) or "understand the heart" (YLT; that is, the fallen heart as the source of one's lack of spiritual wisdom or tendency to do what is unwise and wrong). The last meaning appears to be the most straightforward. Translation teams, however, must carefully examine the support for each of these translations (and perhaps others) to reach their own conclusion.

[6] "Listen, because I speak noble things,
And the opening of my lips *speaks* upright things,[192]

[7] "Because my mouth mutters truth,
But wickedness is an abomination to my lips.[193]

"Listen" (a plural verb) implies the same persons addressed in the previous context, especially the "naïve" and "fools." The Hebrew particle translated here as "because" presents a cause or reason for Wisdom's hearers to pay attention to what she says. The verb, as with earlier verbs in this context, probably indicates a characteristic present tense[194]—in other words, such speech characterizes Lady Wisdom. "Noble things" looks in the Hebrew like the noun "nobles," "princes," or "leaders." However, the context indicates its use as an adjective "excellent" (GNV, ASV, NKJV) or "noble" (RSV, NAS, HCSB, NJPS, ESV) as the attribute of "things" or "words." Versions or commentators using "straightforward," "honest," or "true" depend upon changing the Hebrew text to result in a different word.[195]

When translating Hebrew poetry, translators need to pay close attention to the parallelism of lines and the frequent gapping (ellipsis) of terms used in the first line, but assumed in the second line.

Translators need to supply a verb for the second poetic line, since the author intends for the verb in the first line to serve both lines. Such an ellipsis of the verb in the second line occurs frequently in Hebrew poetry. When translating Hebrew poetry, translators need to pay close attention to the parallelism of lines and the frequent gapping (ellipsis) of terms used in the first line, but assumed in the second line.[196] In place of "the opening of my lips," the translator could use "my mouth." However, as discussed below, it might be desirable to preserve the variety of references to speech.

Verse 7 begins with the same particle expressing reason or cause as we saw in the first line of verse 6. Poetic variation occurs in reference to the speaking. First, in verse 6 the verb "I speak" is used. Then the second line of verse 6 switches to "the opening of my lips" to identify the instrument of speech. Now the writer uses "my palate." Hebrew poets frequently use sets of three variations. Rather than eliminating the variations and smoothing the translation by using the same form throughout (e.g., "I have important things to tell you. Everything I say is right, for I speak the truth" NLT), preserving the variety of expression (keeping "lips" and "palate/mouth") helps to retain the poetic quality of the text.

The second line of verse 7 begins with the Hebrew conjunction attached to a non-verb ("abomination"). Quite often this construction identifies a disjunctive clause expressing a contrast. Since the two lines of this verse appear to make just such a contrast, "but" becomes the preferred translation. In addition, the word order in this noun clause indicates a statement classifying the subject ("wickedness") as "an abomination."[197] The verb "is" must be added to the verbless Hebrew clause in order to make sense in English.

[8] "All the words of my mouth are *spoken* in righteousness;
There is nothing in them twisted or perverse.[198]

[9] "All of them are straight to the one who understands
And upright to those who find knowledge.[199]

Verses 8 and 9 continue with the topic of Wisdom's words addressed in verses 6 and 7. In contrast to the previous stanza focusing on the words spoken, this stanza returns to those whom Wisdom addresses. In verses 4 and 5, they are the "naïve" and "fools." In this stanza, they are the ones who understand Wisdom's instruction and acquire knowledge. Translators face another challenge by the occurrence of a third term for the organ of speech introduced in the first poetic line of verse 8 ("mouth"). It is a different Hebrew word than the one in verse 7 (there, it is literally "palate"). However, the pattern of references provides a solution: "lips" (v. 6b), "palate" (v. 7a), "lips" (v. 7b), "mouth" (v. 8a). The alternating terms indicate that using "mouth" in place of "palate" preserves the pattern better in translation. There does not appear to be any specialized or intended distinction between the two terms when viewed in the overall context. The context also implies the verb "*spoken*," due to the repeated references to the products of speaking.

In the second poetic line of verse 8, the antecedent to the pronominal suffix occurring with "in them" must be the immediately preceding "words." The two adjectives ("twisted or perverse") stand in stark contrast to the first line's "righteousness." No major English version takes these final two words as a hendiadys (two words expressing but one meaning), although translators could consider it a plausible possibility: "crookedly perverse" or "crooked perversity" (the first adjective or noun modifies the second adjective or noun).[200]

The pronominal suffix on "all of them" (v. 9) refers to the same antecedent as the previous pronominal suffix (v. 8): "words." "Straight" (RSV, NRSV, ESV) might also be translated "straightforward" (NEB, REB, NAS, NJPS, NAB) or "right" (DRA, NIV, NIRV). A number of English versions have chosen "plain" (KJV, ASV, NKJV, NJB, NLT) or "clear" (CJB, NET, HCSB, GWT, GNT) based upon the root meaning "that which is directly opposite to" or "right in front of someone"[201]—in other words, that which is in plain sight. The second line's parallel term acts as a synonym ("straight," "on the level," "right," or "upright"). Most English versions choose "right" for this second term.

"The one who understands" (first poetic line of v. 9) arises out of the Hebrew definite article attached to a participle being used as a noun. That construction results in translations like "the one who gains understanding" or "the one who understands." Although the second line's participle occurs in a construction to which the Hebrew definite article cannot be attached, the context suggests it be treated as definite: "to/for the ones who find knowledge" or "to/for those who find knowledge." This is due to the fact that the first participle is singular ("the one who"), but the second is plural ("the ones who" or "those who"). The singular indicates a personal, individual relationship to Wisdom, whereas the plural speaks more generically. Finding knowledge speaks of attaining knowledge, but might also imply the process or search for it.

[10] "Receive my instruction, but do not *receive* silver
And *receive* knowledge rather than choice gold,[202]

[11] "Because wisdom is better than corals
And all desirable things do not become equal to her."[203]

Verse 10 begins with a plural imperative translated by the English versions in two directions: (1) with a more passive concept as "receive" (KJV, DRA, ASV, NKJV, NET) or "accept" (NEB, NJB, NJPS, HCSB), and (2) with a more active concept as "take" (RSV, NAS, NRSV, NASB, ESV, GWT) or "choose" (REB, NCV, GNT, NLT, NIV, NIRV). The seeming ambiguity exists in the semantic range of the Hebrew verb itself. The passive meaning occurs in Elisha's refusal to accept any gifts from Naaman (2 Kings 5:15–20) and of Israel receiving double retribution from Yahweh due to her sins (Isa. 40:2). Yet, the active meaning appears in the description of an eagle taking up and carrying off its young (Deut. 32:11) and of Ishbosheth taking Paltiel's wife, Michal, away from him (2 Sam. 3:15). Every translator wrestles with this kind of semantics problem. The final translation depends upon a number of factors the translation team needs to investigate:

- the context and its overall description of a situation,
- the object of the action and whether it is a gift or plunder, or something else, and
- the occurrence of similar uses elsewhere—(1) within the same author's writings, (2) then, within writings of the same historical period, and, (3) finally, within the broad scope of the Hebrew Bible as a whole.

Sometimes translators will make one choice and later the version's revisers opt for a different translation, as in the case of Proverbs 8:10 with the NEB's "accept" and the REB's "choose." The passive ("accept" or "receive") seems better in this particular context, since Lady Wisdom appears to offer wisdom as a desirable gift of great value—like the gifts brought to the baby Jesus by the wise men (Matt. 2:11). Such a passive meaning for this verb root occurs also in Proverbs 1:3; 2:1; 4:10; 9:7; and 10:8.

Sometimes translators will make one choice and later the version's revisers opt for a different translation, as in the case of Proverbs 8:10 with the NEB's "accept" and the REB's "choose."

"My instruction" presents another word with potentially differing meanings. The positive aspect refers to "instruction," but the negative aspect refers to "discipline" in the sense of chastisement. Since the full stanza speaks of value and reward, the positive meaning offers the better sense. The next clause is verbless and starts with the Hebrew conjunction—thus forming another statement of contrast: "but." A Hebrew negative (*'al*) normally occurring with subjunctive and imperative verbs precedes the noun "silver" (or "money"). Therefore, the author evidently omitted the verb, since the previous verb ("receive" or "accept") serves in this clause as well: "do not *receive* silver." Since the second line refers to "gold," this line should be taken as a reference to "silver," not "money"—the two precious metals compose a common pairing in the Hebrew Bible.

The second line of verse 10 continues the same verb ellipsis: "And *receive* knowledge." The word "knowledge" already made its appearance at the end of verse 9, so translators should use the same word to translate it in both places. In fact, translation teams should determine all translations of the various synonyms for "wisdom," "instruction," "understanding," "prudence," "knowledge," "discretion," and "learning" (these reflect the NASB version) throughout the entire book of Proverbs according to the choices they made for each individual Hebrew term in 1:1–7, the prologue. However, those word equivalents should not be so strictly applied as to ignore potential variations in meanings that might occur for a word in different contexts throughout the book.

A preposition often translated as "from" forms a prefix on the next word. In this context, however, it carries a comparative force equivalent to "more than" (cf. WYC), but better translated as "rather than" or "instead of" in this clause. The word for "gold" forms a familiar word pair with "silver" (see Prov. 3:14; 8:19; 16:16; as well as Ps. 68:13 [Heb. 14] and Zech. 9:3). A participle used as an adjective modifies the word for "gold": "choice gold" (= "chosen gold").

Verse 11 begins with the causal conjunction "because," providing the reason for the statements in verse 10. Since verse 11 forms a subordinate (or dependent) clause to verse 10, the punctuation should demonstrate that relationship (thus the comma in the English above). A comparative clause (using the word "good" together with the comparative preposition) provides the sense of "better than": "wisdom" (the same word as in v. 1, *hokmah*) "is better than . . ." The Hebrew *p^{e}ninim* most likely refers to precious red corals used in jewelry.[204] Terms for various gems and precious stones and metals often require a good deal of research in the receptor language. The body of knowledge and experience for Bible translation astounds first-time translators—they must deal with technical vocabulary in gemology, zoology, botany, architecture, and medicine, just to name some of the fields of knowledge encountered in the pages of Scripture. Fortunately for the SBCL translation team in Bangladesh, Bangladeshis were familiar with Burmese red coral from Myanmar, making our translation task fairly simple. Despite the familiarity with red coral, we still tested the knowledge and awareness of the term for the uneducated as well as the educated.

The body of knowledge and experience for Bible translation astounds first-time translators—they must deal with technical vocabulary in gemology, zoology, botany, architecture, and medicine, just to name some of the fields of knowledge encountered in the pages of Scripture.

Many early English versions lacked adequate resources to understand this gem name occurring only six times in Hebrew wisdom poetry (Prov. 3:15; 8:11; 20:15; 31:10; Job 28:18; and Lam. 4:7). Recognizing the difficulty in Proverbs 8:11, the Wyclif version (WYC) uses "alle the most precious richessis." The Geneva Bible (GNV) chose "precious stones" (perhaps following the Septuagint's *lithōn polutelōn*). And, the Douay-Rheims (DRA) opted for "the most precious things." We must note, however, that DRA represents a translation, not from the Hebrew, but from the Latin Vulgate's *pretiosissimis*. Therefore, DRA's translation for the gem here reflects the same uncertainty and lack of specificity confronting the translators of the Vulgate from Jerome down to the more recent Clementine version. Other, more recent English versions followed suit with simply "jewels" (RSV, NAS, NJB, NRSV, NASB, HCSB, ESV, GNT, GWT). Translation teams might choose to follow the same safe practice. The problem with that, however, is that translators may end up using the same translation for a large number of other equally difficult gem names. This might give the impression that the biblical writers themselves did not use accurate names or could not properly identify the gems.

Other translations go with a red-colored, but inaccurate alternative, "rubies" (KJV, ERV, DBY, YLT, ASV, NKJV, NJPS, NIRV, NET, NLT, NCV, NIVUK, NIV). A few other modern translations opt for the equally inaccurate "pearls" (CJB, CEB). A distinct minority of English versions identify the gem as "coral"/"corals" (ERB, NAB) or "red coral" (NEB, REB). Since Lamentations 4:7 attributes a reddish color to the gem and a different Hebrew word appears to represent the ruby in passages like Exodus 28:17 and Ezekiel 28:13, "corals" appears to be the most accurate translation. In post-biblical Hebrew, the word did ultimately take on the meaning "pearls," but this should not be taken as equivalent to the older use of the word.[205]

The second line of verse 11 speaks of "all desirable things" as a summary of valuable items like silver, gold, and corals. And, the final statement addresses the fact that nothing of value equals wisdom. The translation "become equal to her" understands the verb form to be a dynamic stative expressing a state of becoming, rather than a state of being—perhaps implying the growing value of wisdom through time. An alternate translation could be "all desirable things do not become her equal," or even "all desirable things never become her equal." Most translators will choose to stick with the simplest means of stating this: "are not equal to her" or "are not her equal."

As we complete our analysis of the final two verses of this section of Proverbs 8, Lady Wisdom's direct discourse has not concluded. Her speech continues in verses 12 and following, but takes a different tone and direction, being more descriptive of herself.

Bible translators should record their decisions as they work through a passage of Scripture. After completing their translation, they should review that record (whether written or an audio recording) to identify lessons learned.

> Learning occurs on every project. Lessons learned is the learning gained from the process of performing the project. . . . We learn from our own project experiences as well as the experiences of others. . . . Sharing lessons learned among project team members prevents an organization from repeating the same mistakes and also allows them to take advantage of orga-

> nizational best practices. . . . Lessons learned can be used to improve future projects and future stages of current projects.[206]

The process of record keeping has already begun with the identification and documentation of translation decisions for Proverbs 8:1–11 on the preceding pages. Let's turn next to analysis.

Translators' Lessons Learned

From the discussion about translation choices in Proverbs 8:1–11, we have discovered that clarity and accuracy provide significant challenges to translators. First, resolving translation issues demands giving close attention to the context. Careful examination of the context determines the structure of a text, the flow of the text, and the meanings of both individual vocabulary words and grammatical forms. Second, translators must pay close attention to the little words: particles, conjunctions, negatives, and prepositions. Such words determine relationships between words, phrases, and clauses.

Third, the type or form of literature often controls the usage of both vocabulary and grammar. Hebrew poetry, for example, behaves quite differently from Hebrew prose narrative. Translators must learn the characteristics of the different literary types in the Hebrew Bible in order to properly interpret and translate the text. A variety of elements must be taken into consideration: repetition, parallelism, ellipsis, figurative speech, and personification—just to name a few.

Fourth, clarity of meaning in the original text can sometimes elude the translator—especially when it comes to technical terms (like the identification of specific gems). Occasionally translation teams might conclude that a more general translation provides the wisest choice (such as "jewels" or "precious stones" for "red coral"). On the other hand, they might not have a choice if the language itself does not include a term for a specific species of gem, animal, or plant.

Accuracy and clarity go hand in hand. If a translation lacks clarity (cannot be understood), it cannot be accurate in the minds of the readers. On the other side of the coin, translators cannot accurately represent the original text if they lack a clear understanding of it. In the end, no translation can perfectly represent the original in every aspect of the text. That brings the translator to the desired goal: an essentially literal translation that does not misrepresent the meaning of the text in all of its complexity. In other words, it is essentially accurate, even if some of the meaning within the text remains elusive.

"An essentially literal translation" might not represent the goal for some Bible translation projects. In such cases, the translation team must identify the nature of their goal and develop principles to help them obtain their purpose. Essentially literal Bible translations provide superb versions for in-depth Bible study, but might not always speak directly to the heart of someone encountering the Bible for the first time—especially in a context characterized by biblical illiteracy (lack of basic Bible knowledge) or even an absence of basic religious concepts within Judaism or Christianity. For such individuals, a more dynamic translation might engage their attention and interest. Eventually, as they grow in both biblical and spiritual knowledge, they might prefer to move to an essentially literal version to delve more deeply into the biblical text. No matter the kind of translation, they all still aim for the twin attributes of accuracy and clarity—they just employ a different translation style in their end product. If we agree to the necessity of a variety of Bible versions, we must also pursue the production of diverse Bible versions in any particular language around the world—a single Bible version might not accomplish the full mission.

Every good translation team seeks to

- guard its handling of the text,
- pursue detailed research in all areas of grammar, literary structure, vocabulary, background history, and cultural setting, and
- produce an accurate and clear translation.

CHAPTER 8

WHICH ENGLISH BIBLE VERSION IS BEST?

After learning about translation variability and seeing that simplicity, clarity, and accuracy can be maintained even with different ways to translate the same text, another series of questions come to mind. Which English Bible versions prove best for use in the pulpit? Which ones are best for private Bible study? Pastors, church lay leaders, and individual believers ask about modern Bible translations because they want to use the most accurate Bible translation available. They also desire an English version they can read easily, especially in public reading. Everyone looks for an understandable English Bible translation. With the plethora of so-called "literal" Bible translations available on the market, how is a pastor or church member to know which is the best choice?

Answering these questions requires us to examine at least a few selected examples and to pursue some serious evaluation of a group of English Bible versions recognized widely as good translations. We will focus on the following versions:

- King James Version (KJV)
- New King James Version (NKJV)
- New American Standard Bible (NAS)
- New American Standard Bible Update (NASB)
- English Standard Version (ESV)

- New Revised Standard Version (NRSV)
- New International Version (NIV)
- Christian Standard Bible (CSB)

These eight versions have the greatest potential of being chosen by evangelicals for pulpit, pew, or personal use. For those who are already wondering why the more dynamic NIV appears in this list with the seven more formal translations, the reasons will soon become apparent.

Differentiating Translations

Robert Thomas's *How to Choose a Bible Version*[207] lays out a five-step deviation test for evaluating Bible translations. The technique assigns the following values for different types of deviations:[208]

Changes in order and omissions	= 1
Lexical and syntactical alterations	= 2
Additions	= 4

Omitting words, phrases, or verses from a Bible version might, however, represent a greater deviation from literal translation than some additions. Assigning omissions a value of 1 and additions a value of 4 does not reflect the more serious cases of omission nor does it adequately represent lesser additions. Meanwhile, the area that most affects accuracy (that of lexical and syntactical alterations) receives only a 2-point value in all occurrences.[209] In order to simplify the procedure and to provide a hierarchy within each category of change, I propose a slightly different system of evaluation.

> ***Rather than looking at the analysis as merely a measurement of literalness, the emphasis should be placed equally upon the verification of accuracy (faithfulness to the original languages).***

In the course of examining these eight versions, I attempt to critique them by an objective analysis comparing selected passages with the text in the original languages as well as comparing the versions with each other.

Rather than looking at the analysis as merely a measurement of literalness, the emphasis should be placed equally upon the verification of accuracy (faithfulness to the original languages). Literalness in some cases is quite a different matter in English versions as compared with other language versions. Approaching this as a Bible translator with prior involvement with translation projects in other languages, I find that literalness can be a detriment to accuracy. Translators with only an English Bible translation experience often equate literalness with accuracy. While agreeing that such an equation might fit a majority of the time in the discussion of English translations, I still maintain that there are cases where the equation is not always applicable. The resulting comparison between versions, therefore, reflects both the literalness and the accuracy of the translations.

Accuracy especially comes into play when we deal with idioms in the original language—see our previous discussion in chapter 2. An idiom is an expression that should not be taken literally. Technically an idiom is a word or group of words that has a special meaning not discernible from the parts comprising that word or group of words. Usually an idiom is an expression peculiar to a particular language and conveys a distinct meaning that may be contrary to the meanings of its component parts. Two different languages will rarely have the same idiomatic forms. Therefore, in a deviation test, translations of idioms can be categorized too readily as nonliteral.

It behooves all of us to keep in mind that it is difficult enough to translate the Bible. As difficult as translation might be, however, judging a translation proves even more difficult. Thomas's book goes a long way toward helping us understand that translations do need to be judged or evaluated. Although he and I might use two different modifications of Wonderly's deviation test, the similarity of our results demonstrates that the differences in translations can be significant. Too often translation critics employ subjective criteria too arbitrary to be of value. Indeed, many critical evaluations involve literary criticism more than actual translation criticism.

Too often translation critics employ subjective criteria too arbitrary to be of value. Indeed, many critical evaluations involve literary criticism more than actual translation criticism.

Leland Ryken's *The Word of God in English*[210] presents a superb examination of English Bible versions from the viewpoint of a literary critic. In the national Evangelical Theological Society (ETS) meetings in San Antonio (November 2004), Ryken admitted, however, that he had no background or training in the original languages. Lack of basic exegetical skills hampers his ability to provide a full critique of any English Bible version. Nonetheless, he provides a valuable list of literary criteria worthy of consideration when choosing an English Bible version. However, that choice can experience significant improvement if exegetical accuracy accompanies the literary criteria.

Pastors and lay people need an approach that highlights faithfulness to the original languages and accuracy with regard to meaning. Katharina Reiss's observation deserves our attention. She said, "The judgment of a translation should never be made *one-sidedly* and *exclusively* on the basis of its form in the target language."[211] Therefore, measurement of literary quality alone fails to be sufficient. Most importantly, all Bible translations must be evaluated according to identical principles and standards. At all costs, we must avoid the vague generalities plaguing reviews or promotional materials: "a fluent translation," "clear and understandable," "an uneven translation," "a readable translation," or "this translation reads like the original."

For the purpose of this evaluation we will devote our attention to but one familiar text from each Testament. From these two sample texts I will make observations about the relative faithfulness of each of the selected versions. Such observations must be understood for what they are: limited and selective. It would be hazardous to extrapolate an ultimate characterization of any one version on the basis of these two texts alone. The principles gained through such analysis, however, should provide tools for continuing similar analysis in other sample pericopes. Eventually, given enough research of this nature, a pastor should gain a clear enough analysis to produce a sound recommendation for the people in his congregation.

A grading system for the translations expedites the presentation of a quantitative evaluation. For each verse of each sample text, I have assigned a numerical value equal to the total number of *necessary* English words for an *accurate and literal translation*. Numerical values for each version will be decided by assigning points as follows:

Words that are *both clear and accurate*	= **1.0**
Words that are *relatively accurate but unclear or ambiguous*	= **0.5**
Words that are *inaccurate lexically and/or grammatically*	= **0.0**

Unless a change in word order affects clarity and/or accuracy, that aspect will be ignored, since word order differs inherently between English and Hebrew or Greek. Restructured grammar adversely affecting accuracy and/or clarity will be treated as inaccurate. Adherents to dynamic equivalence may find fault with the strictness with which I apply this principle. Restructuring according to subjective aesthetics is less desirable than restructuring required by the relative absence or non-use of a grammatical structure in the receptor language. For example, rare use of the passive in Bengali requires restructuring many biblical passives as actives. Such restructuring is not for aesthetic purposes—it is directly related to a difference in the structures of the two languages. The average grade a translation receives for the section of biblical text will provide the score by which we might identify the most accurate translation. The higher the score, the more accurate the translation. In order to provide a comparison, I include scores for Today's English Version (TEV), also known as the Good News Translation (GNT), since it tends to be far more free in its translations than the other eight versions being evaluated.

Restructured grammar adversely affecting accuracy and/or clarity will be treated as inaccurate.

This evaluation will produce three items for each verse in the selected biblical passages:

(1) a table showing the wording of each version and each version's grade
(2) observations to explain the evaluation process
(3) a list of principles by which subsequent decisions might be made

At the conclusion of the passage a summary table appears to display the overall grading for each of the versions.

Evaluation of Selected Versions of Psalm 23

In order to simplify the evaluation, I offer a "base" translation representing the original Hebrew text as closely as possible. The "base," therefore, reveals my personal judgment regarding what an accurate and clear essentially literal translation should say—limiting it to the number of words necessary to represent each textual, grammatical, and semantic aspect of meaning. The first number in the second to last column represents the number of words in my translation (representative of each significant element of translatable meaning). The number of words does not bear any direct correlation to the number of words present in the Hebrew or Greek. We already saw that evidence for Psalm 23:1 in the comparative analysis of ancient and modern versions presented in chapter 6.

Obviously, some amount of subjectivity might characterize the translation at times, but the notes I provide should enable readers to understand the reasons for my choices. Disagreements with those reasons could lead to a slightly different evaluation of these passages from individual English versions.

v. 1	**Base**	A psalm by David. YHWH is my shepherd, I do not lack.	12	% **100**
	KJV	A Psalm of David. The Lord is my shepherd; I shall not want.	9.5	**79**
	NKJV	A Psalm of David. The Lord is my shepherd; I shall not want.	9.5	**79**
	NAS	*A Psalm of David.* The Lord is my shepherd, I shall not want.	9.5	**79**
	NASB	A Psalm of David. The Lord is my shepherd, I shall not want.	9.5	**79**
	ESV	A PSALM OF DAVID. The Lord is my shepherd; I shall not want.	9.5	**79**
	NRSV	A Psalm of David. The Lord is my shepherd, I shall not want.	9.5	**79**
	CSB	A Davidic psalm. The Lord is my shepherd; there is nothing I lack.	10	**83**
	NIV	A psalm of David. The Lord is my shepherd, I shall not be in want.	10	**83**
	TEV	The Lord is my shepherd; I have everything I need.	6	**50**

Observations on Verse 1

Other than differences in italicization (NAS) and capitalization (ESV), all except TEV treat the psalm heading the same. Because the TEV omits the heading entirely, it receives a major deduction; omission = -4.0.

Accurate translation recognizes that the Hebrew preposition attached to "David" is a *lamed* (the Hebrew letter composing the preposition) of authorship (compare the same usage in Isa. 38:9; Hab. 3:1).[212] The psalm was written "by David"—"of David" is ambiguous. Ambiguity = -0.5 point.

The verb in the first line of the text is absent, but understood, in the Hebrew noun clause. However, italicization in the KJV and NKJV is unnecessary, as evidenced by the treatment of the remaining translations. No accurate English translation may safely omit the stative verb.

"The LORD" is the traditional rendering of the Tetragrammaton (*YHWH*) first employed by the Septuagint translators because of a misinterpretation and misapplication of the third commandment (see previous discussion in chapter 6).[213] In public reading there is no way for the hearer to know whether the divine title thus represented is *YHWH* (LORD: "Yahweh") or *Adonai* ("Lord"). Translating both with the same word contributes to a confusion of divine names. Ambiguity = -0.5 point.

Employment of a future tense for the Hebrew verb in the second line is due to a doubtful, but traditional, treatment of the imperfect in Hebrew as a present-future tense form. The context of this psalm and of this line (cf. the first line) indicates that the present would be more accurate. Inaccuracy = -1.0 point. CSB's present tense accurately represents the context.

"Want" is ambiguous in English but continues in translations of Psalm 23:1 primarily due to familiarity with the the KJV's rendering of the psalm even among non-Bible readers. A smoother use of "lack" would be "I have no lack," even though it changes the form to imply the negation of a noun ("lack") rather than the Hebrew's negation of the verb. Ambiguity = -0.5 point.

The NIV ("I shall not be in want") and CSB ("I have what I need") exhibit the only substantial attempts to clarify the meaning of "want." The NIV's is accurate and clear, but CSB's, like the TEV's positive ("I have everything I need") for negative in the final line, is unnecessary and misleading. Inaccuracy = -1.0.

Principles Derived from Examining the Versions on Verse 1

Principle #1: Copula verbs understood in Hebrew noun clauses need not be italicized since they are part of an accurate translation into English. This verb is implied in the Hebrew grammar even though not represented by a specific Hebrew word.

Principle #2: Hebrew verb tenses need to be translated by context, not by form.

Principle #3: Ambiguity in the English translation should be avoided as much as possible.

Ambiguity in the English translation should be avoided as much as possible.

Principle #4: Treatment of the Tetragrammaton should not be based upon the erroneous interpretation of the heretical sect of Alexandrian Jews in Egypt in the third century B.C. Clarity rather than confusion in public oral reading ought to characterize a translation's treatment of the divine name.

v. 2	**Base**	In grassy/green pastures He causes me to lie down, Beside calm water He leads me.	15	% **100**
	KJV	He maketh me to lie down in green pastures: he leadeth me beside the still waters.	15	**100**
	NKJV	He makes me to lie down in green pastures; He leads me beside the still waters.	15	**100**
	NAS	He makes me lie down in green pastures; He leads me beside quiet waters.	15	**100**
	NASB	He makes me lie down in green pastures; He leads me beside quiet waters.	15	**100**
	ESV	He makes me lie down in green pastures. He leads me beside still waters.	15	**100**
	NRSV	He makes me lie down in green pastures; he leads me beside still waters;	15	**100**
	CSB	He lets me lie down in green pastures; He leads me beside quiet waters.	14	**93**
	NIV	He makes me lie down in green pastures, he leads me beside quiet waters,	15	**100**
	TEV	He lets me rest in fields of green grass and leads me to quiet pools of fresh water.	12	**80**

Observations on Verse 2

Most versions are unusually accurate throughout. However, the CSB and TEV change the causative ("makes") to a permissive ("lets")—a potentially significant difference for understanding the author's intent. Inaccuracy = -1.0.

Two images advance the sheep metaphor in this verse: "pastures of vegetation" and "waters of rest." The first refers to the fresh green of grass or other edible vegetation. "Green pastures" is an excellent rendering in English. The second refers to water that is not a rushing torrent with cascades and rapids. "Still" and "quiet" are both accurate translations for English.

The TEV substitutes "rest" for "lie down." This is potentially misleading since the Hebrew verbs are different. Ambiguity = -0.5.

The TEV's exchange of "to" for "beside" is potentially accurate, but interpretive. Ambiguity = -0.5.

Expanding the final phrase ("quiet waters" or "still waters"), the TEV's "quiet pools of fresh water" misleads readers as to the actual wording of the original. Inaccuracy = -1.0.

Principles Derived from Examining the Versions on Verse 2

Principle #5: Imagery in Hebrew poetry should be retained as much as possible to convey the Hebrew Bible's poetic richness.

v. 3	**Base**	He revives/restores my soul, He guides me in paths of righteousness for His name's sake.	15	**% 100**
	KJV	He restoreth my soul: he leadeth me in the paths of righteousness for his name's sake.	13	**87**
	NKJV	He restores my soul; He leads me in the paths of righteousness For His name's sake.	13	**87**
	NAS	He restores my soul; He guides me in the paths of righteousness For His name's sake.	14	**93**
	NASB	He restores my soul; He guides me in the paths of righteousness For His name's sake.	14	**93**
	ESV	He restores my soul. He leads me in paths of righteousness for his name's sake.	14	**93**
	NRSV	he restores my soul. He leads me in right paths for his name's sake.	13.5	**90**

	CSB	He renews my life; He leads me along the right paths for His name's sake.	13	**87**
	NIV	he restores my soul. He guides me in paths of righteousness for his name's sake.	15	**100**
	TEV	He gives me new strength. He guides me in the right paths, as he has promised.	10	**67**

Observations on Verse 3

The TEV's interpretive translation ("gives me new strength") risks obscuring the potential reference to conversion in the text. Inaccuracy = -1.0. "Restores," "renews," and "revives" preserve the potential because the action could refer to restoring the soul's spiritual relationship to God or giving new life.[214]

The psalmist employs a different verb for "lead/guide" in this verse as compared to verse 2. That difference ought to be maintained in translation so that the reader understands the writer used another term. The difference produces not only an appreciation for the variety of words used in the psalm, but a question about the possible distinction between the two words and implications for interpretation. Inaccuracy = -1.0.

"Paths of righteousness" proves to be another point of differentiation between the translations. The Hebrew construction represents an indefinite rather than a definite noun phrase. No definite article appears in the text. "The paths of righteousness" is too specific as far as the grammar of the Hebrew is concerned. Inaccuracy = -1.0.

The NRSV's "right paths" presents potential for a different interpretation associated with "correct paths" or "moral paths." Neither has any definite connection to the concept related to the term for "righteousness" in the Hebrew text. "Right paths" seems overly interpretive. Ambiguity = -0.5.

Both "life" (CSB) and "me" (TEV) for "soul" could be considered ambiguous = -0.5.

"As he has promised" (TEV) is interpretive and obscures the original wording ("for his name's sake") badly. Inaccuracy = -3.0 (for three elements of particle, noun, and pronominal suffix).

Principles Derived from Examining the Versions on Verse 3

Principle #6: Different vocabulary words in the same context should be translated by different terms in the receptor language when possible.

Different vocabulary words in the same context should be translated by different terms in the receptor language when possible.

Principle #7: The absence of the definite article ought to be retained in translation unless other contextual or idiomatic factors indicate clearly otherwise.

Principle #8: Interpretive translations should be kept to a minimum.

v. 4	**Base**	Indeed, though I walk in a very dark valley, I do not fear trouble, Because You are with me; Your rod and Your staff, **they** comfort me.	27	**%** **100**
	KJV	Yea, though I walk through the valley of the shadow of death, I will fear no evil: for thou *art* with me; thy rod and thy staff they comfort me.	23	**85**
	NKJV	Yea, though I walk through the valley of the shadow of death, I will fear no evil; For You *are* with me; Your rod and Your staff, they comfort me.	23	**85**
	NAS	Even though I walk through the valley of the shadow of death, I fear no evil; for Thou art with me; Thy rod and Thy staff, they comfort me.	24	**89**
	NASB	Even though I walk through the valley of the shadow of death, I fear no evil, for You are with me; Your rod and Your staff, they comfort me.	24	**89**
	ESV	Even though I walk through the valley of the shadow of death, I will fear no evil, for you are with me; your rod and your staff, they comfort me.	23	**85**

	NRSV	Even though I walk through the darkest valley, I fear no evil; for you are with me; your rod and your staff—they comfort me.	26	**96**
	CSB	Even when I go through the darkest valley, I fear no danger, for you are with me; Your rod and Your staff—they comfort me.	27	**100**
	NIV	Even though I walk through the valley of the shadow of death, I will fear no evil, for you are with me; your rod and your staff, they comfort me.	23	**85**
	TEV	Even if I go through the deepest darkness, I will not be afraid, Lord, for you are with me. Your shepherd's rod and staff protect me.	22.5	**83**

Observations on Verse 4

"The shadow of death" is a Hebrew idiom referring to deep darkness. Inaccuracy = -1.0. The inclusion of "death" as part of the compound word in Hebrew probably indicates that a dark ravine in the Judean highlands was a dangerous place for man or sheep.[215]

There is no definite article for "valley" in the Hebrew text (Principle 7). Both "the darkest valley" and "the deepest darkness" result from attempting to produce a smooth and concise translation in English. Perhaps the mental picture traditionally depicted for this phrase ("the valley of the shadow of death") influences the translation so that death might be preserved as the meaning. Inaccuracy = -1.0.

Omission of "valley" (TEV) obscures the intended metaphor involving a shepherd pursuing errant sheep in a deep, narrow wadi filled with deep shadows and unforeseen dangers. Inaccuracy = -1.0.

The verbs ("walk," fear," "comfort") acquire their present tense by context (Principle 2). Inaccuracy = -1.0.

In the Hebrew, *ra'* ("evil" in most of these versions) in this context refers to "calamity" or "trouble" while the English "evil" implies something moral. The CSB's "danger" actually approximates the sense quite well. The TEV's omission inaccurately represents the psalmist's statement. Inaccuracy = -1.0.

The TEV's provision of an antecedent ("Lord") for the second person masculine singular pronoun in "you are with me" is unnecessary. Inaccuracy = -0.5.

The final line of the verse ("Your rod and Your staff, they . . .") involves a compound nominative absolute (or extraposition) followed by the emphatic personal pronoun ("they") before the verb (bold font shows the emphasis in the base translation). Translators find the emphasis difficult to represent easily and smoothly in English. Careful wording of the construction can help to imply the emphasis by preserving "they" or by using a perfectly legitimate equivalent of the construction: "As for Your rod and Your staff, they do comfort me."

When possible, emphasis ought to be expressed in the translation, but not at the expense of a smooth English translation.

TEV's "protect" for the text's "comfort" inaccurately translates the verb root meaning. Inaccuracy = -1.0.

Principles Derived from Examining the Versions on Verse 4

Principle #9: Hebrew idioms should not be translated word for word, but according to their sense.

Principle #10: When possible, emphasis ought to be expressed in the translation, but not at the expense of a smooth English translation.

v. 5	**Base**	You arrange a table before me in front of my enemies; You refresh my head with oil, My cup overflows.	19	**% 100**
	KJV	Thou preparest a table before me in the presence of mine enemies: thou anointest my head with oil; my cup runneth over.	19	**100**
	NKJV	You prepare a table before me in the presence of my enemies; You anoint my head with oil; My cup runs over.	19	**100**

	NAS	Thou dost prepare a table before me in the presence of my enemies; Thou hast anointed my head with oil; My cup overflows.	18	**95**
	NASB	You prepare a table before me in the presence of my enemies; You have anointed my head with oil; My cup overflows.	18	**95**
	ESV	You prepare a table before me in the presence of my enemies; you anoint my head with oil; my cup overflows.	19	**100**
	NRSV	You prepare a table before me in the presence of my enemies; you anoint my head with oil; my cup overflows.	19	**100**
	CSB	You prepare a table before me in the presence of my enemies; You anoint my head with oil; my cup overflows.	19	**100**
	NIV	You prepare a table before me in the presence of my enemies. You anoint my head with oil; my cup overflows.	19	**100**
	TEV	You prepare a banquet for me, where all my enemies can see me; you welcome me as an honored guest and fill my cup to the brim.	11	**58**

Observations on Verse 5

Again, the context indicates present tense verbs as the best rendition (Principle 2). The NAS and NASB are the only versions choosing to employ the English present perfect ("hast/have anointed"), which makes the action past rather than present. Inaccuracy = -1.0.

TEV's expansion of "in front of my enemies" to say "where all my enemies can see me" contains two inaccuracies: the addition of "all" and the unwarranted restructuring of the statement. Inaccuracies = -2.0.

TEV's interpretive restatement of the second line inserts potentially erroneous cultural detail ("honored guest") and obliterates the psalmist's actual statement. Inaccuracies = -5.0.

The Hebrew verb often translated "anoint" in this verse actually means "make fat." The NEB offers an accurate expanded translation: "thou hast richly bathed my head with oil." Although the Hebrew word is not the normal word for "anoint," the gloss still fits the action. "Refresh" provides the intended outcome of rubbing oil on a guest's head.[216] In the Hebrew, the definite article appears in "with oil" (literally, "with the oil"), but it involves the generic usage with a commodity or with the material used in connection with an action like anointing.[217] Therefore, its absence in English is accurate.

The TEV's exchange of "fill to the brim" for "overflows" employs words that do not represent the original text. The reader would be unable to know what the psalmist actually said. Inaccuracy = -1.0.

Principles Derived from Examining the Versions on Verse 5

No new principles.

v. 6	**Base**	Surely, goodness and loyal love will pursue me my whole life, And I will dwell lifelong in YHWH's house.	19	% **100**
	KJV	Surely goodness and mercy shall follow me all the days of my life: and I will dwell in the house of the LORD for ever.	16	**84**
	NKJV	Surely goodness and mercy shall follow me All the days of my life; And I will dwell in the house of the LORD Forever.	16	**84**
	NAS	Surely goodness and lovingkindness will follow me all the days of my life, And I will dwell in the house of the LORD forever.	16.5	**87**
	NASB	Surely goodness and lovingkindness will follow me all the days of my life, And I will dwell in the house of the LORD forever.	16.5	**87**
	ESV	Surely goodness and mercy shall follow me all the days of my life, and I shall dwell in the house of the LORD forever.	16	**84**
	NRSV	Surely goodness and mercy shall follow me all the days of my life, and I shall dwell in the house of the LORD my whole life long.	17	**89**
	CSB	Only goodness and faithful love will pursue me all the days of my life, and I will dwell in the house of the LORD as long as I live.	17.5	**92**

	NIV	Surely goodness and love will follow me all the days of my life, and I will dwell in the house of the LORD forever.	16.5	**87**
	TEV	I know that your goodness and love will be with me all my life; and your house will be my home as long as I live.	13.5	**71**

Observations on Verse 6

"Only" in the CSB's translation leads to a misunderstanding of the text. Inaccuracy = -1.0.

The TEV's "I know that" for "Surely" misleads readers as to exactly what the psalmist wrote. Inaccuracy = -1.0.

Adding "your" (TEV) to the two descriptive nouns might clarify whose goodness and love are involved, but the text leaves it as an implication that God is behind all such experiences for those who serve Him faithfully. Inaccuracy = -1.0.

The verbs in the context of verse 6 speak of the future because of references to the remainder of the psalmist's life (Principle 2).

That which is translated "mercy," "lovingkindness," and "love" in these versions is the Hebrew *chesed*, referring to "loyal love" or "steadfast love." "Mercy" provides a confusing meaning that really does not fall within the semantic range of the Hebrew word. Inaccuracy = -1.0; "lovingkindness" and "love" are closer = - 0.5.

"Follow" presents a tame and potentially misleading translation of the much more aggressive "pursue" for *radap*, but it is not so much a matter of absolute inaccuracy as ambiguity. Ambiguity = -0.5.

Complete elimination of the preceding verb ("pursue") by the TEV misrepresents the text. Inaccuracy = -1.0.

As in verse 1, the divine name requires a less ambiguous translation for public reading. Ambiguity = - 0.5. The TEV's elimination of the divine name involves an inaccuracy = -1.0.

The TEV's "will be my home" for "I will dwell"[218] misleads readers by restructuring in a way that obscures the original wording of the psalmist. The psalmist is not moving into the tabernacle to make it his permanent home. The meaning is that he can be found there quite frequently—more the idea of being habitually present. Inaccuracy = -1.0.

"Forever" is extremely unfortunate as a translation of "for length of days." The phrase in the base translation uses a phrase meaning "lifelong."

Synonymous parallelism with the preceding phrase ("all the days of my life" or "my whole life") makes the meaning certain. Inaccuracy = -1.0.

Principles Derived from Examining the Versions on Verse 6

No new principles.

Concluding Statistics and Observations for Versions of Psalm 23

The following tabular presentation of the evaluation scores allows readers to compare the selected English versions at a glance.

	Version	Verse-by-Verse Score						Average
		1	2	3	4	5	6	
	KJV	79	100	87	85	100	84	**89.2**
	NKJV	79	100	87	85	100	84	**89.2**
	NAS	79	100	93	89	95	87	**90.5**
	NASB	79	100	93	89	95	87	**90.5**
	ESV	79	100	93	85	100	84	**90.2**
	NRSV	79	100	90	96	100	89	**92.3**
	CSB	83	93	87	100	100	92	**92.5**
	NIV	83	100	100	85	100	87	**92.5**
	TEV	50	80	67	83	58	71	**68.2**

By comparing the scores of the first eight selected English versions with the TEV's scores, one can see at a glance how much more accurate those eight versions tend to be. Those eight versions of at least Psalm 23 neither exemplify free translations nor approximate the methodology of dynamic equivalence. They are more formal in their renderings of the Hebrew text.

Why do the CSB, NIV, and NRSV outscore the KJV, NKJV, NAS, and NASB? Part of the reason in this particular passage entails allowing the first three versions' translators greater freedom in handling this very popular and well-known text. The NKJV, NAS, and NASB basically follow the KJV with little variation, even if the translation proved to be technically inaccurate with regard to the original Hebrew. The high scores in Psalm 23, therefore, ought not be taken as indicative of the tenor of the rest of the Old Testament in these versions. Other factors must be taken into consideration in evaluating these versions. For example, the NIV's penchant for the Septuagint in matters of textual criticism impacts its overall accuracy and translation consistency in the Old Testament. Also, the NIV will tend, at times, to be quite free with the text. Psalm 23's popularity may not have allowed the NIV translators to be as free with it as they might with less familiar or popular portions of the Old Testament. It is possible, in any evaluation system, for a less accurate overall translation of the Bible to excel in both accuracy and clarity in some passages while lacking both qualities in other verses. It just so happens that Psalm 23 reveals the "Achilles' heel" of the KJV/NKJV and NAS/NASB pairings. Newer English Bible versions remaining too faithful to the KJV can end up abandoning accuracy in some passages. Tradition, like politics and commerce, often does not mix well with Bible translation, because accuracy often loses.

It is possible, in any evaluation system, for a less accurate overall translation of the Bible to excel in both accuracy and clarity in some passages while lacking both qualities in other verses.

Examples of accuracy in the NIV when the more literal versions have failed are the reason why its overall final score is higher. At least in Psalm 23, the NIV has been more consistently accurate and literal than the other translations. Accuracy in Psalm 23, however, does not guarantee equal success for accuracy in the remaining translation of the Old Testament.

Evaluation of Versions of Romans 6:8–14

Turning to the New Testament, Romans 6:8–14 serves well as a sample text because (1) it is of similar length to the Old Testament passage just evaluated, (2) it is in a familiar passage, but not as familiar as Psalm 23, and (3) it will allow a comparison with Thomas's deviation values for the epistle to the Romans.[219] The base represents my own translation of the Greek text found in the United Bible Societies' fourth edition, seeking to represent accurately each and every element of significant meaning within the Greek text.

v. 8	Base	But since we died with Christ, we believe that we will also live with Him,	15	**% 100**
	KJV	Now if we be dead with Christ, we believe that we shall also live with him:	14	**93**
	NKJV	Now if we died with Christ, we believe that we shall also live with Him,	14.5	**97**
	NAS	Now if we have died with Christ, we believe that we shall also live with Him,	14	**93**
	NASB	Now if we have died with Christ, we believe that we shall also live with Him,	14	**93**
	ESV	Now if we have died with Christ, we believe that we will also live with him.	14	**93**
	NRSV	But if we have died with Christ, we believe that we will also live with him.	14	**93**
	CSB	Now if we died with Christ, we believe that we will also live with Him,	14.5	**97**
	NIV	Now if we died with Christ, we believe that we will also live with him	14.5	**97**
	TEV	Since we have died with Christ, we believe that we will also live with him.	14.5	**97**

Observations on Verse 8

All the versions match up closely in their translations. The NAS, NASB, ESV, NRSV, and TEV treat the Greek aorist (better translated in this context as "we died") as though it were a Greek perfect ("we have died"). The reader (either on the basis of English grammar knowledge or some knowledge of Greek) might think that the translation implies some sort of continuing result—the normal implication of the Greek perfect. While not entirely incorrect (a person who has died, for example, is still dead), the translations can mislead, because they do not represent the distinction indicated by the Greek verb form. Rodney Huddleston explains,

> The essential difference between the perfect and the past tense is this: the perfect locates the situation within a period of time beginning in the past and extending forward to include the present . . . , whereas the past tense is used where the time of the situation is identified as wholly in the past, as a

> past that excludes the present. With the perfect we have an "inclusive past", with the past tense an "exclusive past".[220]

For example, "have died" might be taken as the beginning of a process in which the believer must continue to die. This verse in and of itself does not give such an implication. Also, translators must take care not to always treat the Greek aorist as a one-time (once for all) action, since that represents an oversimplified approach and an inaccurate understanding of the broad scope of aorist usage. Perhaps this point of discussion borders on the overly technical, but translations of the Bible should be superior examples of proper grammar, since grammar is one of the key conveyors of significant meaning. Ambiguity = -0.5.

Translations of the Bible should be superior examples of proper grammar, since grammar is one of the key conveyors of significant meaning.

Conditional sentences can be notoriously difficult to translate. The first-class condition may reflect either a true condition or a condition assumed to be true for the sake of argument or a condition that is real ("if, and it is" or "since," rather than "if"). Context determines the meaning, and here the third sense seems most consistent. Therefore, translators should give preference to using "since" as the conditional particle—something only the TEV gives among the nine English versions. Ambiguity = -0.5.

A case can be made for always translating *ei* as "if" in English translations and leaving the identification of the type of condition for the reader to determine by context. For some translators this approach avoids requiring the translator to engage in interpretation. However, translation cannot take place without interpretation. For example, even the most literal of English Bible translators would not translate *ek* as "out of" in every occurrence nor *en* as "in" in every occurrence. They would translate both with "by" when the context clearly indicates instrumentality. "By" in such cases is still a literal translation, even if it is the result of contextual interpretation. Likewise, "since" for *ei* in the context of Romans 6:8 is a literal translation based upon a sound interpretation of the text.

Principles Derived from Examining the Versions on Verse 8

Principle #1: Although the aorist must be interpreted by context, care must be taken to avoid giving the readers any implication of a sense contrary to usage in the context.

Principle #2: All Bible translations should adhere to the highest standards of grammatical accuracy in the particular language (English, German, Bengali, Swahili, etc.) that they use.

Principle #3: When possible by context, the translator should make use of the first-class condition for the sake of accuracy.

v. 9	Base	knowing that Christ being raised from the dead no longer dies, death no longer lords over him.	17	% **100**
	KJV	Knowing that Christ being raised from the dead dieth no more; death hath no more dominion over him.	17	**100**
	NKJV	knowing that Christ, having been raised from the dead, dies no more. Death no longer has dominion over Him.	17	**100**
	NAS	knowing that Christ, having been raised from the dead, is never to die again; death no longer is master over Him.	16	**94**
	NASB	knowing that Christ, having been raised from the dead, is never to die again; death no longer is master over Him.	16	**94**
	ESV	We know that Christ being raised from the dead will never die again; death no longer has dominion over him.	15	**88**
	NRSV	We know that Christ, being raised from the dead, will never die again; death no longer has dominion over him.	15	**88**
	CSB	because we know that Christ, having been raised from the dead, no longer dies. Death no longer rules over Him.	16.5	**97**
	NIV	For we know that since Christ was raised from the dead, he cannot die again; death no longer has mastery over him.	13	**76**
	TEV	For we know that Christ has been raised from death and will never die again—death will no longer rule over him.	12.5	**74**

Observations on Verse 9

The initial participle ("knowing") may serve as a causal participle (implying "for" or "because"), but to translate as the NIV, CSB, and TEV disrupts the flow and intrudes an emphasis upon the subjects ("we") rather than on the action itself. If translators (see the ESV and NRSV) separate the participle from the preceding verb ("we believe," v. 8), they ignore the subordinate role of the participle to that verb. Relative inaccuracy = -0.5.

The second participle ("being raised") is an aorist passive that is somewhat difficult to translate into good, smooth English. Therefore, the variations must be allowed except for those like the NIV and TEV that make the participle a regular verb, destroying its subordination to the main verb ("dies"). Inaccuracy = -1.0.

Two identical negatives follow one upon the other in consecutive clauses. These ought to be translated identically (KJV) so as not to destroy the symmetry of the original statement or lead the reader to think that the apostle Paul used two different kinds of negatives in the original language. The NIV's "cannot" inserts the concept of ability without grounds to do so. Inaccuracy = -1.0.

The present tenses ("dies" and "rules") are significant—they indicate the ongoing nature of the situation. Future tenses in translation are not nearly as clear—they are ambiguous = -0.5.

The TEV exhibits a number of departures from better translation choices: "For we know" = -0.5; "has been raised" (changing dependent participle into independent verb) -1.0; "death" instead of "dead" (referring to the dead individuals) = -1.0; future tenses (2x) = -1.0; inconsistent negatives = -1.0.

> ***Disruption of grammatical subordination inaccurately represents the relationships internal to the sentence that enable readers to identify the proper emphasis.***

Principles Derived from Examining the Versions on Verse 9

Principle #4: Greek New Testament writers often use participles to show subordination to a major verb in the sentence. Whenever possible, the subordination should be retained. Disruption of grammatical subordination inaccurately represents the relationships internal to the sentence that enable readers to identify the proper emphasis.

Principle #5: Identical terms in the same context (like the two negatives in v. 9) should be translated the same, unless there are additional particles or collocations indicating otherwise.

Principle #6: Converting present tenses into futures represents a legitimate option only when contextual constraints require. Futures might give basically the same idea, but they will not be identical to a present in many settings. If need be, the translator should err on the side of caution in this particular matter.

v. 10	**Base**	For the *death* He died, He died once for all *time* to sin; but the *life* He lives, He lives to God.	22	% **100**
	KJV	For in that he died, he died unto sin once: but in that he liveth, he liveth unto God.	22	**100**
	NKJV	For *the death* that He died, He died to sin once for all; but *the life* that He lives, He lives to God.	22	**100**
	NAS	For the death that He died, He died to sin, once for all; but the life that He lives, He lives to God.	21	**95**
	NASB	For the death that He died, He died to sin once for all; but the life that He lives, He lives to God.	21	**95**
	ESV	For the death he died he died to sin, once for all, but the life he lives he lives to God.	21	**95**
	NRSV	The death he died, he died to sin, once for all; but the life he lives, he lives to God.	20	**91**
	CSB	For in that He died, He died to sin once for all; but in that He lives, He lives to God.	22	**100**
	NIV	The death he died, he died to sin once for all; but the life he lives, he lives to God.	20	**91**
	TEV	And so, because he died, sin has no power over him; and now he lives his life in fellowship with God.	17.5	**80**

Observations on Verse 10

"Once" has the meaning of "once for all *time*" (cf, CSB) not "once for all *people*." "Once for all" could be ambiguous. In this particular context, only the most careless of readers would misunderstand the meaning. Therefore this potential ambiguity involves no inaccuracy.

By omitting any translation for the Greek particle *gar* ("for"), the NRSV and NIV obscure the logical relationship between verses 8–9 and verse 10. Inaccuracy = -1.0.

Absence of italics to indicate words added to the translation but not actually in the original language misleads readers. It contributes to inaccuracy because the reader comes away thinking those words (e.g., "death" and "life": NAS, NASB, ESV, NRSV, NIV, CSB) are in the original text. Preachers do not always check the original Greek and tend to focus on every single word. Thus, they could make a nonexistent word (in the original text) into a major preaching point just because it is in the version from which they are preaching. Inaccuracy = -1.0.

Italicization provides translators with a valuable tool for signaling to the reader what words have been added in translation but do not occur in the original language.

For the TEV, "And so" is an adequate rendering of *gar*. "Because" expresses a new relationship created by restructuring the grammar of the verse and misleading the reader as to the content of the original; inaccuracy = -1.0. "Sin has no power over him" is an equally misleading restructuring; inaccuracy = -1.0. "Now" is also an inaccuracy = -1.0; "his life" is unnecessarily interpretive = -0.5. "In fellowship with God" is very interpretive, eliminating the meaning "with regard to God's will" or "for God's purpose"; inaccuracy = -1.0.

Principles Derived from Examining the Versions on Verse 10

Principle #7: Italicization provides translators with a valuable tool for signaling to the reader what words have been added in translation but do not occur in the original language.[221]

Principle #8: Overly interpretive translations make exegetical decisions for the reader that are not necessarily implicit in the text. When more than one potential interpretation of the grammar exists in a passage's context, the translators should attempt a translation that allows for a legitimate variety of interpretations.

v. 11	Base	So also you count yourselves, on the one hand, to be dead to sin but, on the other hand, to be alive to God in Christ Jesus.	27	% **100**
	KJV	Likewise reckon ye also yourselves to be dead indeed unto sin, but alive unto God through Jesus Christ our Lord.	24	**89**
	NKJV	Likewise you also, reckon yourselves to be dead indeed to sin, but alive to God in Christ Jesus our Lord.	25	**93**
	NAS	Even so consider yourselves to be dead to sin, but alive to God in Christ Jesus.	26	**96**
	NASB	Even so consider yourselves to be dead to sin, but alive to God in Christ Jesus.	26	**96**
	ESV	So you also must consider yourselves dead to sin and alive to God in Christ Jesus.	26.5	**98**
	NRSV	So you also must consider yourselves dead to sin and alive to God in Christ Jesus.	26.5	**98**
	CSB	So, you too consider yourselves dead to sin, but alive to God in Christ Jesus.	26	**96**
	NIV	In the same way, count yourselves dead to sin but alive to God in Christ Jesus.	26	**96**
	TEV	In the same way you are to think of yourselves as dead, so far as sin is concerned, but living in fellowship with God through Christ Jesus.	24	**89**

Observations on Verse 11

The coordinating function of *men . . . de* in the Greek could be exegetically significant by indicating with clarity a "both/and" situation ("on the one hand . . . but on the other hand"). "Indeed" (KJV/NKJV) misleads by supplying an emphatic conjunction not adequately representing the Greek particles. Employing only the second particle ("but") implies a contrast between two situations that might not be coexistent. Inaccuracy = -1.0. Translating the second as "and" (ESV and NRSV) comes very close to expressing the coordination, but could be ambiguous. Ambiguity = 0.5.

"Through" (KJV) for the preposition *en* is overly interpretive and misleading. Inaccuracy = -1.0. "Our Lord" (KJV and NKJV) is most likely a textual addition without adequate support to retain.[222] Inaccuracy = -1.0.

A translation will only be as accurate as its textual base.

The TEV's translation of the first half of verse 11 is unnecessarily expansionistic, but not terribly inaccurate. "But" = -1.0; "living in fellowship with God" = -1.0; "through" = -1.0.

Principles Derived from Examining the Versions on Verse 11

Principle #9: Text critical problems need to be properly resolved in order to establish a firm base for translation from the original languages. A translation will only be as accurate as its textual base.

v. 12	Base	Therefore, do not let sin reign in your mortal body, so that you obey its lusts.	16	% **100**
	KJV	Let not sin therefore reign in your mortal body, that ye should obey it in the lusts thereof.	15.5	**97**
	NKJV	Therefore do not let sin reign in your mortal body, that you should obey it in its lusts.	15.5	**97**
	NAS	Therefore do not let sin reign in your mortal body that you should obey its lusts,	15.5	**97**
	NASB	Therefore do not let sin reign in your mortal body so that you obey its lusts,	16	**100**
	ESV	Let not sin therefore reign in your mortal bodies, to make you obey their passions.	14.5	**91**
	NRSV	Therefore, do not let sin exercise dominion in your mortal bodies, to make you obey their passions.	14.5	**91**
	CSB	Therefore do not let sin reign in your mortal body, so that you obey its desires.	16	**100**
	NIV	Therefore do not let sin reign in your mortal body so that you obey its evil desires.	15.5	**97**
	TEV	Sin must no longer rule in your mortal bodies, so that you obey the desires of your natural self.	12.5	**78**

Observations on Verse 12

The plural pronoun ("your") indicates that the singulars ("dominion," "body," and "its") should be understood as distributive, applying to each and every individual and/or "body." Due to the ambiguous nature of "your" in English (it can be singular or plural), the distributive singulars may be translated literally without fear of obscuring the original plurality of "your." "Bodies" (ESV, NRSV, TEV) contributes to a potential misunderstanding that the passage has a corporate (referring to an assembly of believers), rather than a distributive (individual believers) focus. Ambiguity = -0.5.

Modality exists as an exegetically significant factor in the grammar of the text. "Should obey" in the KJV, NKJV, and NAS uses the modal auxiliary verb "should" to imply moral necessity. However, the context does not indicate such a mood for the infinitive. In the older KJV English the subjunctive following a "that" indicating result is expected, but not in more recent English. Ambiguity = -0.5.

Translators must take great care not to obscure, remove, or alter the modality of the text when it clearly places responsibility for action or inaction upon the individual(s) referred to in the context.

The ESV's and NRSV's "to make you obey" inaccurately represents the result clause. Causation is not indicated by the context and the result about which the text speaks is not guaranteed. Inaccuracy = -1.0.

The NIV's "evil desires" comprises an interpretive expansion for which "evil" should be in italics. Minor interpretive direction = -0.5.

The TEV's omission of "therefore" is an inaccuracy = -1.0. "Sin must no longer rule" represents restructuring that destroys the personal responsibility indicated by the wording of the Greek; inaccuracy = -1.0. "Of your natural self" creates an artificial and inaccurate dichotomy between "bodies" and "natural self" = -1.0.

Principles Derived from Examining the Versions on Verse 12

Principle #10: Translators must take great care not to obscure, remove, or alter the modality of the text when it clearly places responsibility for action or inaction upon the individual(s) referred to in the context.

v. 13	Base	Do not present your members *as* weapons[223] of unrighteousness for sin, but rather present yourselves to God, as alive from the dead, and your members as weapons of righteousness to God.	31	% **100**
	KJV	Neither yield ye your members *as* instruments of unrighteousness unto sin: but yield yourselves unto God, as those that are alive from the dead, and your members *as* instruments of righteousness unto God.	30.5	**98**
	NKJV	And do not present your members *as* instruments of unrighteousness to sin, but present yourselves to God as being alive from the dead, and your members *as* instruments of righteousness to God.	30.5	**98**
	NAS	and do not go on presenting the members of your body to sin *as* instruments of unrighteousness; but present yourselves to God as those alive from the dead, and your members *as* instruments of righteousness to God.	29.5	**95**
	NASB	and do not go on presenting the members of your body to sin *as* instruments of unrighteousness; but present yourselves to God as those alive from the dead, and your members *as* instruments of righteousness to God.	29.5	**95**
	ESV	Do not present your members to sin as instruments for unrighteousness, but present yourselves to God as those who have been brought from death to life, and your members to God as instruments for righteousness.	29.5	**95**
	NRSV	No longer present your members to sin as instruments of wickedness, but present yourselves to God as those who have been brought from death to life, and present your members to God as instruments of righteousness.	26	**84**
	CSB	And do not offer any parts of it to sin as weapons for unrighteousness. But as those who are alive from the dead, offer yourselves to God, and all the parts of yourselves to God as weapons for righteousness.	28.5	**92**

	NIV	Do not offer the parts of your body to sin, as instruments of wickedness, but rather offer yourselves to God, as those who have been brought from death to life; and offer the parts of your body to him as instruments of righteousness.	25.5	**82**
	TEV	Nor must you surrender any part of yourselves to sin to be used for wicked purposes. Instead, give yourselves to God, as those who have been brought from death to life, and surrender your whole being to him to be used for righteous purposes.	23	**74**

Observations on Verse 13

"No longer" (NRSV) misrepresents the text especially in light of the same English negative in the immediately preceding context (v. 9). The Greek negative is not the same as in verse 9, but uses the negative at the beginning of verse 12. Inaccuracy = -1.0.

"The members of your body" (NAS/NASB, cf. the NIV's "parts of your body" and the CSB's "parts of it") will lead readers to understand "your" as a singular pronoun, since the addition of "body" in the singular can indicate such a meaning. This detracts from the Greek's plural pronoun. Inaccuracy = -1.0.

The CSB's "any parts" and "all the parts" are both added concepts not present in the text. Inaccuracy = -1.0 for each.

The ESV's and NRSV's "who have been brought from death to life" is a misleading interpretive expansion erroneously focusing attention on the agent by means of the passive translation when the agent is not the focus in this text. Inaccuracy = -1.0.

The NRSV's "wickedness" might be an acceptable translation, but unnecessarily detracts from the carefully constructed word pair ("unrighteousness" and "righteousness") in the original language. Ambiguity = -0.5.

The adversative *alla* ("but") is stronger than *de*, and, in some contexts like this one, needs to be correspondingly strengthened to "but, on the contrary" or "but rather" (NIV), or even "instead" (TEV). Ambiguity = -0.5.

The NRSV's insertion (without italics) of a third "present" (cf. the NIV's "offer") misleads the reader as to the wording of the original and proposes a three-part logical division of the verse (not presenting, presenting yourself, and presenting your bodily members) when the grammar indicates only a two-part logical division (not presenting and presenting). Inaccuracy = -1.0.

The NIV's overall translation is a bit expansionistic, but not always in the direction of inaccuracy or in a way that is misleading. However, it makes nearly all the same mistakes as the NRSV.

The TEV's "surrender" implies a combat-related action not conducive to the context; ambiguity = -0.5. Perhaps the TEV's translators thought military terms like "weapons" might indicate the author's intent involved extending the metaphor to the action of presenting itself. However, the better procedure would be to assume the apostle Paul could have and would have used a military-related verb if that were his intent. In the area of biblical interpretation, one might refer to this type of approach as trying to make a metaphor "walk on all four legs." Bible students do well to keep a metaphor's implications to the single truth the writer intends it to specify.

Translators should avoid clever turns of phrase in an attempt to extend the original writer's metaphor beyond the limits of its actual statement.

Additional problems with the TEV include the following: "Give yourselves" seeks to provide variety (in place of "present") rather than accuracy; inaccuracy = -1.0. The second "surrender" has the same problem as the NRSV's threefold "present" and the NIV's threefold "offer"; inaccuracy = -1.0. "Any part" and "whole being" commit the same error as the CSB; inaccuracy = -1.0 each. The additions of "to be used for" and "purposes" inadequately represent the original text; ambiguity = -1.0 each. "Wicked" is the same error as the NRSV, detracting from the word pair of the original text; ambiguity = - 0.5. "Who have been brought from death to life" commits the same error as the ESV and NRSV; inaccuracy = -1.0.

Principles Derived from Examining the Versions on Verse 13

Principle #11: Additions expressive of totality ("any," "all," "whole") must be limited to those situations where either lexical or grammatical factors demand such a translation.

Principle #12: Translators should avoid clever turns of phrase in an attempt to extend the original writer's metaphor beyond the limits of its actual statement.

v. 14	Base	For sin will not lord over you; for you are not under law[224] but rather under grace.	17	% 100
	KJV	For sin shall not have dominion over you: for ye are not under the law, but under grace.	17	100
	NKJV	For sin shall not have dominion over you, for you are not under law but under grace.	17	100
	NAS	For sin shall not be master over you, for you are not under law, but under grace.	17	100
	NASB	For sin shall not be master over you, for you are not under law but under grace.	17	100
	ESV	For sin will have no dominion over you, since you are not under law but under grace.	17	100
	NRSV	For sin will have no dominion over you, since you are not under law but under grace.	17	100
	CSB	For sin will not rule over you, because you are not under law but under grace.	17	100
	NIV	For sin shall not be your master, because you are not under law, but under grace.	17	100
	TEV	Sin must not be your master; for you do not live under law but under God's grace.	13	76

Observations on Verse 14

Most of the versions merely fail to indicate the strength of the adversative *alla* ("but rather"), which appears to present a significant contrast in this particular context. However, translation of the strong adversative in such a clear and concise contrast becomes unwieldy and potentially misleading when a translator attempts to utilize "but rather" or "but, on the contrary" with every use of *alla*. Therefore, it is not inaccurate to retain the simple English "but" in this example. Translators should not always attempt to insert commentary—some elements of meaning are better left to commentators and preachers.

The NIV's wording might appear to be a restructuring by taking "your" (plural) as a possessive ("your master") rather than as the object ("master you"). However, if it represents restructuring, so do NAS/NASB with their "be master over you" (still using "master" as a noun, not a verb). Both are legitimate and equally accurate optional translations of the verb and the pronoun in the genitive case.

The TEV eliminates the transitional particle *gar* ("for"/"because"); inaccuracy = -1.0. "Must" as a subjunctive does not convey the same concept as the indicative "will"; inaccuracy = -1.0. "Live" exhibits an interpretive rendering that does not represent the wording of the original nor leave the option for other meanings; inaccuracy = -1.0. "God's" is an unnecessary addition and misleading with regard to the underlying Greek text; inaccuracy = -1.0.

Principles Derived from Examining the Versions on Verse 14

Principle #13: Translators should not attempt to insert commentary—some elements of meaning are better left to commentators and preachers.

Concluding Statistics and Observations for Versions of Romans 6:8–14

Version	Verse by Verse Score							Average
	8	9	10	11	12	13	14	
KJV	93	100	100	89	97	98	100	**96.7**
NKJV	97	100	100	93	97	98	100	**97.9**
NAS	93	94	95	96	97	95	100	**95.7**
NASB	93	94	95	96	100	95	100	**96.1**
ESV	93	88	95	98	91	95	100	**94.3**
NRSV	93	88	91	98	91	84	100	**92.1**
CSB	97	88	95	98	100	92	100	**95.7**
NIV	97	76	91	96	97	82	100	**91.3**
TEV	97	74	80	89	78	74	76	**81.1**

Tabulated results from this study reveal a nearly identical overall measurement to Thomas's Romans chart[225]—an indication of the relative accuracy of the system even with some adjustments and a different user with his own potential for subjectivity. We can now compare the order of ranking for both Old Testament and New Testament from our evaluations of Psalm 23 and Romans 6:8–14. The versions rank as follows:

Psalm 23		Romans 6:8–14		Overall	
1. CSB	92.5	**1.** NKJV	97.9	**1.** CSB	94.1
2. NIV	92.5	**2.** KJV	96.7	**2.** NKJV	93.6
3. NRSV	92.3	**3.** NASB	96.1	**3.** NASB	93.3
4. NASB	90.5	**4.** CSB	95.7	**4.** NAS	93.1
5. NAS	90.5	**5.** NAS	95.7	**5.** KJV	93.0
6. ESV	90.2	**6.** ESV	94.3	**6.** ESV	92.3
7. NKJV	89.2	**7.** NRSV	92.1	**7.** NRSV	92.2
8. KJV	89.2	**8.** NIV	91.3	**8.** NIV	91.9
9. TEV	68.2	**9.** TEV	81.1	**9.** TEV	74.7

Ties in scoring were resolved by referring to the known characteristics of a version regarding its text-critical methodology in the Old Testament (in other words, faithfulness to the Masoretic text rates higher than a lack of overall faithfulness to the Masoretic text). Of course, the deviation tests conducted for this study are first of all very limited and secondly only one means of evaluating a version. Before a pastor, church, or lay person chooses a Bible version, each must consider a number of factors. There's the matter of choosing the older English with "thee"/"thou" and *-st*/*-th* words (like "hast," "anointest," "dieth," and "liveth") or the more modern English that excludes the older forms (making the NKJV and NASB more desirable than either the KJV or NAS). Some prefer the old style versification without paragraph format. Others prefer the paragraph format, since it more accurately conveys the structure of the text. Accuracy in paragraphing must also be evaluated, however, since the presence of paragraphing does not guarantee translators have accurately formatted the text. Translation theory and text-critical philosophy need research as well. Both of these factors are normally explained in the translators' introduction to each version.

The Issue of Gender-inclusive Language

Another factor to influence choice involves the treatment of gender. Although there is legitimate reason for indicating when "man" is truly generic (= humankind), each version's degree of consistency will indicate the translators' concern for accuracy. The following samples demonstrate the problem in that regard. Note that both New Testament passages are citing one or both of the Old Testament passages. The column on the right indicates the number of passages in which the translators of a version employed gender-specific terminology and the number of passages that employed gender-inclusive terminology.

Version	Psalm 62:12/ Proverbs 24:12	Romans 2:6	Matthew 16:27	Specific/ Inclusive
CSB	each ... his a person ... his	each one ... his	each ... he	0/4
NKJV	each one ... his *each* man ... his	each one ... his	each ... his	1/3
KJV	every man ... his *every* man ... his	every man ... his	every man ... his	4/0
NASB	a man ... his man ... his	each person ... his	every man ... his	3/1
NAS	a man ... his man ... his	every man ... his	every man ... his	4/0
ESV	a man ... his man ... his	each one ... his	each person ... he	2/2
NRSV	all ... their all ... their	___ ... each one's	everyone ... ___	0/4
NIV	each person ... he each person ... he	each person ... he	each person ... he	0/4
TEV	everyone ... his you ... you	every person ... he	everyone ... his	0/4

The NKJV, NASB, and ESV stand out as inconsistent even when the identical text is being represented in the four separate passages. The CSB, NRSV, NIV, and TEV have stuck with gender-inclusive in these texts, but each would have to be checked further to find out if any actually distorts truly gender-specific passages. The KJV and NAS remained gender-specific in spite of the clear genderless meaning of this particular text. Obviously, pastors will wish to pursue this topic more systematically before choosing a particular version for pulpit and/or pew use.

For each single-verse proof regarding inaccuracy in a version, one could probably find twice as many proofs of accuracy—and vice versa. A shotgun approach will never reveal the true dimensions of a version's integrity and accuracy. Whole passages need to be carefully evaluated and compared between versions in order to identify the true character of the version.

Conclusion

This brief and limited analysis serves but as an example of the type of research that someone needs to pursue in order to decide on a particular Bible version for pulpit, pew, or personal reading. One might choose the easy road by just accepting the conclusions of excellent volumes like Thomas's *How to Choose a Bible Version*. Or, one might choose to look even deeper into the matter and involve others in his search for the best translation. For churches, this process should not be hasty. One to two years for church leaders to research and discuss the matter will prove well worth the time and effort. Church leaders spending that much time in the Word together may well find spiritual reward and benefit beyond their expectation.

Among other factors, church leaders need to consider the literacy level of their congregation for reading English. Congregations made up of a majority of people speaking English as a second language might need to consider a version aimed at a lower level of English proficiency. The Bible version used in the pulpit and in the classrooms can be more literal than translations used in personal study. Pastors and teachers have the opportunity in public preaching and group Bible studies to explain the more difficult readings. Personal Bible study might more readily adopt a variety of translations without causing division and confusion, if individuals are willing to anchor themselves with solid literal translations and sound exegetical commentaries during the process of study.

No Bible translation is perfect. Many translations are disturbingly imperfect—above and beyond what one might expect out of an objective translation based upon the original text. Evangelicals need to stay vitally involved in the production of Bible translations, and evangelical churches need to make wise choices with regard to pulpit and/or pew versions. Lazy translations produce lazy expositors and lazy readers. Imperfect translations can contribute to the production of imperfect interpretation and flawed theology. No one should take the task lightly.

CHAPTER 9

WHAT DOES IT TAKE TO BE A BIBLE TRANSLATOR?

PREPARATION FOR A MINISTRY IN BIBLE translation requires a love for the Bible and commitment to a task involving far more detail than one might imagine. Developing oneself into a good translator involves both formal and informal education. It all begins with a conviction that it is God's will for an individual to pursue just such an enterprise. That conviction will keep a translator going when the way forward seems irreversibly blocked.

Calling and Conviction

It is not true that God leads only great authors or skilled linguists into Bible translation. Many effective Bible translators began as unlikely candidates for their task. Consider the testimony of Julie Fehr. Julie could never visualize herself as a missionary, because she proved inept at learning languages. She dropped French in her Canadian high school and her attempt to learn German at the University of British Columbia was not a shining success. At Bible college she would have flunked out of her first year of New Testament Greek except for the gracious intervention of her professor. After college the Lord led Julie to go to Gabon, Africa, as a missionary. Reversing her high school experience with French, Julie completed studies in that same language to prepare for her ministry in Francophone Africa. When she arrived on the field, her missionary colleagues agreed to assign Tsogo as the tribal language she needed to learn next.

No complete New Testament existed for the Tsogo, who had been praying for one for years. Even though Julie was just beginning Tsogo study, her use thrilled the tribe's members who saw her as a potential Bible translator for the New Testament. However, she was uncertain that God was leading her to be involved in such a work. She was overwhelmed by her immersion into this strange culture and its language. According to Julie, "I used to cry myself to sleep . . . . When you can't speak the language, you're like a child and less than a dog. People yelled at the dog in Tsogo and the dog would respond. They'd talk to me and I wouldn't know what they were saying."[226]

> ***Without God's grace and His empowerment, no one can accomplish anything of worth in Bible translation ministries.***

During her furlough from the field, Julie continued to struggle with the difference between the Tsogo people's confidence in her ability to translate the New Testament and her own low estimate of her abilities. By the time her furlough came to a close, however, the Holy Spirit had changed her heart and given her a clear understanding of what the Tsogo church could be like if they had the New Testament in their own language. After all, with God all things are possible, right? With God even a high-risk language student could translate the New Testament. That is when she committed herself to the Tsogo translation. Twenty years later the Tsogo New Testament had been translated, printed, dedicated, and distributed. Julie still cannot believe that God would allow someone like her to participate in such a significant project.[227] Many Bible translators can identify with Julie's struggles and feelings of inadequacy. Without God's grace and His empowerment, no one can accomplish anything of worth in Bible translation ministries.

Paul wrote to the Corinthians that his confidence for ministry was obtained through Christ. As he put it, "Not that we are adequate in ourselves to consider anything as coming from ourselves, but our adequacy is from God, who also made us adequate *as* servants of a new covenant, not of the letter but of the Spirit; for the letter kills, but the Spirit gives life" (2 Cor. 3:5–6 NASB). Every pioneer church planter and evangelist must rely upon the wisdom and power of God for success in their ministries. Bible translators are not exempt. They, too, must depend upon the Lord and His Spirit. In fact, the spiritual preparation for Bible translation is arguably the most important. Without being in tune with the Lord and ultimate Author of the Word of God, a translator will have difficulty producing an adequate and accurate translation.

Clues to a Calling

To admit to the necessity of God's empowerment is a simple matter. Far more difficult, however, is the arrival at the conviction that He has indeed called *me* to serve Him as a Bible translator. How do people determine whether God is leading them into Bible translation as a ministry? What steps should be taken? What are the keys to gaining an understanding of one's calling?

A natural ability in language acquisition and skill in the use of one's own language often provide clues regarding God's leading into a ministry involving high levels of communication in another language. However, other personal skills and characteristics must accompany linguistic skill or make up for its lack. Foremost to a Bible translator's success will be personal humility. Einstein listened as a distinguished astronomer said, "To an astronomer, man is nothing more than an insignificant dot in an infinite universe." He replied, "I have often felt that, but then I realize that the insignificant dot who is man is also the astronomer."[228] Einstein's observation applies equally to the Bible translator. Humble individuals learn a new language more readily, because they are able to laugh at their own mistakes while learning and do not object to others correcting their pronunciation, vocabulary, and grammar. In addition, humility makes it possible for a translator to work well with the other members of the translation team—both foreign and national. Pride obstructs one's view of their work and does not deal well with the long and painstaking process of editing translation draft after translation draft.

Bible translators must possess an unquenchable thirst for everything biblical.

Bible translators must possess an unquenchable thirst for everything biblical: biblical backgrounds (geography, history, and culture), biblical theology, and, of course, biblical languages. In addition to these, a good Bible translator seeks to learn as much as possible about the history of Bible translation from the ancient versions through to the present—including Bible versions in languages other than English. Success often comes by learning from the experiences of other translators and translation teams. In order to prepare oneself for everything biblical, a lot of reading and study must take place. In today's information-rich environment, potential Bible translators can collect resources in digital format rather than amassing a vast library. Physical volumes are difficult (and expensive) to transport and to preserve in potentially inhospitable climates. Digital resources also prove handy for the search function accompanying them, since many superb hard copy volumes lack proper indexes by which to access information efficiently.

The following starter list of biblical resources barely scratches the surface but will give an idea of the types of volumes Bible translators find useful.

Bible Backgrounds. Many Bible students tend to gravitate to a few popular single-volume contributions to the topic of Bible backgrounds, especially cultural backgrounds. Although those volumes too often present outdated or inaccurate material, they do contain some helpful information. The following, however, offer more dependable associations and descriptions.

Arnold, Clinton E., ed. *Zondervan Illustrated Bible Backgrounds Commentary: New Testament*, 4 vols. Grand Rapids: Zondervan, 2002.

King, Philip J., and Lawrence E. Stager. *Life in Biblical Israel.* Library of Ancient Israel. Louisville: Westminster John Knox Press, 2001.

Walton, John H., ed. *Zondervan Illustrated Bible Backgrounds Commentary: Old Testament*, 5 vols. Grand Rapids: Zondervan, 2009.

Bible Dictionaries and Encyclopedias. The large number of Bible dictionaries and encyclopedias may give the impression that they provide unnecessary duplication. However, they do differ from one another in theological persuasion and the presence or absence of up-to-date data. Much can be gained by comparing several of these resources. The valuable IVP Bible Dictionary series (four volumes each for Old Testament and New Testament) should head every Bible translation team's list of resources, together with the following:

Barry, John D., ed. *The Lexham Bible Dictionary*. Bellingham, WA: Lexham Press, 2016.

Elwell, Walter A., ed. *Baker Encyclopedia of the Bible*, 4 vols. Grand Rapids: Baker Publishing Group, 1997.

Freedman, David Noel, ed. *The Anchor Bible Dictionary*, 6 vols. New Haven, CT: Yale University Press, 1992.

Yamauchi, Edwin M., and Marvin R. Wilson. *Dictionary of Daily Life in Biblical and Post-biblical Antiquity*. Peabody, MA: Hendrickson Publishers, 2017.

Bible Atlases and Historical Geographies. In this category there exists no lack of resources. Two older works should not be ignored. Denis Baly's *The Geography of the Bible: A Study in Historical Geography*, rev. ed. (New York: Harper & Row, 1974), though out of print, provides one of the best introductions to Israel's physical geography ever published. And, George Adam Smith's *The Historical Geography of the Holy Land*, 3rd ed. (London: Hodder and Stoughton, 1895), remains available in multiple reprints. Smith's volume presents a well-written observant traveler's description of what he was seeing on the ground in the Israel of his day. Below are some of the best of current volumes.

Aharoni, Yohanan, Michael Avi-Yonah, Anson F. Rainey, and Ze'ev Safrai. *The Carta Bible Atlas*, 4th ed. Jerusalem: Carta, 2002.

Bimson, John J., ed. *Baker Encyclopedia of Bible Places: Towns and Cities, Countries and States, Archaeology and Topography*. Grand Rapids: Baker, 1995.

Brisco, Thomas V. *Holman Bible Atlas: A Complete Guide to the Expansive Geography of Biblical History*. Nashville: Holman Reference, 2014.

Currid, John D., and David P. Barrett. *Crossway ESV Bible Atlas*. Wheaton, IL: Crossway, 2010.

Schlegel, William. *Satellite Bible Atlas: Historical Geography of the Bible*. N.p.: William Schlegel, 2013.

Bible Commentaries. Good commentaries provide a great deal of information for grammatical, literary, and lexical analysis (word studies).

Bible translators should gather, read, and refer often to as many of the better exegetical commentaries as possible. While researching translation problems by means of commentaries, the team should keep an accurate record of every element that has potential exegetical and expository significance. Observe how commentators explain the significance of each element of the text. The most consistently reliable commentary series include the following (in alphabetical order).

- Baker Commentary on the Old Testament (BCOT)
- Baker Exegetical Commentary (BEC)
- *Expositor's Bible Commentary* (*EBC*)
- Evangelical Exegetical Commentary (EEC)[229]
- Kregel Exegetical Library (KEL)
- New American Commentary (NAC)
- New International Commentary on the New Testament (NICNT)
- New International Commentary on the Old Testament (NICOT)
- New International Greek Testament Commentary (NIGTC)
- NIV Application Commentary (NIVAC)
- Tyndale New Testament Commentaries (TNTC)
- Tyndale Old Testament Commentaries (TOTC)
- Word Biblical Commentary (WBC)
- Zondervan Exegetical Commentary on the New Testament (ZECNT)
- Zondervan Exegetical Commentary on the Old Testament (ZECOT)

The newer series (EEC, BCOT, BEC, KEL, ZECNT, and ZECOT) continue to produce volumes as they work their way through the entire Bible. Translation teams should stay alert to the availability of new volumes. An excellent series does not guarantee that each volume treats the text in the same way or with consistency interpretatively. Bible translators should also acquire independent commentaries, which are sometimes superior to those within a series. Below are just a few select examples of significant non-series volumes:

Finley, Thomas J. *Joel, Amos, Obadiah*. Wycliffe Exegetical Commentary. Chicago: Moody Press, 1990.[230]

Hoehner, Harold W. *Ephesians: An Exegetical Commentary*. Grand Rapids: Baker Academic, 2002.

Hughes, Philip Edgcumbe. *A Commentary on the Epistle to the Hebrews.* Grand Rapids: Eerdmans, 1977.

Thomas, Robert L. *Revelation 1–7: An Exegetical Commentary.* Chicago: Moody Press, 1992.

Thomas, Robert L. *Revelation 8–22: An Exegetical Commentary.* Chicago: Moody Press, 1995.

Unger, Merrill F. *Zechariah: Prophet of Messiah's Glory.* Grand Rapids: Zondervan Publishing House, 1963.

New Testament Use of the Old Testament. Although the first resource below might be difficult to find, it will reward the diligence of a determined Bible translator with its user-friendly format and attention to detail.

Archer, Gleason L., and G. C. Chirichigno. *Old Testament Quotations in the New Testament.* Chicago: Moody Press, 1983.

Beale, G. K., and D. A. Carson, eds. *Commentary on the New Testament Use of the Old Testament.* Grand Rapids: Baker Academic, 2007.

Exegetical Guides. One of the more recent developments in exegetical aids consists of several series of exegetical guides providing both micro- and macro-syntactic information for detailed analysis of the original language texts for both the Old and New Testaments. All of theses series continue to produce occasional volumes as they develop a full collection. Bible translators will find them of immense value. (The Lexham publications are digital resources through Logos Bible Software.)

Baylor Handbook on the Greek New Testament (BHGNT). Waco, TX: Baylor University Press.

Baylor Handbook on the Hebrew Bible (BHHB). Waco, TX: Baylor University Press.

Köstenberger, Andreas J., and Robert W. Yarbrough, eds. *Exegetical Guide to the Greek New Testament.* Nashville: B&H Academic.

Mangum, Douglas, ed. *Lexham Bible Guide.* Bellingham, WA: Lexham Press.

See also,

Andersen, Francis I., and A. Dean Forbes. *The Hebrew Bible: Andersen-Forbes Phrase Marker Analysis.* Bellingham, WA: Lexham Press, 2009.

Deppe, Dean. *The Lexham Clausal Outlines of the Greek New Testament: SBL Edition*. Bellingham, WA: Lexham Press, 2011.

Lukaszewski, Albert L., and Mark Dubis. *The Lexham Syntactic Greek New Testament*. Bellingham, WA: Lexham Press, 2009–.

History of Bible Translation. Although most English language histories focus on the history of the English Bible, some resources look at a broader history. A variety of biographies have also been written about Bible translators like Jerome (Latin Vulgate), Martin Luther (German Bible), William Tyndale (English Bible), John Wyclif (English Bible), Myles Coverdale (English Bible), Adoniram Judson (Burmese Bible), William Carey (a number of Bibles for the multilingual Indian sub-continent), and many others around the world. All are worth reading, since each reveals the lessons to be learned from those who have gone before us in this ministry.

Ackroyd, P. R., et al., eds. *The Cambridge History of the Bible*, 3 vols. Cambridge: Cambridge University Press, 1963–70.

Paget, James Carleton, et al., eds. *The New Cambridge History of the Bible*, 4 vols. Cambridge: Cambridge University Press, 2012–16.

Bible Translation Helps. The UBS Helps for Translators series (a series of translation handbooks) together with the journal *The Bible Translator* present invaluable information for Bible translators around the world. Our Bangladesh team referred to these resources over and over again.

Learning a Second Language

For nearly fifty years of teaching biblical languages, traveling in many countries, and working with individuals with multilingual skills, I have observed three types of language learners: (1) the audio learner—the individual who picks up a language by hearing it spoken and imitating its sounds and voice inflections, (2) the visual learner—the one who needs to see the language in writing and look at its structure grammatically, and (3) the kinesthetic learner—the person who slowly and painfully approaches the language through repetition, memorizing self-produced vocabulary cards, and creating games to help cement the language into their thinking. Interestingly, people with musical, mathematical, or engineering backgrounds seem to exhibit traits of audio learners—perhaps due to having an ear for musical harmony or a mind trained to look for patterns, equations, and consistency.

The ability to build interpersonal relationships also affects one's language capabilities. Shy and introverted people might do well as visual learners immersed in grammars and books, but they often resist using a new language for fear of making mistakes or facing disapproving listeners. Successful language learners sometimes find a group of children with whom to converse and try out new words and sentences. Children in every culture can be naughty and delight to trick the unwary foreigner into using unacceptable slang or even vulgar language, so a dependable adult mentor can help navigate the social pitfalls while acquiring the language.

Academic Training

As with most technical vocations, a certain amount of academic training forms the foundation for acquiring, building, and honing the biblical skills necessary for the work of Bible translation itself. Very few people can prepare themselves through a regimen of independent reading and personal study. First of all, self-study eliminates interaction with both experienced practitioners and one's student peer group. Group learning in a classroom setting serves to expose the student to working in a social environment for a set of common goals. Enrichment takes place through class discussions and group interaction. Any tendency toward extremism or fanaticism faces appropriate challenges and correctives. Academic education develops research techniques, communication and writing skills, as well as significant interpersonal relationships. Formal education directs students to the best resources, introduces them to different viewpoints, develops good reasoning, and provides a disciplined approach to studies encouraging completion in a timely fashion.

As with most technical vocations, a certain amount of academic training forms the foundation for acquiring, building, and honing the biblical skills necessary for the work of Bible translation itself.

Since Bible translation inherently demands biblical knowledge, theological seminaries and Bible colleges offer the best academic venues. Students preparing for Bible translation ministries should consider taking a general course of study by enrolling in a wide range of subjects, rather than plotting a specialized course of study—at least in the bachelors and/or masters level courses. A second masters degree and a doctorate will normally require specialization, if the potential Bible translator decides to attain the highest academic qualifications. A general course of study should include equal amounts of credit hours for Old and New Testaments (together with the biblical languages of Hebrew, Aramaic, and Greek), as well as incorporating such subjects as theology, hermeneutics, apologetics, church history, Bible backgrounds (geography, history, archaeology, culture), spiritual life, and ministry-related courses.

The final area above (ministry-related courses) might come as somewhat of a surprise to some. Why take the time to fulfill coursework in ministry-related topics like church planting, evangelism, pastoral ministries, and Christian education? Bible translations serve the churches—the Bible comprises the chief doctrinal and practical guide for the church. Without the Bible in their heart language, people cannot turn to the Word of God itself to evaluate their own lives before God, preach biblical sermons, teach the Bible in the church or in the home, or evangelize lost family members and neighbors. Bible translators who isolate themselves from the active ministries of the local church will fail to produce a Bible version usable throughout the church's ministries.

In the normal Bible college or theological seminary two subject areas are apt to be missing: linguistics and cross-cultural communication. Potential candidates for Bible translation must either seek a school offering these two alongside the usual biblical studies curriculum or plan to obtain some specialized training in nearby institutions offering such courses. Many Bible translators obtain their training in these two areas by enrolling in a Summer Institute of Linguistics program (Graduate Institute of Applied Linguistics, Dallas, TX; Moody Bible Institute, Chicago, IL; Houghton College, Houghton, NY; Biola University, La Mirada, CA; University of North Dakota, Grand Forks, ND), or get such subjects in their mission agency's preparatory programs (e.g., the Ethnos360 [formerly New Tribes] Missionary Training Center in Roach, MO). The Master's Seminary in Sun Valley, CA recently opened its Tyndale Center for Bible Translation to provide students with linguistics training under experienced Bible translators.

Determination and Dedication

A stern constitution and a sanctified stubbornness are good qualities in a Bible translator. Most translators also serve in full-time ministry as pastors, teachers, or missionaries. Their translation efforts are often subject to a huge number of interruptions for a variety of purposes, including personal health and circumstances. Consider the case of Martin Luther as he was immersed in the translation of the New Testament into German. In a letter to Melanchthon on July 13, 1521, Luther confessed: "For the last eight days I have written nothing, nor prayed nor studied, partly from self-indulgence, partly from another vexatious handicap."[231] The vexations of which he spoke were the earthly ailments of constipation and piles. As John Piper observed regarding such interruptions, however, "That stressful visit that interrupted your study may well be the very lens through which the text will open to you as never before."[232]

Too often I had opportunity to experience that same mixed blessing during our fifteen years of missionary service in Bangladesh. Everything from church problems to bloody dysentery interrupted our progress. At times the interruptions were so numerous that I despaired of ever completing the task God had set before our translation team. If no major catastrophes interrupted us, a casual inquirer might drop in to ask about the message we preached. These were, in reality, golden opportunities to test our translation firsthand with native Bengali speakers. If inquirers could not understand our gospel, how could we expect future readers of our translation to understand the result of our labors?

Now that we have examined the qualifications for being a Bible translator, the next chapter deals with individuals fitting into a Bible translation team. Great teams succeed in a joint task when they have set parameters for their project. Bible translation teams working with any language achieve their lofty goals when the team has established guidelines by which the team operates.

CHAPTER 10

PREPARING FOR THE PROJECT: ESTABLISH TRANSLATION PRINCIPLES

Because of my fifteen-year relationship to the translation work in Bangladesh, the preceding chapters of this book include a number of illustrations from and statements about the Standard Bengali Common Language (SBCL) translation. Identical principles are being applied to all of the so-called "common language" translation projects under the auspices of the Association of Baptists for World Evangelism (ABWE) in Bangladesh. Those projects include the Muslim Bengali Common Language Bible (MBCL), the Chakma Common Language Bible (CCL), and the Tripura Common Language Bible (TCL). Other projects are underway for both Mro and Marma.

Criticizing Bible translations is one of the church's favorite intramural sports. Many translators could have completed their projects in much less time had they not had to respond to critics every step of the way. However, criticism is inherent in the process of Bible translation. After all, if no one is going to read a translation because it offends its readers, it is hardly worth continuing with the project. Ronald Knox observed that Bible translation draws a much broader array of criticisms than the translation of any other work of literature:

> If you translate, say, the *Summa* of St. Thomas, you expect to be cross-examined by people who understand philosophy and by people who understand Latin; no one else. If you translate the Bible, you are liable to be cross-examined by anybody; because everybody thinks he knows already what the Bible means. And the form which these questions take is a very interesting one; nearly always it is, 'Why did you *alter* such and such a passage?' Why did I *alter* it—when you say you are going to translate the Bible, it is assumed that you do not mean to do anything of the kind. It is assumed that you mean to revise existing translation, with parts of which we are all familiar; altering a word here and a word there, like a compositor correcting proofs with a pair of tweezers. The more you plagiarize from the work of previous interpreters, the better your public will be pleased.[233]

Criticizing Bible translations is one of the church's favorite intramural sports.

It is unfortunate that some critics choose to ignore reality when they attack various Bible translations. Few take the time, to begin with, to discover the facts firsthand before they rush into print or into the pulpit with misinformation and unfounded judgments.[234] Others fail to use a consistent standard of evaluation for all translations. In the 1950s and 1960s, there were some critics of the RSV who evaluated it by one set of standards while judging the KJV by another set of standards. Robert L. Goddard speaks quite plainly about this disconnect in the minds of translation critics:

> When reading the Authorized Version, a person is supposed to exercise sufficient common sense to correct any manifest errors. If one verse is rendered in such a way as to contradict other verses, the reader is supposed to understand that the former does not really mean what it appears to mean. If the pronoun "it" is used with reference to the Holy Spirit, the reader is not to be upset; but should substitute "He" as he reads. When he reads "For he hath made him to be sin for us who knew no sin," he is not to accuse the version of denying the sinfulness of man, but is to understand that the phrase "who knew no sin," contrary to all laws of English grammar, modifies "him," not "us."
>
> When the same reader opens the Revised Standard Version, a strange thing happens. He suddenly loses all sense of reason, and becomes completely unable to protect himself from the slightest mistranslation. If

> one verse is translated so as to contradict the rest of Scripture, the reader now immediately rejects the latter and clings to the former. If the phrase "through his blood" is not found in Colossians 1:14, he concludes that the Revised Standard Version offers a bloodless religion. The fact that the blood of Christ is mentioned in many other places has no weight with him.[235]

The SBCL translation team has had its share of armchair critics. Such critics are not a modern-day plague. Jerome (fourth century A.D.) encountered many critics of his Latin Vulgate translation. His letter to Sunnias and Fretela responding to their questions about his translation of key verses in the Psalter makes fascinating reading. From the days of the early church, the last clause of Psalm 23:5 has been a matter of contention. In one of his letters Jerome spilled a lot of ink to defend various decisions he made in his Latin translation. Writing to Sunnias and Fretela, he argued that the Greek *to poterion sou* ("your cup") is in error, and other versions—the Greek Septuagint, the Hebrew, and all expositors—follow the Hebrew *kosi* ("my cup"), which is equivalent to Jerome's *calix meus* ("my cup").[236] By referring to other versions, perhaps Jerome meant the first- and second-century Greek versions by Aquila and Theodotion who both used *poterion sou.*[237] Interestingly, the Targum's *kalidi* ("my cup") is probably a loanword from the Greek *kalux* or the Latin *calix* (from which English obtained our word "chalice").

> ***"I have always held in esteem a holy simplicity but not a wordy rudeness. He who declares that he imitates the style of apostles should first imitate the virtue of their lives; the great holiness of which made up for much plainness of speech."***
>
> **— Jerome**

In spite of the critics, the Vulgate became so highly respected that it was the primary source consulted for the English Bible translation project funded by King James of England. In fact, some verses and parts of verses in the KJV were available to the translators only through the Latin Vulgate since they were not to be found in any existing Greek manuscript. Jerome responded to his critics in a way that some embattled modern Bible translators might do well to imitate. He wrote, "I have always held in esteem a holy simplicity but not a wordy rudeness. He who declares that he imitates the style of apostles should first imitate the virtue of their lives; the great holiness of which made up for much plainness of speech."[238]

Bible translations produced by a single individual are always subject to the whims and quirks of that translator. He or she works independently to produce the kind of translation they desire. Versions that find their way into the church for consistent usage normally reflect the labor of a team of translators. Give-and-take in the normal everyday process of translating Scripture goes a long way to prevent unique and/or prejudiced readings. When William Carey produced the first Bengali translation, it never attained widespread usage. Estrangement from his fellow missionaries through the translation process caused this sad state of affairs. In the end, his translation died because his own missionary colleagues refused to continue to use it in their evangelizing, preaching, and teaching. Instead, William Yates began a brand new translation in Bengali after the death of Carey in 1834. Had Carey included more of his colleagues in the development of translation principles and in the discussion of difficult texts and touchy theological issues, his translation might have survived to this present day.

In order to guard the integrity of a modern Bengali Bible translation begun in 1965, the SBCL project operated under very strict principles approved by all the missionaries in the Bangladesh Field Council of ABWE. Those principles include the following:

1. The Bangladesh Field Council and the translation team hold to biblical inerrancy and the verbal, plenary inspiration of Scripture.
2. All members believe that each individual will be held accountable before God for any addition to, any deletion from, or any other perversion of the Scriptures as given by God originally.
3. So-called "biblical relativism" which utilizes cultural substitutes for theologically important details is unacceptable. For example, the SBCL does not substitute sacrificial pigs or camels for sacrificial lambs. Nor does the translation substitute "gallows" for "cross." Examples of such unacceptable translations include the Cotton Patch Version in the United States and productions like the Mariner's Version of Psalm 23.

4. The control over what the SBCL translation says in its final form is not shared with any other group. The Bangladesh Field Council of ABWE has sole control over the text of the translation. Legal written agreements with all Bible societies (the United Bible Societies and the Bangladesh Bible Society) carefully define the ownership of the text and permit its distribution. The two Bible societies are vitally involved in funding, printing, and distribution.

Why is this kind of documentation necessary? Even the best and most closely knit translation teams will encounter disagreements. Basic standards and guiding principles resolve major issues and save valuable time—not to mention team unity. Such principles also help preserve consistency throughout the translation. And, as mentioned above in regard to William Carey's translation, having a wider group in agreement regarding the standards and principles contributes toward a broader acceptance and use of the finished product.

Even the best and most closely knit translation teams will have disagreements. Basic standards and guiding principles resolve major issues and save valuable time—not to mention team unity.

Documentation also should assign and protect rights of revision and distribution. A translation team's worst nightmare is to work long and agonizingly to produce a translation that someone else hijacks, revises with unacceptable readings, or distributes. That hijacked product basically would violate the standards and principles under which the original team labored.

Bible societies also need to protect themselves. If they are going to invest money, workforce, and time into a translation project, they need to be assured that the translation team will uphold an acceptable translation philosophy and methodology. The United Bible Societies provide funds, consultants, translation resources, printing, and distribution for Bible translations worldwide. It is a significant ministry both in size and accomplishments. Such a ministry requires excellent communication, coordination, and transparent agreements.

Working with a local Bible society can also prove beneficial. The Bangladesh Bible Society paid a stipend to checkers for the SBCL project, provided opportunities for the translation team to meet with and discuss the translation with national Christian leaders, arranged for the printing of the Bible (portions, New Testaments, and complete Bibles), and aided in the distribution of printed copies. Eventually, one of our translation team members served for years as one of the leaders of the Bangladesh Bible Society.

Oops, How Did That Happen?

No matter how detailed a Bible translation project makes its guidelines and procedures, something unforeseen will arise. For example, shortly after completing the third draft of the book of Genesis for the SBCL, we sent the manuscript to the Bangladesh Bible Society for distribution to the checkers who lived in various locations throughout the country. When we received their comments, we revised the draft, typed it again on mimeograph stencils, printed copies, and sent a copy to the Bible society so they could see our progress. Within a short time we received word that the Bible society had printed a thousand bound copies for distribution and sales. However, we were not yet satisfied with our latest draft. When I received a copy of the printed booklet, I began reading and stopped after a mere five verses. I was astounded. An extra day had somehow been inserted in the seven-day creation account—the translation had a total of eight days for creation!

As I investigated the insertion of an extra day in Genesis 1, I discovered that several events had led to this little translation fiasco. First, I was a new member of the translation team and still in Bengali language training. Therefore, we asked one of the nationals to read the Bengali draft and produce a back-translation into English on cassette tape for my benefit and checking. His back-translation gave no hint of any problem whatsoever. When I took the published text to him and asked why he had translated it in a way that hid the problem, he said that he had assumed that the team knew what we were doing, so he back-translated it with the meaning that he knew it should be—not how the meaning appeared to be in the draft from which he was reading. *Lesson #1:* If it is necessary to temporarily employ someone to produce a back-translation for any new team member, provide them with enough training to accomplish the task with complete objectivity and without assumptions having the potential for adverse effects.

Then I discovered that the reason for the inserted error involved the experienced national team members' misunderstanding of why the text in Genesis says, "And there was evening and there was morning, one day" (Gen. 1:5 NAS). Those two team members assumed that the ancient Hebrews would speak of a day the way Bangladeshis do—morning first, then the evening. Therefore, they reasoned, the first mention of "evening" must be the end of the first day, while the first mention of "morning" was the start of a second day. And, with that we now had two days in Genesis 1:5, not just one. *Lesson #2:* Provide full explanation for all team members for such things as the Hebrew concept regarding a day and how the ancient Hebrews identified a day.

Having handled the immediate team process and the issues we had uncovered, the next step had to be resolving the early publication of a manuscript. *Lesson #3:* Establish a system for identifying the status of translation drafts passed on to the Bible society, checkers, fellow missionaries, national pastors, and any potential publisher. I ordered a hand stamp with accompanying ink pad that read, "Not Finalized." From that time on, every manuscript we sent out bore that stamp until we were ready for it to be published.

Translation Teams and Local Churches

Where does a Bible translation find its most significant home? Many would probably respond to this question by indicating the personal relationship individual people have with God's Word. Each person who experiences the new birth (conversion) does so "through the living and enduring word of God" (1 Peter 1:23 NASB; see, also, James 1:18). As a direct result of the new birth, new believers ought to desire the Word of God so they may grow spiritually (1 Peter 2:2). So, there is no question that a Bible translation has great significance for individual believers.

God's design, however, includes the creation of communities of believers in local assemblies for the purpose of proclaiming the gospel, edifying believers, and stimulating "one another to love and good works" (Heb. 10:24 ESV). Thus, the local church serves as the center for expository preaching to build up believers and as the launch pad for the proclamation of the gospel concerning Jesus Christ. Without the written Word of God in translation, the church has no charter, no doctrine, no direction, and no original history. Local churches need the Word of God in order to fulfill their God-given role in the programs of redemption and kingdom.

Without the written Word of God in a translation, the church has no charter, no doctrine, no direction, and no original history.

The church's set of functions (see Eph. 4:11–16) requires that the assembly of believers also possesses a significant role in the production of Bible translations. Each translator must be actively serving in a local congregation. Without that context, translators risk being out of touch with the assembly and its individual believers. The translation team must keep the church in mind as it seeks to accurately translate the Scriptures. A Bible translation the church cannot use makes the translation project a failure. Lay people and pastors should be among the checkers for every Bible translation project. Their input needs to form a coordinated body of information together with the input of biblical scholars and linguists. And, of course, the core translation team itself must include national believers who serve in local churches—no team should be made up solely of foreign missionaries or scholars.

Our translation teams in Bangladesh possessed several advantages. First, our teams included highly trained national believers in the realm of the Bengali language (grammar and literature) as well as those who served actively in their local churches. They had also taught young people, so they were aware of the language of young people in Bangladesh. Second, our teams included women who understood the challenges of the language of women better than the male members of the teams. Third, our mission hospital provided highly trained medical personnel with whom we could discuss matters like the identification and translation of biblical diseases. Fourth, biblical language experts also served on the teams, bringing to the table their expertise in Hebrew, Aramaic, and Greek. In addition, some team members had background in zoology, botany, and agriculture.

A Bible translation project's guidelines and principles must identify the process of engaging local churches in the project. That might require a fair amount of teaching about that process and its principles. A reconciliation committee must be assigned the task of resolving translational disagreements between local churches and the core team. The translation reconciliation committee requires guidelines by which to make its final decision regarding any disputed translation. For the SBCL project, one such guideline stipulated that each reading should follow the majority of sound evangelical scholars, unless clear and overwhelming evidence existed to the contrary. In our case, the reconciliation committee involved all of our adult missionaries serving in Bangladesh at the time of the committee's meeting. It was expected that the missionaries would come to the meeting having already consulted with key national church leaders about the translation matter. Ideally, such leaders should be regular members of the translation reconciliation committee, because any sound interpretation still must come across accurately to national readers in their own language and culture. No missionary, regardless of extensive years of service or language ability, can ever match the native-born nationals' knowledge of that language and culture.

Bible Translators among the Sheep

Jeramie Rinne, attempting to describe the relationship of church lay elders to the congregation, observes that the elders must smell like sheep. The principle applies to Bible translators as well. Rinne writes,

> [The] shepherd is *among* the sheep. He's not off somewhere else. He is walking in the midst of the animals, touching them and speaking to them. He knows them because he lives with them. As a result, he even smells like sheep.
>
> Maybe, instead of visualizing literal shepherds, simply think of Jesus. In the Gospels, we find Jesus constantly *among* the people. Except for periods of private prayer, it seems Jesus spent all his time with his disciples, as well as with the crowds. He touched, taught, and trained people wherever he went. The Good Shepherd not only laid down his life for the sheep, but he also spent his life with them.[239]

Bible translation cannot take place outside the people and environment of the receptors. Translators need to live among the people, speak the language, experience the culture, and know the full context. Such knowledge cannot be gained secondhand or by remaining remote.

That does not require every Bible translator to live in poverty and disease, or to inhabit a jungle hut. But, at some time during the translator's work in the field, he or she must experience such conditions at least for a time. Someone might know mentally that most Bangladesh villagers use cow urine as an antiseptic when cleaning their homes (especially the restroom facilities). However, nothing compares to actually experiencing it firsthand with its odor permeating one's clothing and hair. The experience awakens a new understanding of the significance of Mosaic legislation and its insistence upon purification by means of fresh water (see Lev. 15:13) in the midst of an agricultural people who also may have used cow or camel urine as a household antiseptic.

Additional Translation Principles

In chapters 2, 3, and 4, we looked at a number of the translation principles followed by the SBCL team in Bangladesh. The following list offers an abbreviated and generalized summary of those principles discussed in more detail in those chapters.

- The meaning of the original text takes precedence over the form. Contextual consistency has priority over verbal consistency. A word in the Hebrew or Greek may have a different meaning in a different context—that difference should be carefully observed.
- Common language should take priority over dialectal, literary, or technical language. Words and constructions understood by everyone take precedence over those known only to the highly educated or to those from but one region of the country.
- The language (especially vocabulary, as compared to grammar) of people in the 25–35 age group is to have priority over people older than 35 and younger than 25.
- In a society like Bangladesh, publicly dominated by men, the language used by women should have priority over the language used by the men. Such a guideline might not apply to other societies (like in the United States or Canada). The point means the translation should serve those with the least education in any society.
- The language utilized in the translation must be understood by non-Christians as well as Christians, if it is to be used in evangelism.
- Reference to participants in a narrative should be made clear according to the proper receptor language pattern.
- Redundant expressions (such as "saying said," "answering said," or "dreamed a dream") should be avoided.
- The employment of emphasis must be in accord with proper receptor language usage. Hebrew, Aramaic, and Greek normally utilize changes in word order to indicate points of emphasis.
- Forms of addressing people uncommon or objectionable to the people in the receptor language should be avoided.

- If they are available in the receptor language, proper distinctions between the honorific and the familiar forms for pronouns and verbs must be accurately utilized even though the biblical languages use no such forms.
- No original language term (in Hebrew, Aramaic, or Greek) should be automatically translated by just one and the same receptor language term in all contexts.
- Figurative language and idioms may be replaced by parallel figures or idioms in the receptor language only when it causes no historical or cultural difficulty and only when the new figure or idiom has the same meaning in the receptor language.
- Retain the form whenever a literal translation produces an accurate, meaningful, and natural expression in the receptor language.
- Retain details of culture (customs, vocations, clothing, foods, and ceremonies), geography (places and features, climate and weather elements), and history (nations, empires, and events), even if they are not within the range of common knowledge for the receptor language peoples. However, add classifiers or determinatives that make the terms identifiable in accordance with receptor language usage (for example, "Jordan *River,*" "Bethany *village,*" "Antioch *city,*" or "*King* Hezekiah").
- Retain words having symbolic value within the theological framework of the Bible (such as the "Lamb of God," "blood," and "cross").
- Every effort should be made to reflect the different styles of language found in different parts of Scripture.
- In general, the level of language should be neither too formal nor too casual or slangy.

In other words, the formation of translation principles covers two major areas: (1) the process of team translation and (2) the guidelines for actual translation choices within the language itself. The ones mentioned above might require expansion for clarity in regard to each distinctly different Bible translation project. Additional principles should also be identified to more completely cover the specific requirements of the receptor language as compared to the original Hebrew, Aramaic, and Greek. No team member should be left out of the identification, discussion, and determination of the guiding principles for the project.

CHAPTER 11

A FINAL REQUEST

Only the original manuscripts themselves were perfect, free of error. They were produced under the direct superintendence of the Holy Spirit. No subsequent copy, edition, or version (ancient or modern) has been perfect. Sinful men, who are in no way perfect, produced and continue to produce them all.

John Eliot, a British missionary who worked among the native Americans from 1631 to 1690, involved himself in translating the Bible into one of the indigenous languages. He found himself unable to translate the word "lattice" in Judges 5:28. Describing the object as best he could to some native American friends, Eliot received what he thought was an appropriate translation. Years later Eliot discovered, to his great amusement and consternation, his rendering of the verse read: "The mother of Sisera looked out at a window, and cried through the *eel-pot*."[240] The error came about because of an anachronistic understanding of "lattice" as some sort of window-fitting woodwork with spaces through which a person might look. The native Americans constructed their eel pots of sticks with spaces between each stick in the structure. Eliot thought it might give his informants the conceptual form of a lattice. He understood that he was referring to the concept, not to the specific object before them. They did not understand that the function and structure of the lattice for a window would be quite different.

Errors will occur in Bible translations. Consider how easily a mistake might occur in the process of translation. Different manuscripts of Acts 17:6 in the Latin Vulgate have two different renderings. One has *orbem* ("world") and another has *urbem* ("city"). Both fit the context. They are very similar in sound. A copyist made a very understandable error when he wrote *urbem* instead of *orbem*. No one is more aware of this fact than someone involved in that demanding task. Those who are dedicated to producing an accurate and faithful rendering of God's Word in a language other than their mother tongue dread such errors. Much time must be spent checking and rechecking the translation. National and missionary translators must read every word, every phrase, every verse, each punctuation mark—both silently and aloud, individually and together. Every question must be asked—and answered. The process can be grueling and take a lot more time than a team originally plans.

Bible translators come to realize that they are totally dependent upon God for the wisdom required for such an overwhelming responsibility. With that humility also comes the realization translators need the prayers of God's people for a Bible translation project to succeed. Success will be measured first of all by the integrity of the translation to the biblical text. It will also be measured by its understandability and usability. Bengali does not need another translation like William Carey's, which no one wanted to use and ended up as just another exhibit in museums.

In the late 1970s, after the SBCL New Testament had been published in its first edition, one Bangladeshi church leader made the following statement: "I praise God for the new Bible translation. The old translation was too hard to understand, but now we have no excuse for not obeying God." That succinctly presents the ultimate argument for a common language translation. That may also be the reason why God used common languages for the Old and New Testaments in their original forms—so that people might be without excuse.

Dear reader, *pray* for Bible translators—men and women who walk in the footsteps of Ezra, the first recorded Bible translator (Neh. 8:1–8). Out of the world's 7,000-plus languages, approximately 6,400 still do not possess a complete Bible (Old and New Testaments)—over 90 percent. The need remains great and the opportunities continue to grow as one culture and language after another experiences the impact of the gospel concerning Jesus Christ. The ministry of Bible translation requires the wisdom and energy of God Himself for those who engage in such a task.

Human wisdom and strength alone can never produce the inexpressible glory of divine truth in expressible words that bring inexpressible joy.

How Can You Pray?

God desires His people to pray as they seek to be obedient to Him. As a loving Father, He loves to hear the requests of His people with regard to their service in His vineyard to produce fruit to His glory.

- Pray for God to lead men and women into Bible translation ministries.
- Pray for guidance and wisdom to find national believers willing to partner with international missionaries.
- Pray for Christians willing to leave their own culture and language to immerse themselves into a totally different culture and language for the purpose of the gospel.
- Continue praying for Bible translation teams as they form and establish a procedure that will keep them faithful to an accurate and understandable translation of God's Word.
- Pray for God's daily protection for the translation team from the dangers encountered in different areas of our fallen world.
- Pray for unity and harmony among the members of the Bible translation team.
- Pray for steadfast dedication to the grueling task of transferring the meaning of the ancient biblical languages into the challenging puzzle of a receptor language.
- Pray for adequate financial support for the translators, their resources, national readers to check the translation team's product, accuracy in transcribing the translation, printing and publishing arrangements, and storage and distribution of the final copies of the newly translated Bible or portions thereof.
- Pray for the churches to be blessed by the new translation with individual believers growing spiritually and with the proclamation of the gospel of Jesus Christ to those who have not yet heard.

Someone will ask, "Why do we need to translate the Bible into other languages? Can't people learn and use an already completed version in one of the major languages of the world?" The answer comes within the written Word itself when biblical writers reveal that God draws to Himself people "from every tribe and language and people and nation" (Rev. 5:9 ESV). John the apostle wrote of a vision in which he

> looked, and behold, a great multitude that no one could number, from every nation, from all tribes and peoples and languages, standing before the throne and before the Lamb, clothed in white robes, with palm branches in their hands, and crying out with a loud voice, "Salvation belongs to our God who sits on the throne, and to the Lamb!" (Rev. 7:9–10 ESV)

For such a vast group of people with differing origins to believe the gospel of Christ requires the Word of God in their own languages. Each person who becomes a Christian by faith has been "born again not of seed which is perishable but imperishable, *that is,* through the living and enduring word of God" (1 Peter 1:23 NASB).

In all practicality, the very first necessity for the spread of the gospel to any people group consists of the Bible in their language. People need to hear the gospel in their language. They require a Bible revealing that gospel in its fullest expression—in their own language. Evangelism cannot proceed without a translation of the gospel message. Churches cannot be planted without the possession of God's written Word in the language of the people so they can be taught and edified and sent into their own communities to serve Christ.

The Lasting Legacy

Long after the Bible translator or translation team has completed their work. Long after the missionaries have returned home. Decades after the translators have entered the presence of their Savior. Generations after the first publication of a Bible translation in a new language, the Bible continues on to produce spiritual fruit. Its words convert, instruct, encourage, strengthen, guide, and comfort generations of believers yet unborn. No other book possesses such power and potential.

Nearly twenty years after the completion of the SBCL and MBCL, I received a request from Germany for a Bengali Bible for a new Christian from Bangladesh. What a joy to package the Muslim-language version and send it out for that young man. He continues to grow in his faith through God's written revelation. Eventually, he hopes to return to Bangladesh to carry the message of Christ to his family and friends who remain in that country. This cycle will repeat itself until the Lord Jesus returns. What a privilege to have been allowed by God to be part of the translation teams who labored for decades to produce both the SBCL and MBCL for Bengali-speaking people. Every member of those teams would gladly give their lives to perform that life-changing task all over again. There is no greater gift to leave behind than the Bible, God's Word. No greater legacy can be found than bringing the Bible into another language for yet another people.

Bible translation is a gospel-proclaiming, church-planting, church-guiding, and Christ-glorifying work.

What can you do to keep the ministry of Bible translation expanding to reach every people in every language? You can pray, give, encourage people to enter that area of Christian ministry, train them for that ministry, support them financially, and send them forth to do the work. Perhaps God desires for you to be the one to prepare and to go. Bible translation is a gospel-proclaiming, church-planting, church-guiding, and Christ-glorifying work. Without it you would not have come to Christ for salvation. Without it you would have no church to attend, no preaching to hear, and no service to perform.

ENDNOTES

Dedication

1. Moritz G. Saphir, in *A Treasury of Jewish Humor*, ed. by Nathan Ausubel (Garden City, NY: Doubleday & Company, Inc., 1951), 127.

Chapter 1: Because They Understand

2. Clifton Fadiman, ed., *The Little, Brown Book of Anecdotes* (Boston: Little, Brown, 1985), 197–98.
3. David Daniell, *William Tyndale: A Biography* (New Haven, CT: Yale University Press, 1994), 58. Daniell also reminds us, "that during the English Reformation, lay men and women were so hungry for the Bible in English that they were often prepared to die for it" (100).
4. The Greek translation of the Old Testament began with the Pentateuch (Moses's five books). For over a century a variety of Jewish translators continued the project until its completion. This process resulted in a Greek translation displaying diverse translation philosophies and methodologies. Despite the diversity, the Septuagint generally reflects a desire to communicate the meaning of the Hebrew Bible in the Greek understood by the common people of that time.
5. For an excellent introduction to the study of the Septuagint, see Karen H. Jobes and Moisés Silva, *Invitation to the Septuagint*, 2nd ed. (Grand Rapids: Baker Academic, 2015).
6. Analyses of New Testament writers' uses of the Septuagint reveal a number of differences between some of their quotes and the Septuagint text. Sometimes differences occur between New Testament writers citing the same reference. For example, Mark's Gospel normally reflects the same Septuagint text as Matthew and Luke use, but occasionally departs from one or both. Such departures show up in the quotations of Exodus 20:13–17; Deuteronomy 6:4; and Psalms 21[22]:3 and 109[110]:1. See Henry Barclay Swete, *The Gospel according to St. Mark*, Classic Commentaries on the Greek New Testament (New York: MacMillan, 1898), lxxvii–lxxx.
7. F. C. Conybeare and St. George Stock, *Grammar of Septuagint Greek: With Selected Readings, Vocabularies, and Updated Indexes* (1905; repr., Peabody, MA: Hendrickson Publishers, 1995), 19–20.
8. Jobes and Silva, *Invitation to the Septuagint*, 107.
9. Ibid., 107–14, 184–89.
10. John Wycliffe, quoted in "Why Wycliffe Translated the Bible into English," *Christian History* 2, no. 2 (1983): 26.
11. Henry Knighton, quoted in "Why Wycliffe Translated the Bible into English," *Christian History* 2, no. 2 (1983): 26.

12. Albert C. Baugh and Thomas Cable, *A History of the English Language*, 3rd ed. (Englewood Cliffs, NJ: Prentice-Hall, 1978), 191–95
13. Pastors in Wyclif's era (last half of the 14th century) characteristically served as absentee pastors of multiple parishes or benefices (permanent ecclesiastical appointments with property and income). Wyclif criticized them for these practices; see G. R. Evans, *John Wyclif: Myth and Reality* (Downers Grove, IL: InterVarsity, 2005), 93–95. According to E. H. Broadbent, *The Pilgrim Church* (London: Pickering & Inglis Ltd., 1931), 103 and 139, the corruption of the clergy resulted from the efforts of men to obtain influential posts providing monetary gain. Herbert B. Workman, *The Church of the West in the Middle Ages* (London: Charles H. Kelly, 1898), 54–58, the well-known church historian, declares the many examples of corrupt clergy are no exaggeration of the depravity running rampant in the Western church of the Middle Ages.
14. Baugh and Cable, *A History of the English Language,* 205.
15. Daniel Boorstin, *The Discoverers* (New York: Random House, 1983), 523.
16. John H. P. Reumann, *The Romance of Bible Scripts and Scholars: Chapters in the History of Bible Transmission and Translation* (Englewood Cliffs, NJ: Prentice-Hall, 1965), 58. Cf. Matthew H. Black, "The Printed Bible," in *The Cambridge History of the Bible*, ed. S. L. Greenslade (Cambridge: Cambridge University Press, 1963), 3:423: "It has been calculated that altogether 8,000–10,000 copies were printed: which indicates a considerable market, when it is remembered that early editions probably cost (as Vulgates also must have cost) the equivalent of a town house, or fourteen fattened oxen. From the evidence of bequests, most vernacular Bibles were owned by laymen—which is what one would expect."
17. Reumann, *The Romance of Bible Scripts and Scholars*, 72–73.
18. Some readers might cite sign language for the deaf as an exception. However, the signs may be understood as being "read" by the deaf. Likewise, Braille is "read" even though the organ of perception becomes the finger tips.
19. Glen G. Scorgie, "Introduction and Overview," in *The Challenge of Bible Translation: Communicating God's Word to the World*, eds. Glen G. Scorgie, Mark L. Strauss, and Steven M. Voth (Grand Rapids: Zondervan, 2003), 20.
20. J. P. Louw and Eugene A. Nida, eds., *Greek-English Lexicon of the New Testament Based on Semantic Domains*, 2nd ed., 2 vols. (New York: United Bible Societies, 1989), 811 (§91.6).
21. Ibid.
22. A. T. Robertson, *A Grammar of the Greek New Testament in the Light of Historical Research* (Nashville: Broadman Press, 1934), 1149. Cf., also, Daniel B. Wallace, *Greek Grammar Beyond the Basics: An Exegetical Syntax of the New Testament* (Grand Rapids: Zondervan Publishing House, 1996), 673.
23. Robertson, *A Grammar of the Greek New Testament*, 1149.
24. "It ought to be preserved in the translation."—A. T. Robertson, *Word Pictures in the New Testament*, 6 vols. (Nashville: Broadman Press, 1930), 3:178.
25. H. G. Liddell, *An Intermediate Greek-English Lexicon Founded upon the Seventh Edition of Liddell and Scott's Greek-English Lexicon*, electronic ed. (Oak Harbor, WA: Logos Research Systems, Inc., 1996), 181. See BDAG, 222: *dē* was used with "exhortations or commands, to give them greater urgency." Wallace, *Greek Grammar Beyond the Basics*, 761 lists *dē* as a "true emphatic conjunction."
26. D. A. Carson, "The Limits of Functional Equivalence in Bible Translation—and Other Limits, Too," in Scorgie, Strauss, and Voth, *The Challenge of Bible Translation*, 73.
27. Martha L. Carter and Keith N. Schoville, eds., *Sign, Symbol, Script: An Exhibition on the Origins of Writing and the Alphabet* (Madison: University of Wisconsin–Madison, 1984), 42. See, also, F. F. Bruce, *The Books and the Parchments: Some Chapters on the Transmission of the Bible*, 3rd rev. ed. (Westwood, NJ: Fleming H. Revell Company, 1963), 52–53.
28. Sijbolt Noorda, "New and Familiar: The Dynamics of Bible Translation," in *Bible Translation on the Threshold of the Twenty-First Century: Authority, Reception, Culture and Religion*, eds. Athalya Brenner and Jan Willem van Henten, JSOTSup 353, The Bible in the 21st Century 1 (London: Sheffield Academic Press, 2002), 14–15.

29. George Steiner, *After Babel: Aspects of Language and Translation*, 3rd ed. (Oxford: Oxford University Press, 1998), 66.
30. Leland Ryken, *The Word of God in English: Criteria for Excellence in Bible Translation* (Wheaton, IL: Crossway Books, 2002), 219.
31. Gleason L. Archer and G. C. Chirichigno, *Old Testament Quotations in the New Testament* (Chicago: Moody Press, 1983), 123.
32. Charles R. Taber, "Hermeneutics and Culture—An Anthropological Perspective," in *Down to Earth: Studies in Christianity and Culture*, eds. John R. W. Stott and Robert Coote (London: Hodder and Stoughton, 1981), 87.
33. Quoted in Kim Beaty, "Take Off the Lid!" *In Other Words* 17, no. 5 (1991): 5.
34. For the life, testimony, and ministry of Viggo Olsen, read his book *Daktar: Diplomat in Bangladesh* (repr.; Grand Rapids: Kregel Publications, 1996).

Chapter 2: Common Language for Common People

35. Thomas Pyles, "Some Characteristics of American English and Their Backgrounds," in *The World of Language: A Reader in Linguistics*, eds. N. Hudspeth and Donald F. Sturtevant (New York: American Book Company, 1967), 171.
36. J. S. M. Hooper, *Bible Translation in India, Pakistan and Ceylon*, 2nd ed., revised by W. J. Culshaw (London: Oxford University Press, 1963), 27.
37. Ryken, *The Word of God in English*, 67–68.
38. Edward Finegan and Niko Besnier, *Language: Its Structure and Use* (San Diego: Harcourt Brace Jovanovich, 1989), 416.
39. "Meat," in *The Compact Edition of the Oxford English Dictionary* (1971; repr., Oxford: Oxford University Press, 1985), 1:1755.
40. B. K. Kuiper, *The Church in History* (Grand Rapids: Eerdmans, 1964), 222.
41. Daniell, *William Tyndale*, 284.
42. Jeremy Punt, "Translating the Bible in South Africa: Challenges to Responsibility and Contextuality," in Brenner and Van Henten, *Bible Translation on the Threshold of the Twenty-First Century*, 119.
43. Bruce M. Metzger, *The Bible in Translation: Ancient and English Versions* (Grand Rapids: Baker Academic, 2001), 150–51.
44. Daniell, *William Tyndale*, 113.
45. Ibid., 135.
46. Ronald Knox, *The Trials of a Translator* (New York: Sheed & Ward, 1949), 18–19.
47. Samuel K. Workman, *Fifteenth Century Translation as an Influence on English Prose*, Princeton Studies in English 18 (Princeton, NJ: Princeton University Press, 1940), 9.
48. A chiasm is a literary device presenting parallel elements in an inverted (or mirror image) order: A-B-B'-A', for example. Psalm 19:1 (v. 2 in Hebrew) presents an A-B-C-C'-B'-A' order.
49. Studies focusing on such technical theological terms include Ben Kuwitzky, "The Semantics and Translation of Technical Terms: A Case Study on ἀπόστολος," *Journal of Translation*, 12, no. 1 (2016): 1–12 and David Hill, *Greek Words and Hebrew Meanings: Studies in the Semantics of Soteriological Terms*, Society for New Testament Studies Monograph Series (Eugene, OR: Wipf and Stock, 2000).
50. Steiner, *After Babel*, 90.
51. Daniell, *William Tyndale*, 137.
52. Ibid.
53. Adele Berlin, "On Bible Translations and Commentaries," in Brenner and Van Henten, *Bible Translation on the Threshold of the Twenty-First Century*, 181. We will discuss more on the issue of interpretive translation in chapter 3.
54. Ryken, *The Word of God in English*, 79–102 ("Seven Fallacies about Translation") and 103–19 ("Eight Fallacies about Bible Readers").
55. Ibid., 125.

56. George Steiner points out that "[a] true reader is a dictionary addict" (*After Babel*, 25). This is even more applicable for a translator.
57. Desiderius Erasmus quoted in J. F. Mozley, *William Tyndale* (New York: Macmillan Company, 1937), 34; cited in Daniell, *William Tyndale*, 67.
58. Daniell, *William Tyndale*, 43.
59. Ibid., 1.
60. Ann Cornelisen, "The Widow Fascide," in *Other Fields, Other Grasshoppers: Readings in Cultural Anthropology*, ed. L. L. Langness (New York: J. B. Lippincott Company, 1977), 179.
61. Steiner, *After Babel*, 41–42.
62. For a detailed and enlightening discussion of biblical idioms and their impact on interpretation and translation, see Andrew David Naselli, *How to Understand and to Apply the New Testament: Twelve Steps from Exegesis to Theology* (Phillipsburg, NJ: P&R Publishing, 2017), 66–68.
63. Knox, *The Trials of a Translator*, 113.

Chapter 3: Semantics and Context in Bible Translation

64. William Morris, ed., *The American Heritage Dictionary of the English Language* (Boston: Houghton Mifflin, 1979), 951.
65. Robert L. Thomas, *How to Choose a Bible Version: An Introductory Guide to English Translations* (Fearn, UK: Mentor/Christian Focus Publications, 2000), 98–99.
66. Weston W. Fields, "The Translation of Biblical Live and Dead Metaphors and Similes and Other Idioms," *Grace Theological Journal* 2, no. 2 (1981): 192–93.
67. This citation of the original 1611 KJV helps us understand that even that very popular translation has undergone changes in the process of its publication and use. The most trustworthy translations are those that have been periodically revised to keep up with changes in the language and also the improvement of our knowledge of the original languages.
68. Clyde Kluckhohn, *Mirror for Man: The Relation of Anthropology to Modern Life* (New York: McGraw-Hill Book, 1949), 154–55. Kluckhohn also offered another example from personal experience: "I asked a Japanese with a fair knowledge of English to translate back from the Japanese that phrase in the new Japanese constitution that represents our 'life, liberty, and the pursuit of happiness.' He rendered, 'license to commit lustful pleasure'" (ibid., 154).
69. For recent studies in semantics, biblical languages, and Bible translation, see the following (listed chronologically, starting with the latest: Ingrid Faro, "Semantics," in *The Lexham Bible Dictionary*, eds. John D. Barry, et al. (Bellingham, WA: Lexham Press, 2016); Ben Kuwitzky, "The Semantics and Translation of Technical Terms: A Case Study on ἀπόστολος," *Journal of Translation*, 12, no. 1 (2016): 1–12; Gene L. Green, "Lexical Pragmatics and Biblical Interpretation," *Journal of the Evangelical Theological Society* 50, no. 4 (2007): 799–812; David H. Aaron, *Biblical Ambiguities: Metaphor, Semantics and Divine Imagery* (Boston: E. J. Brill, 2002); David Hill, *Greek Words and Hebrew Meanings: Studies in the Semantics of Soteriological Terms*, Society for New Testament Studies Monograph Series (Eugene, OR: Wipf and Stock, 2000). Classic studies in the field of semantics and biblical languages include D. A. Carson, *Exegetical Fallacies* (Grand Rapids: Baker Academic, 1996) and Moisés Silva, *Biblical Words and Their Meaning: An Introduction to Lexical Semantics* (Grand Rapids: Zondervan Publishing House, 1983).
70. Clyde Kluckhohn, "The Gift of Tongues," in Hudspeth and Sturtevant, *The World of Language*, 27.
71. "The Translators to the Reader," in *The Holy Bible 1611 Edition: King James Version* (repr., Nashville: Thomas Nelson Publishers, 1982).
72. NAS and NASB inexplicably retain "children of Israel" only in Deuteronomy 1:3.
73. Knox, *The Trials of a Translator*, 13.
74. Gen. 15:1; Deut. 28:66; 1 Sam. 20:21; 2 Sam. 4:9; 22:6, 20; 1 Kings 5:4; 18:9; Pss. 3:3; 18:4, 5, 19; 22:5, 15; 26:12; 27:1; 31:4; 34:7; 49:5; 91:3, 5; 107:26; 116:3, 6; 121:7; Prov. 7:23; 10:17; 13:14; Isa. 21:15; 38:17; Jer. 38:24; Lam. 3:47; Jonah 1:4, 5, 7; Hab. 2:9; Zech. 9:16.
75. *HALOT*, 295, 492, 713 (cf. 755), 922, 1270.

76. Knox, *The Trials of a Translator*, 37–38. As one example of the most recent English versions, CSB uses "danger" in Pss. 23:4; 57:1; 119:109; 138:7; Prov. 1:33; 3:25; 19:23; 22:3; 27:12; Eccl. 12:5; Luke 8:23; Rom. 8:35; 1 Cor. 15:30; 2 Cor. 11:26. Thus, some English versions exhibit improvements in such cases.
77. Gregory Rabassa, "No Two Snowflakes Are Alike: Translation as Metaphor," in *The Craft of Translation*, eds. John Biguenet and Rainer Schulte (Chicago: University of Chicago Press, 1989), 1.
78. Mildred Larson, *A Manual for Problem Solving in Bible Translation* (Grand Rapids: Zondervan Publishing House, 1975), 106. This example from Matthew 21:33 and the examples in John 6:35 and 10:12 from Central and South American Indian languages are presented by Larson as problems to be solved by translators. The purpose of her translation manual is to provide an awareness of the types of problems to be encountered, not the solutions to those problems. The principles involved in finding solutions are contained in the companion volume: John Beekman and John Callow, *Translating the Word of God* (Grand Rapids: Zondervan Publishing House, 1974). Chapter 13 (191–211) of that volume contains an extensive discussion of the handling of lexical equivalence problems. A third volume in this set is Kathleen Callow, *Discourse Considerations in Translating the Word of God* (Grand Rapids: Zondervan Publishing House, 1974).
79. Geo. B. Eager, "Bread," in *ISBE*, 1:516.
80. See F. W. Farrar, "Brief Notes on Passages of the Gospels: II. The Camel and the Needle's Eye," *The Expositor* 3, no. 5 (1876): 369–80.
81. Cf. D. A. Carson, "Matthew," in *EBC*, 8:425 and W. D. Davies and Dale C. Allison, Jr. *A Critical and Exegetical Commentary on the Gospel according to St. Matthew*, 3 vols., ICC (New York: T&T Clark International, 2004), 3:51–52.
82. D. A. Carson, "The Limits of Dynamic Equivalence in Bible Translation," *Notes on Translation* 121 (1987): 11–12.
83. Ibid., 10.

Chapter 4: Simplicity and Clarity in Bible Translation

84. Many examples of the common vocabulary of New Testament Greek have been collected by James Hope Moulton and George Milligan, *The Vocabulary of the Greek New Testament* (repr., Grand Rapids: Eerdmans, 1972) For a handy collection of some of these sources, see George Milligan, *Selections from the Greek Papyri* (repr., Freeport, NY: Books for Libraries Press, 1969) It includes annotated Greek texts and English translations as well as a Scripture index.
85. Donald Guthrie, *New Testament Introduction*, 4th ed. (Downers Grove, IL: InterVarsity, 1990), 382. Luke employs a literary form of the common Greek in Luke 1:1–4 and in Acts 1:1–5 and 17:16–34.
86. On the subject of medical language in Luke's Gospel, see Henry J. Cadbury, *The Style and Literary Method of Luke*, HTS 6 (repr., Cambridge: Harvard University Press, 1969).
87. For a brief but informative description of New Testament Greek, see J. Harold Greenlee, "The Language of the New Testament," in *EBC*, 1:409–16. A more technical description of the history and nature of Koine Greek and its relationship to the New Testament can be found in Robertson's *A Grammar of the Greek New Testament in the Light of Historical Research*, 49–139.
88. The following sources provide additional information about the Hebrew and Aramaic languages of the Old Testament: G. Douglas Young, "The Language of the Old Testament," in *EBC*, 1:197–208; and, Bruce, *The Books and the Parchments*, 33–57.
89. Greenlee, "The Language of the New Testament," 416.
90. Cf. John MacArthur, *Galatians*, MacArthur New Testament Commentary (Chicago: Moody Press, 1983).
91. The year of publication applies to the year of original publication or to the year of the particular reprint, as fits each case best.
92. These types of translations will be discussed in chapter 6. Since Psalm 23 is very familiar, I have reserved it for that discussion.

93. For an examination of the impact of the Hebrew definite article on determining whether the Hebrew *ʾadam* refers to "the man" or to "Adam," see William D. Barrick, "Old Testament Evidence for a Literal, Historical Adam and Eve," in *Searching for Adam: Genesis and the Truth about Man's Origin*, ed. Terry Mortenson, 17–51 (Green Forest, AR: Master Books, 2016), 28–30.
94. BDAG, 20.
95. The discussion in Robertson, *A Grammar of the Greek New Testament in the Light of Historical Research*, 771–74 reveals *pas* in the Greek can carry both "all" and "every" with or without a definite article, in either singular or plural or forms. Being singular and without the definite article in 1 John 1:9, the more traditional grammarian might argue for "every" in this verse.
96. Dave Brunn, *One Bible, Many Versions: Are All Translations Created Equal?* (Downers Grove, IL: IVP Academic, 2013), 189–90.
97. E.g., Roland E. Murphy, "A Brief Note on Translating Proverbs," *Catholic Biblical Quarterly* 60, no. 4 (1998): 621–25.
98. Knox, *The Trials of a Translator*, 43.
99. Murphy, "A Brief Note on Translating Proverbs," 623.

Chapter 5: Theology and Bible Translation

* This chapter presents a revision of a study I previously published as "The Integration of OT Theology with Bible Translation," *Master's Seminary Journal* 12, no. 1 (2001): 15–31. This revised material is used with the permission of that journal's editor and the journal's publication committee.

100. Howard Rheingold, *They Have a Word for It: A Lighthearted Lexicon of Untranslatable Words and Phrases* (Los Angeles: Jeremy P. Tarcher, 1988), 5.
101. *Pace* Burton Raffel, "Translating Medieval European Poetry," in *The Craft of Translation*, ed. John Biguenet and Rainer Schulte (Chicago: University of Chicago Press, 1989), 28.
102. The OT was written in two languages: Hebrew and Aramaic. Unfortunately, the latter tends to be the ignored child in the biblical language curriculum of Bible colleges and seminaries. Since schools seldom require Aramaic, students graduate with MDiv and ThM (or their equivalents) without any ability to read Daniel 2:4–7:28 in the original language.
103. The debate over gender-inclusive language in Bible translation is a recent theologically charged example involving the biblical employment of identical phraseology carrying vastly different intended meanings. Cf. D. A. Carson, *The Inclusive Language Debate: A Plea for Realism* (Grand Rapids: Baker Books/Leicester, UK: Inter-Varsity Press, 1998); Wayne Grudem, *What's Wrong with Gender-Neutral Bible Translations?* (Libertyville, IL: Council on Biblical Manhood and Womanhood, 1997).
104. Millard J. Erickson, *Christian Theology* (Grand Rapids: Baker, 1995), 917–18. See, also the discussion of reprobation in William G. T. Shedd, *Dogmatic Theology*, 3 vols., Classic Reprint Edition (1888; repr., Grand Rapids: Zondervan, 1971), 1:419.
105. Patrick D. Miller Jr., "Syntax and Theology in Genesis XII 3a," *Vetus Testamentum* 34, no. 4 (1984): 472.
106. Christopher Wright Mitchell, *The Meaning of* BRK *"To Bless" in the Old Testament*, SBLDS 95 (Atlanta: Scholars Press, 1987), 33. See also Gordon J. Wenham, *Genesis 1–15*, WBC 1 (Waco, TX: Word Books, 1987), 277.
107. Miller, "Syntax and Theology in Genesis XII 3a," 473.
108. Ibid., 474.
109. Ibid., 475.
110. Ibid., 474.
111. Wenham, *Genesis 1–15*, 276. See also Allen P. Ross, *Creation and Blessing: A Guide to the Study and Exposition of Genesis* (Grand Rapids: Baker Books, 1996), 264.
112. In and of itself, this distinction between synonyms for "curse" is theologically significant. Cf. Miller, "Syntax and Theology in Genesis XII 3a," 472–76.

113. The verb stem is a Niphal.
114. A detailed listing of the proponents of these various views is available in Michael A. Grisanti, "The Missing Mandate: Missions in the Old Testament," in *Missions in a New Millennium: Change and Challenges in World Missions*, eds. W. Edward Glenny and William H. Smallman (Grand Rapids: Kregel Publications, 2000), 60–62nn 16–18. As for his own conclusion in the matter, Grisanti states that his essay "makes no attempt to provide a final answer to this question. It does assume that a passive nuance is a legitimate and common option for the *Niphal* stem" (ibid., 60n15).
115. For a scholar who follows this interpretation, see Robert B. Chisholm Jr., *From Exegesis to Exposition: A Practical Guide to Using Biblical Hebrew* (Grand Rapids: Baker Books, 1998), 85. Cf., also, Josef Scharbert, "ברך," in *TDOT*, 2:296–97.
116. Steven William Boyd, "A Synchronic Analysis of the Medio-Passive-Reflexive in Biblical Hebrew" (PhD diss., Hebrew Union College, Jewish Institute of Religion, 1993), 10.
117. Cf. Daniel C. Arichea Jr., "Taking Theology Seriously in the Translation Task," *Bible Translator* 33, no. 3 (1982): 309.
118. The Hebrew verb stem is a Hithpael.
119. *IBHS*, 395 (§23.6.4a). Waltke and O'Connor declare that "it is not surprising that the stems are occasionally confounded" (ibid.).
120. Cf. Boyd, "A Synchronic Analysis," 11–12.
121. Claus Westermann, *Genesis 12–36: A Commentary*, trans. John J. Scullion (Minneapolis: Augsburg, 1985), 151–52.
122. Mitchell, *The Meaning of* BRK, 31–36. Cf., also, C. A. Keller, "ברך," in *TLOT*, 1:274: "Yet the usage of this conjugation—in contrast to the pu. and hitp.—probably emphasizes its specific meaning. It indicates an action completed on the subj., without viewing the subj. itself (hitp.) or another person (pu.) as the author of the action . . . . *brk* ni. means, then, 'to experience blessing, participate in blessing,' etc. . . . Gen 12:3b means, then, 'by you shall all the families of the earth gain blessing.'" Unfortunately, the problem is ignored completely by John N. Oswalt, "ברך," in *TWOT*, 1:132–33.
123. Michael L. Brown, "ברך," in *NIDOTTE*, 1:760.
124. Westermann, *Genesis 12–36*, 152. Also, Wenham, *Genesis 1–15*, 278.
125. Victor P. Hamilton, *The Book of Genesis: Chapters 1–17*, NICOT (Grand Rapids: Eerdmans, 1990), 374.
126. E. A. Speiser, *Genesis*, 2nd ed., AB 1 (Garden City, NY: Doubleday, 1978), 86.
127. Walter C. Kaiser Jr., *Mission in the Old Testament: Israel as a Light to the Nations* (Grand Rapids: Baker Books, 2000), 19–20.
128. Brown, "ברך," *NIDOTTE*, 1:760.
129. Kaiser, *Mission in the Old Testament*, 20. Michael A. Grisanti clearly argues the theological significance of the passive in his doctoral dissertation, "The Relationship of Israel and the Nations in Isaiah 40–55" (PhD diss., Dallas Theological Seminary, 1993), 296–303.
130. Cf. Brown, "ברך," *NIDOTTE*, 1:760; Kaiser, *Mission in the Old Testament*, 19–20.
131. Piel, Pual, and Hithpael are all classified as intensive stems in biblical Hebrew.
132. Grammarians describe such repeated actions as iterative (= repeated) or pluralative (= one or more objects for which the action is accomplished). Cf. *HBI*, 26 (Piel, §2.1.4b), 27 (Pual, §2.1.5b). The Hithpael is basically the reflexive of the Piel, thus partaking of the various usages of that stem, including the iterative. See Paul Joüon, *A Grammar of Biblical Hebrew*, trans. and rev. T. Muraoka, Subsidia Biblica 14/I (Rome: Pontifical Biblical Institute, 1996), 159 (§53*i*). For a fuller discussion of the iterative meaning for Hithpael, see *IBHS*, 426–29 (§26.1.2).
133. Biblical Hebrew simple verb stems are the Qal and Niphal and tend to be non-iterative or non-pluralative.
134. The Qal stem for ברך is utilized throughout Genesis 23.
135. Since ברך takes a pluralative meaning in the intensive stems with a plural object, the Pual occurs in Genesis 25:10.
136. In Genesis 28:14, the object of a second ב-preposition phrase is the collective "your seed/offspring." The second phrase is delayed in the sentence, coming after the object of the verb.

137. Niphal of *brk* (ברך) modified by the preposition ב with a singular pronominal suffix (2 ms in Gen. 12:3 and 28:14, 3ms in 18:18).
138. The verbs in these cases are the Hithpael followed by the preposition ב with the collective "your seed/offspring." The intensive verb stem might, therefore, take the pluralative concept that applies the action to a plurality of objects.
139. Although this distinction in the patriarchal blessing formula is consistent within the Pentateuch (the Hithpael form of ברך in Deut. 29:18 is not a use of this formula), the two occurrences of the formula outside the Pentateuch (Jer. 4:2 and Ps. 72:17) involve the Hithpael with a 3ms pronominal suffix on ב. These later adaptations of the patriarchal blessing include several significant variations of the earlier original formula (cf. Mitchell, *The Meaning of* BRK, 55–57, 72–73, 94, 103). Mitchell notes the distinctive employment of the Hithpael with "in your descendants" (ibid., 55–56), but does not mention any association with an iterative or pluralative meaning for the verb. John H. Sailhamer, "Genesis," in *EBC*, 2:114 also concludes that the key is the iterative of the Hithpael employed with the nominal object (as compared to the pronominal object accompanying the Niphal): "the Hithpael [can be read] as iterative when the promise is envisioned with respect to the future 'seed'—the blessing will continue (iterative) to be offered to the nations through the seed of Abraham" (ibid.).
140. *Contra* Chisholm, *From Exegesis to Exposition*, 85; Scharbert, "ברך," *TDOT*, 2:296–97.
141. Grisanti, "The Missing Mandate," 49; referring to the Niphal and Hithpael stems of the Hebrew verb.
142. Cf., also, 2 Kings 22:20/2 Chronicles 34:28.
143. Charles L. Feinberg, "אסף," *TWOT*, 1:60.
144. An impressive array of scholars (some of them not so evangelical) hold this position: Ronald B. Allen, "Numbers," in *EBC*, 2:872–73; Robert G. Boling, *Judges: Introduction, Translation and Commentary*, AB 6A (Garden City, NY: Doubleday, 1975), 72; A. B. Davidson, *The Theology of the Old Testament*, International Theological Library (1904; repr., Edinburgh: T&T Clark, 1961), 500; Walter C. Kaiser Jr., *Toward an Old Testament Theology* (Grand Rapids: Academie Books/Zondervan, 1978), 99; C. F. Keil and F. Delitzsch, *The Pentateuch*, 3 vols., trans. James Martin, Biblical Commentary on the Old Testament (repr., Grand Rapids: Eerdmans, 1971), 1:263; Derek Kidner, *Genesis: An Introduction and Commentary*, TOTC (Downers Grove, IL: InterVarsity Press, 1973), 150, 212; H. C. Leupold, *Exposition of Genesis*, 2 vols. (1942; repr., Grand Rapids: Baker, 1970), 1:485–86, 2:694–95; Gustav Friedrich Oehler, *Theology of the Old Testament*, trans. George E. Day (1883; repr., Minneapolis: Klock & Klock Christian Publishers, 1978), 170; James Orr, "Immortality in the Old Testament," in *Classical Evangelical Essays in Old Testament Interpretation*, ed. Walter C. Kaiser Jr. (Grand Rapids: Baker, 1972), 255; Richard D. Patterson and Hermann J. Austel, "1, 2 Kings," in *EBC*, 4:284; Gordon J. Wenham, *Numbers: An Introduction and Commentary*, TOTC (Downers Grove, IL: InterVarsity Press, 1981), 153; Kyle M. Yates, "Genesis," in *Wycliffe Bible Commentary*, eds. Charles F. Pfeiffer and Everett F. Harrison (Chicago: Moody Press, 1962), 30. In the Berkeley version, the translation footnote to Numbers 20:24 reads, "An intimation of life after death." The Berkeley translation team included Gleason Archer Jr., S. Lewis Johnson, William Sanford LaSor, J. Barton Payne, Samuel J. Schultz, Merrill F. Unger, Leon J. Wood, and Martin J. Wyngaarden. While it is virtually certain that there may have been differences of opinion among the translators, the footnote remains.
145. Walther Eichrodt, *Theology of the Old Testament*, 2 vols., trans. J. A. Baker (Philadelphia: Westminster Press, 1967), 2:213; Feinberg, "אסף," *TWOT*, 1:60; and Judah J. Slotki, "Judges," in *Joshua-Judges*, ed. A. Cohen, rev. A. J. Rosenberg (London: Soncino, 1987), 170.
146. John Gray, *I & II Kings: A Commentary*, 2nd ed., OTL (Philadelphia: Westminster Press, 1970), 88; Eric M. Meyers, "Secondary Burials in Palestine," *Biblical Archaeologist* 33, no. 1 (1970): 2–29. Cf. I. Cornelius, Andrew E. Hill, and Cleon L. Rogers Jr., "אסף," *NIDOTTE*, 1:470; and Slotki, *Judges*, 170.
147. Cf. Kaiser, *Toward an Old Testament Theology*, 99. For a taste of the debate involved with this Old Testament quotation in the New Testament, see Richard T. Mead, "A Dissenting Opinion about Respect for Context in Old Testament Quotations," in *The Right Doctrine from the Wrong Texts? Essays on the Use of the Old Testament in the New*, ed. G. K. Beale (Grand Rapids: Baker Books, 1994), 153–63 (esp. 160).

148. Arichea, "Taking Theology Seriously in the Translation Task," 316.
149. Ross, *Creation and Blessing*, 362.
150. *HBI*, 22 (§1.8.3a).
151. Cf., also, Victor P. Hamilton, *The Book of Genesis: Chapters 18–50*, NICOT (Grand Rapids: Eerdmans, 1995), 45, 47.
152. Eichrodt, *Theology of the Old Testament*, 2:190.
153. Gordon J. Wenham, *Genesis 16–50*, WBC 2 (Dallas: Word Books, 1994), 59.
154. Ibid., 35.
155. See also, Meredith G. Kline, "The Feast of Cover-Over," *Journal of the Evangelical Theological Society* 37, no. 4 (1994): 498.
156. Augustus Hopkins Strong, *Systematic Theology: A Compendium Designed for the Use of Theological Students*, 3 vols. in 1 (1907; repr., Valley Forge, PA: Judson Press, 1967), 318.
157. James A. Borland, *Christ in the Old Testament*, rev. ed. (Fearn, UK: Mentor/Christian Focus Publications, 1999), 152. Others who note this same distinction in the text include: David L. Cooper, *The God of Israel*, rev. ed. (Los Angeles: Biblical Research Society, 1945), 23; and Oehler, *Theology of the Old Testament*, 133. Oehler granted the existence of some sort of distinction being made in Genesis 19:24, but did not think that, in and of itself, it supports the view of identifying the one manifestation directly with the Logos, the Son of God, the second person of the Godhead.
158. Hamilton, *Genesis: Chapters 18–50*, 46. Westermann represents those who think that the repetitive reference to Yahweh is awkward and due to a merging of two different accounts (*Genesis 12–36*, 306).
159. Cf. Arichea, "Taking Theology Seriously in the Translation Task," 309–16. Arichea discusses three factors: "(1) unjustified theologizing by the translator; (2) making translational decisions in the light of one's own theology, and (3) insufficient exegetical follow-through" (ibid., 309). See also a brief response to Arichea's article: Michel Bulcke, "Note: The Translator's Theology," *Bible Translator* 35, no. 1 (1984): 134–35.

Chapter 6: Translating the Shepherd Psalm's First Verse

160. The Hebrew text reads as follows: יְהוָה רֹעִי לֹא אֶחְסָר (*YHWH ro‘iy lo’ ’echsar*).
161. In order to enable a wide range of people to read transliterated language examples in this volume, I have used a simplified system rather than a technical system. Those more technically trained in the various languages using scripts different from English script will readily convert those words into their original scripts in their own minds as they read. Some clarification is in order regarding pronunciation. In the transliterations *ch* represents a guttural like that used in German (as in *kirche*; sounds like clearing one's throat). When *ē* occurs, it should be pronounced as in Spanish (e.g., *señor*).
162. *IBHS*, 55 (§3.3.4e).
163. SBCL = Standard Bengali Common Language Bible. The author was a linguistic and exegetical consultant for this translation project in Bangladesh from 1981 until 1996.
164. The word "shall" occupies nineteen columns of discussion in the *Oxford English Dictionary*, providing a fascinating survey of its background and use from its earliest attested uses in the English language to its use in the twentieth century. *The Compact Edition of the Oxford English Dictionary: Complete Text Reproduced Micrographically* (1971; repr., Oxford: Oxford University Press, 1985), 2:607–13.
165. William Morris, ed., *The American Heritage Dictionary of the English Language* (Boston: Houghton Mifflin Co., 1979), 1189–90.
166. J. N. D. Kelly, *Jerome: His Life, Writings, and Controversies* (New York: Harper & Row, 1975), 89.
167. Ibid., 158.
168. Ibid., 286.
169. Jean Steinmann, *Saint Jerome and His Times*, trans. Ronald Matthews (Notre Dame, IN: Fides Publishers, 1959), 189.
170. Ibid., 199.

171. Yehezkel Kaufmann, *The Religion of Israel from Its Beginnings to the Babylonian Exile*, trans. and abridged. Moshe Greenberg (Chicago: University of Chicago Press, 1960), 148–49.
172. R. Laird Harris, "The Pronunciation of the Tetragram," in *The Law and the Prophets: Old Testament Studies Prepared in Honor of Oswald Thompson Allis*, ed. John H. Skilton (Nutley, NJ: Presbyterian and Reformed Publishing, 1974), 215.
173. Louis F. Hartman, "God, Names of," in *Encyclopaedia Judaica*, ed. Cecil Roth (Jerusalem: Keter Publishing House, 1971), 7:680. For examples of the Christian writers to whom Hartman refers, including Theodoret of Cyros and Clement of Alexandria, see Harris, "Pronunciation," 223.
174. For readers desiring to learn more about the problems of textual criticism in the Old Testament, the following sources are recommended: William D. Barrick, "Current Trends and Tensions in Old Testament Textual Criticism," *Bible Translator* 35, no. 3 (1984): 301–8; James Barr, *Comparative Philology and the Text of the Old Testament with Additions and Corrections* (repr., Winona Lake, IN: Eisenbrauns, 1987).
175. "A" = "certain"; "C" = moderate uncertainty ("difficulty in determining which variant should be in the text"); "D" = "uncertain."
176. Zane C. Hodges and Arthur L. Farstad, *The Greek New Testament according to the Majority Text* (Nashville: Thomas Nelson, 1982).

Chapter 7: The Ultimate Challenge of Bible Translation

177. Speiser, *Genesis*, lxiii.
178. Ibid., lxiv.
179. v. 1a: הֲלֹא־חָכְמָה תִקְרָא, *halo'-chokmah tiqra'*
v. 1b: וּתְבוּנָה תִּתֵּן קוֹלָהּ, *ut^{e}vunah tittēn qolah*
180. See the discussion of the gnomic present in chapter 6 with regard to the JB's translation of Psalm 23:1.
181. See William D. Reyburn and Euan McG. Fry, *A Handbook of Proverbs*, UBS Handbook Series (New York: United Bible Societies, 2000), 176.
182. See *HALOT*, 826 (1,g).
183. v. 2a: בְּרֹאשׁ־מְרוֹמִים עֲלֵי־דָרֶךְ, *b^{e}ro'sh-m^{e}romim '^{a}ley-darek*
v. 2b: בֵּית נְתִיבוֹת נִצָּבָה, *beyt n^{e}tiyvot nitstsavah*
184. See *HALOT*, 388 (5.a.i).
185. v. 3a: לְיַד־שְׁעָרִים לְפִי־קָרֶת, *l^{e}yad-sh^{e}'ariym l^{e}piy-qaret*
v. 3b: מְבוֹא פְתָחִים תָּרֹנָּה, *m^{e}vo' p^{e}tachiym taronnah*
186. Michael V. Fox, *Proverbs1–9: A New Translation with Introduction and Commentary*, AYBC 18A (New Haven, CT: Yale University Press, 2008), 265.
187. Reyburn and Fry, *A Handbook of Proverbs*, 177.
188. v. 4a: אֲלֵיכֶם אִישִׁים אֶקְרָא, *'^{a}leykem 'iyshiym 'eqra'*
v. 4b: וְקוֹלִי אֶל־בְּנֵי אָדָם, *w^{e}qoliy 'el-b^{e}ney 'adam*
189. v. 5a: הָבִינוּ פְתָאיִם עָרְמָה, *haviynu p^{e}ta'yim 'ormah*
v. 5b: וּכְסִילִים הָבִינוּ לֵב, *uk^{e}siyliym haviynu lēv*
190. Fox, *Proverbs1–9*, 268.
191. Reyburn and Fry, *A Handbook of Proverbs*, 178.
192. v. 6a: שִׁמְעוּ כִּי־נְגִידִים אֲדַבֵּר, *shim'u kiy-n^{e}giydiym '^{a}dabbēr*
v. 6b: וּמִפְתַּח שְׂפָתַי מֵישָׁרִים, *umiptach s^{e}patay meyshariym*
193. v. 7a: כִּי־אֱמֶת יֶהְגֶּה חִכִּי, *kiy-'^{e}met yehgeh chikkiy*
v. 7b: וְתוֹעֲבַת שְׂפָתַי רֶשַׁע, *w^{e}to'^{a}vat s^{e}patay resha'*
194. See note 180 above.
195. Crawford H. Toy, *A Critical and Exegetical Commentary on the Book of Proverbs*, ICC (New York: C. Scribner's Sons, 1899), 162.
196. Wilfred G. E. Watson, *Classical Hebrew Poetry: A Guide to Its Techniques*, JSOTSup 6 (Sheffield: Sheffield Press, 1986), 303–6.
197. *HBI*, 41 (§3.1.1b).

198. v. 8a: בְּצֶדֶק כָּל־אִמְרֵי־פִי, *b^{e}tsedeq kol-'imrey-piy*
v. 8b: אֵין בָּהֶם נִפְתָּל וְעִקֵּשׁ, *'eyn bahem niptal w^{e}'iqqēsh*
199. v. 9a: כֻּלָּם נְכֹחִים לַמֵּבִין, *kullam n^{e}kochiym lammēviyn*
v. 9b: וִישָׁרִים לְמֹצְאֵי דָעַת, *w^{e}yshariym l^{e}mots^{e}'ey da'at*
200. *HBI*, 20 (§1.8.3).
201. *HALOT*, 698–99.
202. v. 10a: קְחוּ־מוּסָרִי וְאַל־כָּסֶף, *q^{e}chu-musariy we'al-kasep*
v. 10b: וְדַעַת מֵחָרוּץ נִבְחָר, *w^{e}da'at mēcharuts nivchar*
203. v. 11a: כִּי־טוֹבָה חָכְמָה מִפְּנִינִים, *kiy-tovah chokmah mipp^{e}niyniym*
v. 11b: וְכָל־חֲפָצִים לֹא יִשְׁווּ־בָהּ, *w^{e}kol-ch^{a}patsiym lo' yishwu-vah*
204. *HALOT*, 946.
205. For more discussion of the meaning of *p^{e}ninim*, see Toy, *Proverbs*, 68 (commentary on Prov. 3:15) and Reyburn and Fry, *A Handbook of Proverbs*, 81 (regarding Prov. 3:15).
206. Sandra F. Rowe and Sharon Sikes, "Lessons Learned: Taking It to the Next Level" (paper presented at PMI Global Congress 2006—North America, Seattle, WA and Newtown Square, PA: Project Management Institute, 2006); https://www.pmi.org/learning/library/lessons-learned-next-level-communicating-7991, accessed 22 September 2018. This paper includes an attractive and informative flow chart mapping the following stages: Identify, Document, Analyze, Store, and Retrieve. Rowe and Sikes recommend project facilitators ask three key questions from participants: (1) What went right? (2) What went wrong? (3) What needs to be improved? Bible translation teams will find the same three questions very helpful in evaluating their project.

Chapter 8: Which English Bible Version Is Best?

207. Thomas, *How to Choose a Bible Translation*, 91–95.
208. Ibid., 93. Thomas derives his system from that of William Wonderly as described in Eugene A. Nida, *Toward a Science of Translating: With Special Reference to Principles and Procedures Involved in Bible Translating* (Leiden, Netherlands: Brill, 1964), 187–88.
209. Thomas's assigned values are not the same as those indicated by Wonderly's evaluation method. Wonderly's system assigns a value of 1 for the simplest change in order, omission, addition, and lexical and syntactical alteration. He assigns a value of 2 to those changes that are a little more complex in all of these categories. The value of 4 he assigns to the most radical changes in each of the categories.
210. Ryken, *The Word of God in English*.
211. Katharina Reiss, *Translation Criticism—The Potentials and Limitations: Categories and Criteria for Translation Quality Assessment*, trans. Erroll F. Rhodes (Manchester, UK: St. Jerome Publishing / New York: American Bible Society, 2000), 9. "Target language" refers to the language being translated into the receptor language.
212. The *lamed* of authorship is really nothing more than the *lamed* of agency; cf. Bill T. Arnold and John H. Choi, *A Guide to Biblical Hebrew Syntax* (Cambridge: Cambridge University Press, 2003), 114. In the psalm titles, the verb (viz., "written") is elided—not an uncommon occurrence in the use of prepositions in biblical Hebrew; cf. *IBHS*, 224–25 (§11.4.3.c–e). For the significance of the psalm inscriptions, see Bruce K. Waltke, "Superscripts, Postscripts, or Both," *Journal of Biblical Literature* 110, no. 4 (1991): 583–96.
213. Hartman, "God, Names of," 7:680.
214. Derek Kidner, *Psalms 1–72*, TOTC (Downers Grove, IL: InterVarsity Press, 1973), 110. Kidner explains, "It may picture the straying sheep brought back, as in Isaiah 49:5, or perhaps Psalm 60:1 (Heb. 3), which use the same verb, whose intransitive sense is often 'repent' or 'be converted' (*e.g.* Ho. 14:1f.; Joel 2:12). Psalm 19:7, by its subject (the law) and by the parallel verb ('making wise'), points to a spiritual renewal of this kind, rather than mere refreshment. On the other hand, *my soul* usually means 'my life' or 'myself'; and 'restore' often has a physical or psychological sense, as in Isaiah 58:12, or using another part of the verb, Proverbs 25:13, Lamentations 1:11, 16, 19. In our context the two senses evidently interact, so that the retrieving or reviving of the sheep pictures the deeper renewal of the man of God, spiritually perverse or ailing as he may be."

215. Robert G. Bratcher and William D. Reyburn, *A Handbook on Psalms*, UBS Handbook Series (New York: United Bible Societies, 1991), 233.
216. *HALOT*, 234.
217. GKC, 406–7 (§126*n*).
218. A textual problem exists with regard to "I dwell." The Hebrew form can be taken as a form of either *shuv* ("return") or *yashav* ("dwell," "reside"). See Charles A. Briggs and Emilie Briggs, *A Critical and Exegetical Commentary of the Book of Psalms*, 2 vols., ICC (New York: C. Scribner's Sons, 1906–7), 1:211. Briggs and Briggs argue effectively that "return" seems out of touch with the context "which emphasizes presence in the house and not absence from it."
219. Thomas, *How to Choose a Bible Translation*, 96.
220. Rodney Huddleston, *Introduction to the Grammar of English*, Cambridge Textbooks in Linguistics (Cambridge: Cambridge University Press, 1984), 158. See also Sidney Greenbaum, "Perfect," in *The Oxford Companion to the English Language*, ed. Tom McArthur (Oxford: Oxford University Press, 1992), 759–60. Greenbaum confirms this distinction.
221. For an excellent discussion of the use of italics in Bible translation, see Jack Lewis, "Italics in English Bible Translation," in *The Living and Active Word of God: Studies in Honor of Samuel J. Schultz*, eds. Morris Inch and Ronald Youngblood, 255–70. (Winona Lake, IN: Eisenbrauns, 1983).
222. See Bruce M. Metzger, *A Textual Commentary on the Greek New Testament* (New York: United Bible Societies, 1971), 513.
223. A. T. Robertson, *Word Pictures in the New Tes*tament, 6 vols., electronic ed. (Nashville: Broadman Press, 1930–33; Bellingham, WA: Logos Bible Software, 1933), Rom. 6:13. Robertson says, "Old word for tools of any kind for shop or war (John 18:3; 2 Cor. 6:7; 10:4; Rom. 13:12). Possibly here figure of two armies arrayed against each other (Gal. 5:16–24)."
224. *Nomos*, "law," refers to the Mosaic law, not to law in general. New Testament writers often omit the Greek definite article in prepositional phrases. See Thomas R. Schreiner, *Romans*, Baker Exegetical Commentary on the New Testament 6 (Grand Rapids: Baker Books, 1998), 325.
225. Thomas, *How to Choose a Bible Translation*, 96.

Chapter 9: What Does It Take to Be a Bible Translator?

226. Carmelyn Lois P. Acena, "Is This God Speaking Your Language?" *Mission Today 96* (Evanston, IL: Berry Publishing Services, 1996), 79.
227. Ibid., 78–80.
228. Fadiman, *The Little, Brown Book of Anecdotes*, 188.
229. Lexham Press is an imprint of Faithlife Corporation, producer of Logos Bible Software. Lexham publishes EEC volumes in digital format first and later in hard copy. All Lexham Press titles mentioned in the resource lists for this chapter are available in digital format compatible with Logos Bible Software
230. After only about a half dozen volumes, Moody dropped the Wycliffe Exegetical Commentary series. The EEC comes nearest to both the evangelical stance and exegetical depth of that discontinued series.
231. Luther quoted in E. G. Rupp and Benjamin Drewery, eds., *Martin Luther: Documents of Modern History* (New York: St. Martin's Press, 1970), 72–73.
232. John Piper, *The Legacy of Sovereign Joy: God's Triumphant Grace in the Lives of Augustine, Luther, and Calvin*, The Swans Are Not Silent 1 (Wheaton, IL: Crossway Books, 2000), 106.

Chapter 10: Preparing for the Project: Establish Translation Principles

233. Knox, *The Trials of a Translator*, 106–7.
234. For questions about translating the Bible into foreign languages that critics have failed to answer satisfactorily, see Charles R. Wood, "The Question of Preservation," *Faith for the Family* (1981): 13–14.

235. Robert Leonard Goddard, "An Objective Evaluation of the Accuracy of the Revised Standard Version in the Translation of the New Testament" (ThD diss., Dallas Theological Seminary, 1955), 8–9.
236. J. P. Migne, ed., *Patrologiae Latinae: S. Hieronymus*, Patrologiae Cursus Completus: Series Latina Prior 22 (Paris: Garner Fratres, 1877), 1:843 (Epist. 106).
237. Fridericus Field, ed., *Origenis Hexaplorum*, 2 vols. (Hildesheim, Germany: Georg Olms Verlags-burchhandlung, 1964), 2:121.
238. "Letter LVII. To Pammachius on the Best Method of Translating," in *St. Jerome: Letters and Select Works*, vol. 6 in Select Library of Nicene and Post-Nicene Fathers of the Christian Church (Second Series), trans. Philip Schaff and Henry Wace (Grand Rapids: Eerdmans, 1954), 118.
239. Jeramie Rinne, *Church Elders: How to Shepherd God's People Like Jesus*, 9Marks: Building Healthy Churches (Wheaton, IL: Crossway, 2014), 36.

Chapter 11: A Final Request

240. Fadiman, *The Little, Brown Book of Anecdotes*, 189.

SCRIPTURE INDEX

NAME AND TOPIC INDEX

T